Date Due

Feb 19/93			
Mar 15/93			
Oct 28/96			
OCT 22 1996			
MAR _ 2 1998			
NOV 20 1998			
Nov. 27.			

THE RITES
OF MAN

By the Same Author

Rosalind Miles

THE RITES OF MAN

Love, Sex and Death
in the Making of the Male

132-922634

GraftonBooks
A Division of HarperCollins*Publishers*

GraftonBooks
A Division of HarperCollins*Publishers*
77–85 Fulham Palace Road,
Hammersmith, London W6 8JB

Published by GraftonBooks 1991

Copyright © Rosalind Miles 1991

British Library Cataloguing in Publication Data

Miles, Rosalind
  The rites of man: love, sex and death
  in the making of the male
  1. Masculinity
  I. Title
  305.31

ISBN 0–246–13474–7

Phototypeset by Computape (Pickering) Ltd,
North Yorkshire

Printed in Great Britain by
HarperCollinsManufacturing Glasgow

For my son Conrad

in Lucy Stone's last words
to her daughter –

'Make the world better'

Contents

The greatest enemy of man is man.
Robert Burton,
The Anatomy of Melancholy (1621)

Acknowledgements

During the preparation of this book men from all over the world agreed to be interviewed, spoke to me on the phone, or contributed notes, letters, diaries, or extracts from their writings. Others worked with me in their professional capacity, sharing their expertise and shaping my conclusions. For the openness and generosity of all, which quite belied the common view that men do not care to talk about these things, to all my most grateful thanks.

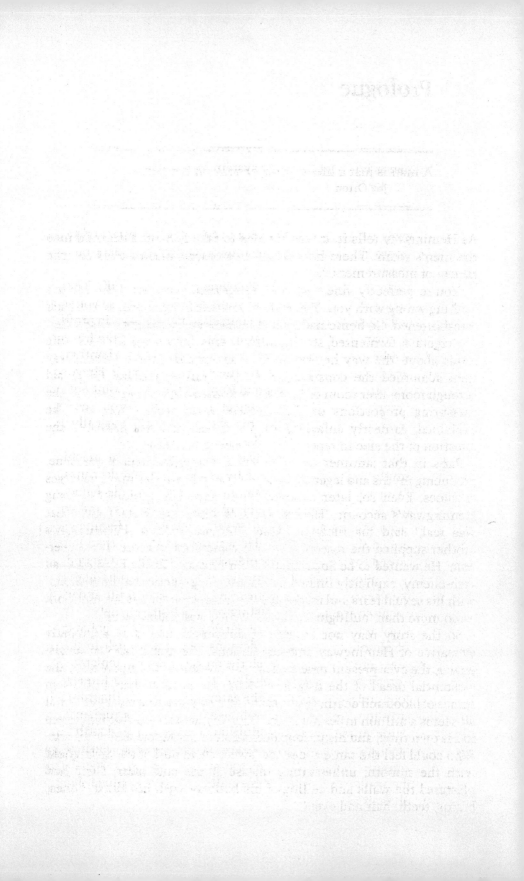

Prologue

A man is just a life-support system for his penis.
Joe Orton

As Hemingway tells it, it was his idea to take F. Scott Fitzgerald into the men's room. There he held an impromptu master-class on 'the matter of measurements'.

'You're perfectly fine,' he told Fitzgerald. 'You are OK. There's nothing wrong with you. You look at yourself from above, so you look foreshortened. Go home and look at yourself in the mirror – in profile.'

Fitzgerald, tormented, so Hemingway says, by a taunt from his wife Zelda about 'the way he was built', was not convinced. Hemingway then adjourned the consultation to the Louvre, guiding Fitzgerald through room after room of Greek and Roman statues to point out the reassuring proportions of the classical male nude. 'You see,' he explained, earnestly enlarging on his thesis, 'it's not basically the question of the size in repose. It's the size it *becomes* . . .'[1]

Paris in that summer of 1929 was a shameless dream machine, producing myths and legends as casually as other cities make sausages or shoes. Even so, later commentators have had trouble believing Hemingway's account. 'He lost track of what was fantasy and what was real,' said his lifelong friend William Walton. Hemingway's brother supplied the reason why: 'He wanted to be more than Superman. He wanted to be Superman's older brother.' Zelda Fitzgerald, an arch-enemy, explicitly linked Hemingway's 'professional he-man act' with his sexual fears and inadequacies, and dismissed his life and work as no more than 'bullfighting, bullslinging, and bullshitting'.[2]

So the story may not be true of Fitzgerald. But it is poignantly evocative of Hemingway and his demons: the naïve faith in penis-power, the ever-present urge to flash the credentials of machismo, the existential dread of the fallible phallus, the need to lose himself in games of blood and death. Now, at the gateway to a new millennium, it all seems a million miles away. Hemingway was an anachronism even in his own time, and his unique definition of manhood died with him. Who could feel the same about the 'sweet clean pull of the Springfield with the smooth, unhesitating release at the end' after 'Papa' had plastered the walls and ceiling of his hallway with his blood, bones, brains, teeth, hair and eyes?

Yet the Hemingway theme lingers on, surfacing in strange places, uneasy echoes and chilling reminders. As a long-distance lorry-driver in the north of England, one of the undisputed 'knights of the road', Peter Sutcliffe had this macho boast prominently displayed in the window of his cab:

> In this truck is a man whose latent genius if unleashed would rock the nation, whose dynamic energy would overpower those around him. Better let him sleep!

Sutcliffe lived to 'rock the nation' with a vengeance, when, as the 'Yorkshire Ripper', he committed the extensive catalogue of murders and mutilations over the period between 1975 and 1981 that have made him Britain's most notorious killer. But inside the coolly professional and apparently passionless exterminator lay the quivering, festering psyche of a man who had had to live since early teens with the nickname 'Peter No-Dick', and whose every waking day was therefore just another variant on the ultimate male nightmare.

From the world of darkness I did loose demons and devils with the power of scorpions to torment.
Charles Manson,
New York Times, 9.2.86

Killers, like clothes, go out of fashion. Who now remembers the Black Panther, the Shoemaker, or the down-home slaughterboys of Truman Capote's *In Cold Blood* (1966)? The twentieth-century public has supped full of horrors: its fickle appetite demands a varied diet, and frequent changes in the menu. So the suppliers keep them coming: a pack-rape and sodomization from Central Park, New York, a werewolf in rural France, a fatal homosexual gang-bang in London's West End.

As one horror-movie scenario sweeps another from the headlines, it is easy to lose count. But it is not so easy to dismiss a growing sense that things used to be different, that the tide of violence is rising. And those who look beyond their own concerns and their own country, who try to connect the private with the public and the particular with the general, may well feel that they are witnesses in a final wave of violent male activity world-wide. Extremes of terror govern the way we live now: of a million million world incidents darkening our *fin de siècle*, a handful of events culled at random from a three-month period at the dawn of the 1990s show the brutally haphazard impact of violence in the world today:

● In France, seven-year-old Céline Jourdan is tortured, raped and killed by an assailant unknown. A senior Paris barrister, Maître Henri Leclerc, attempting a reconstruction of the crime, is attacked, stripped naked, covered with a paste of mustard and flour and savagely beaten by a village mob.

● In Northern Ireland, two Belfast men, Alan McMeekin and Ian Coulter, lifelong friends and members of the same Orange lodge, shoot and kill one another after an evening's friendly drinking.

● In South Africa, Barend Strydom, 'the King of the White Wolves', a former police officer, grinned and laughed as he strolled round Pretoria shooting blacks 'for target practice' at point-blank range. Of his 23 victims, 16 died.

● In Los Angeles, Richard Ramirez, 'the Night Stalker', was sentenced to die in the gas chamber for the murder of 12 people. 'You maggots make me sick,' he told the court. 'I am beyond your experience.'

● In China, a Shandong farmer, Liu Chun San, finding his wife pregnant with what the soothsayer promised would be a boy, throws his four-year-old daughter down a well, smoking a cigarette while he waits for her to drown.

● In India, a 28-year-old widow, Shakuntala Devi, is honoured nation-wide for committing 'suttee' after her husband's death. Uttar Pradesh police later established that Shakuntala had been placed on the funeral pyre four hours after her husband's cremation, covered in blood and with a broken neck.

● In England, the publication of Salman Rushdie's *The Satanic Verses* provokes death threats, public violence, bookstore bombings. Ayatollah Khomeini dies in Teheran amid violent public disorder. London graffiti crow 'KHOMEINI GOT FUCKED. FUCK ISLAM. RUSHDIE WAS RIGHT.'

● In America, T-shirts reading 'STAND FOR AMERICA – RAPE AN IRANIAN WOMAN' keep alive the slogan first seen on placards outside the White House during the Iranian hostage crisis. Says Rap Brown, 'Violence is as American as cherry pie.'

Everyone has a favourite story of modern violence, cruelty or horror. But the welter of anecdotal evidence supports a broader reality: today's violence is a rising tide. This is not simply a question of more sexual crimes being reported in our less judgemental age, but applies equally to muggings and violent assaults on male victims, which they have never had any reason to conceal. Throughout the western world, the number of crimes of violence and sexual offences has shown an unprecedented increase in the last generation. In the US alone, 'between 1971 and 1980, the number of reported major crimes increased by 41 per cent. During the same period, the number of major violent crimes against the person increased by 47 per cent.' This trend is replicated in all countries we call 'advanced' and very many of those which have not yet been accorded this dignity. It is also powerful enough to cut across counter-trends: countries like Britain which show a fall in criminal offences overall still show an upsurge in crimes of sex and violence.[3]

Government statistics supply the facts behind the dinner-table *frissons*: 'the US 1990 "crime clock" shows that one violent crime occurs every 21 seconds', 'in Britain in 1988 the most serious offences of violence increased by 16 per cent', 'America has had a 20 per cent increase in violent crime in all major metropolitan areas', British recorded rapes in the 1990s 'will not necessarily sustain' the annual rise of over 20 per cent recorded since the early 1980s. As the third millennium of western civilization approaches, its achievement for its citizens may be summed up in one stark apposition: 'the chance of being a violent crime victim is now greater than that of being in a traffic accident.'[4] No one is safe. No one is free. This is our world.

At current crime rates, almost every one of us will be a victim of violent crime, attempted or completed, during his or her lifetime. Many of us will be victimized more than once – some three or more times.

US Department of Justice Report to the Nation (1988)

More violence means more victims. Modern victims suffer not simply more exposure to violence, but new kinds of victimization, bizarre, sadistic extremes of violent behaviour. Late twentieth-century technology makes possible the kind of cruelty literally inconceivable to 'Bluebeard' Gilles de Rais, 'Vlad the Impaler', or 'Dracula' Countess Elisabeth Bathory. Apart from the professional torturers of countries like South Africa, China and Iran, those for whom the joy of pain is just a hobby have found hours of fun in the electric drill, the cattle prod, the stun gun, the laser beam, the bacon slicer, the chain saw. When mass murderer 'Pee Wee' Gaskins, awaiting the electric chair in South Carolina in 1989 for killing 37 people, rigged up a prison 'telephone' and blew the head off a fellow-prisoner incautious enough to approximate his ear to the receiver/detonator, he was doing it for 'sheer enjoyment', said the State Prosecutor, Jim Anders.

Contemporary killing is not simply more hi-tech, more instrumentalized, more inhuman. Violence has become alienated in another important way too, as crime after crime demonstrates a central voyeurism whose pornographic desire to be both watcher and participant is at least as strong as the urge to rape, maim or kill. Sharon Patyk Komlos was returning to her home in Boca Raton, Florida, one night in 1980, when she was shot and blinded by a gunman in an overtaking car. Within moments, help was at hand: an ex-Vietnam para-medic helped her to his car and drove her to hospital. As they entered the building Komlos realized that she was not in a hospital, and that her good Samaritan was none other than the assailant himself.

Over the next twelve hours, the attacker repeatedly stabbed, raped, sodomized and tried to suffocate her, finally leaving her for dead. After Komlos's escape and his arrest, it emerged that the rapist, who was neither a Vietnam veteran nor a medic, had previous convictions for exactly this procedure. His method was to create a road traffic accident, in which he could star as the hero hurrying to the rescue of the female in distress, then shift the scene to an indoor location to unreel his sado-pornographic fantasies with himself in the leading role.

This is no isolated phenomenon. 'It's a product of our times,' commented a senior British police officer. 'Every psycho sees himself as the star of his own movie. They like to watch themselves, and have others watching them: their own group, as in gang rape – the media – the world.' Hence another new phenomenon of our times, the attention-attack: on John Lennon, on Ronald Reagan, on Larry Hagman, on Steffi Graf. 'They can gas me, but I am famous,' boasted Sirhan Sirhan. 'I have achieved in one day what it took Robert Kennedy all his life to do.' The illusion of star-power can even tip over into the delusion of being a star-maker: John W. Hinckley Jr asserted, 'Jodie Foster may continue to ignore me for the rest of her life, but I have made her one of the most famous actresses in the world.'[5]

Some fifty millions have died at the hands of psychiatri-
cally normal males since 1900. We are the death sex.
Philip Hodson,
Men: An Investigation (1984)

Not all violence is 'sexual' in the sense of an act designed to produce
sexual gratification or release. But all violence is sexual in the most
basic meaning of the word, determined by sex as breasts or testes are.
Women may get angry, threaten and scream, lash out in fury or seek
murder and revenge. Only men habitually prey on those weaker than
themselves, stalk the night in search of the lonely victim, hunt one
another in packs, devise initiation rituals, exquisite tortures, pogroms
and extermination camps, delight in Russian roulette, 'running the
gauntlet', 'Chicken' (James Dean's last ride), and all the world's
never-ending games of fear, pain and death. 'The insane cruelty man
has inflicted on other men, the thousands of lives destroyed or ruined,
passes belief,' observed historian A. L. Rowse. 'Women have not
behaved to each other like that.'[6]

For males, violence is sexual in another way too: it is inextricably
bound up with the masculine sense of self, and sexual self. London
clinical psychologist Carol Sellars sees violent men as frantic to assert
manhood in a society which repeatedly castrates their every initiative:
'They have been kicked, time and again, and now they are kicking
back. They feel they have no control over their lives. The only time
they feel in control is when they're being violent.' After the murder of
his brother Blake in Chicago, journalist Brent Staples attacked with
bitter authority 'the circumstances in which black men in their teens
and twenties kill one another with such frequency'. Death may come
from stepping on the wrong toe, crossing a territorial line, saying 'I dare
you' to a man with a gun: 'With a touchy paranoia born of living
battered lives, they are desperate to be *real* men.'[7] Not infrequently the
desperation can override any meaning, let alone motive, behind the
act: when John Smith, aged 30, and Peter Harrison (18) were found
guilty of the 'motiveless murder' of another man in 1988, the victim
had been so violently beaten and trampled that he could only be
identified by his fingerprints, the jury was told.

But violence cannot simply be explained away as the product of
deprivation. As the legions of women nursing bruised bodies and
cracked ribs in well-appointed executive homes could testify, successful men can be violent too. When the high-earning, high-flying lawyer
Joel Steinberg was indicted for the murder of his six-year-old adopted

daughter Lisa in Manhattan in November 1987, author Susan Brown-miller summed up the reaction of the whole of New York: 'This is my community. No, no. This sort of thing just does not happen among middle-class people.' But Steinberg was guilty of more than one fatal blow to his child's head. For years he had been regularly assaulting Lisa's adoptive mother, his live-in lover, so violently that only the merest chance dictated that he was facing one murder charge, not two.

Hedda Nussbaum appeared before a US grand jury with the cauli-flower ears, mushed-up mouth and vacant, has-been stare of a punch-drunk boxer. A video made at the time of Steinberg's arrest showed that lumps of her hair had been torn from her scalp, which was also covered in cigarette burns. Her nose had been pulverized so often that its bridge had been destroyed. Her back and thighs were disfigured with numerous ulcerated, gangrenous bruises. Hospital records showed that she had received in-patient treatment for a broken jaw, ruptured spleen, nine broken ribs, and an apparently endless succession of skull fractures, nine in one year alone. Steinberg's favourite weapon, his metal exercise bar, had been used so often and so hard on Nussbaum that it was bent out of shape.

Massive public attention focused on the woman Nussbaum. Why did she stay with Steinberg, when as an educated professional she had the money and power to leave? Why did she allow the attacks on the child? Why did she fail to inform the police? In the flurry of questions, which spread ever wider in the agonized post-mortem (why didn't the police prevent it? The school? The child-care professionals?) one question never seemed to arise. No one, but no one, asked why *he* did it.

No one asks a question when they think they know the answer: when a ready-made explanation exists into which the problem can be filed away and forgotten. '[Steinberg] is dismissed as a madman or a monster,' commented Marilyn French. 'We dismiss him because we understand him.' For French, though, the opposite of this comforting dismissal is true. Far from being crazy, a pervert or a fiend, in other words inhuman, atypical, an aberrant and exceptional case, Steinberg was both normal and typical. He was, in fact, *'the man who was simply being a man'*.

> Every recent authoritative study of the psychology of
> the rapist shows that there is no measurable difference
> between the rapist and men in general
>   Ken Livingstone MP

Not every man carries within him the seeds of the sadist or tyrant: most men never set foot on the path that leads a bright youth to the adult destiny of a Caligula, a Dr Mengele, or an Idi Amin. But today and throughout history 'becoming a man' is inescapably involved at some level with violence, either as perpetrator or victim. 'Masculinity is *predicated* on violence,' says London psychotherapist Adam Jukes, leader of a team working with violent men, and author of the long-term study *Men Who Hate Women* (1990). 'It's part of the formation of every male as they grow up. If you're not "a man", what are you? The fear of that fear is at the core of male identity: it's quite peculiar to people with penises. "Masculinity" is our escape from that.'

But as in all the best psychological thrillers, the escape route leads back into the game. 'Our culture insists on every boy "being a man",' comments Jukes. 'Why have men pitched it so high?' Between Rambo and Wall Street, between the fight against cholesterol and the right to eat quiche, the agenda has never been more demanding. Heavy demands (more sexiness, more success) call forth extreme responses: the more fragile the masculinity, the more violent the extremes of self-definition. 'No wonder men are paranoid,' Jukes concludes. 'It's awful to be so scared.'

And that 'fear of fear', the system of masculinity, is built on yet more fear, the systematic engendering of fear in others: in women and children, but most of all, in other men. For men are 'the death sex' in another way too: not only the main perpetrators of violence but its chief victims. The mass media drum up mass hysteria over violated virgins and helpless old ladies viciously mugged: the reality is that in the world today, for every woman who is violently assaulted, there are three or four men; for every 5000 US female homicides in 1987, there were 15,000 male; and for US males between 15 and 34 throughout the 1980s, homicide was the second most likely cause of death, exceeded only by fatal accidents.[8]

In human terms, men, not women, are 'glassed' in bar-room brawls, slashed in the subway, anally raped in prisons, in the armed forces, in any one of a thousand dingy rooms off the 'meat rack' of Piccadilly or Times Square. Current clients of Survivors, London's leading male rape support agency, range in age from 4 to 70, and include a man who was raped by twelve men in turn at a party, and one who was raped with a broken bottle. Suicides among the 'Survivors', both successful and unsuccessful, are routine, and denial and disbelief continue to be the most common response to the crime that dares not speak its name.

At the nexus where violence, sexuality and the need 'to be a man' meet and mesh, there are many such victims. Today's crisis of violence is a crisis of masculinity, and its parameters spread far wider than ever the crime figures will tell. 'We've been betrayed,' says David Jaglom, New York divorce lawyer and divorced father of four children. 'Men today are baited like bears in a ring: women bleed us to give what they then discover they don't want. The tragedy is, it's the good guys, the hippy-thinking seventies men who helped women make that voyage of discovery, and they're the ones getting dumped right now.'

This grief surfaces again and again in the modern man's confessional litany of betrayal: 'women lie and lie', 'they cheat', 'she fooled me', 'you wouldn't believe how she let me down', and most bleakly of all, 'it starts in the playground. Any little girl of six will sell the pass, and the whole of the male sex with it.' International success, a business empire, a Rolls or a Ferrari, a Bel-Air mansion, a box at Ascot or the Met, all pale into nothingness as man after man stares at his hands and tells the story of how he found out that women didn't need what he had been trained to give. 'We're shafted twice over,' said a British professor whose brilliant public career is everything that his shambolic private life is not. 'We're nutcrackered between the old style of breadwinner/ head of the household and the new "participant fatherhood" – so when it goes wrong, we're not skilled enough to look after our children, and not distant enough not to care.'

For the dislocated man, 'woman' (like 'Reds' or 'faggots' in times past) constitutes a shorthand for an uneasy sense of a profound, almost indescribable and certainly irreversible social change. 'Masculinity' has always been essentially a contract between men and men. As sub-contractors, however, women were vital to the scheme of things. But over the last twenty years or so, women have had their own contracts to reconsider and redraw, and suddenly all the old deals are off. A decade or two of feminism has not only changed the world for women: it has produced a crisis of response for the thinking man. How in this brave new post-patriarchal world is he to 'be a man' when all the time-dishonoured props, scripts, prerogatives and perks have been abolished or swept away?

Inevitably the current crisis of male identity, sexuality and violence is accompanied world-wide by an epidemic of divorce. Contrary to the widespread notion of marriages mutually 'breaking down', the vast majority of petitions for divorce are brought by wives. The majority of divorced men are therefore left with strong feelings of being 'dumped', 'abandoned', and 'betrayed'. Many of these men will use violence against their former wife, especially against a rival male or supplanter. 'No bloke is going to sleep with my wife on my side of the bed,' said David Holmes of Woking, after being found guilty of burning his estranged wife and her boyfriend to death in 1988 in a 'horrific' petrol attack. The need to reclaim territory, to restore ego, to hit back, to return pain and humiliation with compound interest – to be a man – is overwhelming. 'Killing,' says Brent Staples, 'is only machismo taken to the extreme.'

Killing may be the extreme of the cult of masculinity. But where masculinity is the norm ('*cojones*', 'balls', 'spunk') violence can never be far behind. Every supposedly genderless society in reality displays a clear picture of considerable socialization of its males towards violence, argues Harvard professor Harry Brod, 'learned in gangs, sports teams, military training, media images, at the hands (literally) of older males, and in the messages of acceptance that "boys will be boys" when they fight.' Accordingly, while it is commonly held that 'a strong sense of oneself as masculine is essential to a male's mental health', Brod continues, 'such a self-conception may be harmful to his physical as well as to his mental health. Stress in men's lives is caused not so much by the individual's failure to socialize properly as a male, but by the contradictory demands of the male sex role itself.'[9]

Often these strains become intolerable. 'I wanted to die and I didn't want to die,' said restaurateur Peter Langan after an attempt to set fire to himself and his wife early in 1989 resulted in the explosion in which he was fatally injured. By any standards a successful businessman, and a friend of stars like Michael Caine who was also his business partner in his famous brasseries in London and Los Angeles, Langan had for many years relied heavily on alcohol to see him through the course of every day, so much so that to concerned friends the fatal accident only short-circuited the much messier process of what seemed to be a determined long-term suicide by self-poisoning. On the night of the fire Langan had persuaded his wife to make love to him 'one last time' in a vain attempt to dissuade her from persisting with her plans for divorce. Afterwards he threatened her with a petrol bomb, then set fire to himself and the house after she escaped. As he lay dying he whispered, 'Susan, it was meant for me.' His last words were to implore her not to leave him.

Arguably Langan's is a special case, his suicide complicated both in the question-mark over his intentions and the confusion of its execution. But more and more men in recent years are unequivocally going for the suicide option pure and simple. In France, government figures show that suicide among males has more than doubled in the last twenty years, while in England the suicide rate among young men, which has been accelerating sharply for the last seven years, is now 70 per cent higher than it was in 1972. Men at every age are more vulnerable to suicide than women, as they are to other stress-related disorders like ulcers and hypertension. By contrast, women who are failing to cope with life are more likely to sink under the weight of events, turn their distress inwards and succumb to depression than to seek a violent finale: women rarely crash cars, jump off bridges, shoot themselves, or blow themselves up. In sum, for whatever reason, the suicide rate among women in Britain has remained constant over the last decade, while distress calls from women, the Samaritans report, have in fact decreased.

It is a tragic reality of all western cultures, however, that young men are now those who are most at risk. In France, suicide is most common in the age group 15–25, exactly the age group in which suicides by youths in the US have tripled in the period since 1950. From the 'marvellous boy' Chatterton, the eighteenth-century poet, to the bleakly twentieth-century Jan Palach, young males on the brink of manhood have all too often failed the final transition to adulthood, and have chosen instead to make the last great leap into the dark. The latest figures show the continuation of 'an absolutely clear trend', said Stephen Platt of the Medical Research Council's Psychiatric Unit in Edinburgh, and one against the general tendency: 'the rates for all other age groups are going down or holding steady.'[10] And behind every statistic is a young man lost. After telling his father in 1990 that he was upset that electrified rail lines killed badgers, John Shotter, aged nineteen, of Eastleigh in Hampshire, threw himself under a train on the line.

Masculinity, it seems, has never been more fragile, even as it has never been more demanding, more potent, more exorbitant. 'It is both bizarre and sad that we gain sustenance from something so hated and feared,' muses Normandy veteran Nelson Bryant, recalling the horrors of combat and his nightmare memories of 'screaming men'.[11] On this and every other piece of evidence available today, 'masculinity', manhood, machismo, is a luxury we can no longer afford. No civilization worthy of that name allows its citizens to go on killing and maiming one another: no society which values its individual members can permit its males to go on damaging and killing themselves. Since World War II, millions of men lucky enough to have escaped that holocaust have deformed or sacrificed their own lives and those of others in pursuit of their own myth of maleness. In the wider sphere, every crisis of aggression in the private world of personal emotion finds its counterpart on the global scale: as if longing for World War III, the males of country after country translate local hostility into a nationalist pride, and as a consequence the wars of Ireland, Iran, Israel, Beirut, Cambodia, Sri Lanka and Afghanistan grind on, men killing, men dying, *ad infinitum*.

To despairing observer and wretched participant alike, civil and international wars have never seemed so bitter, so long-drawn-out, so intransigent as those marking the dying throes of this most aggressive of centuries. In our era, where men have never worked harder to impose and maintain their power, whether personal, political, military or sexual, never before has it all seemed so complex, so impossible, so out of reach. This realization, however, simply stimulates efforts of greater violence, the escalation of hostilities. 'Men say they fight for a cause,' observes Philip Hodson, 'but that cause is their own identity, an external source of power which they cannot find in themselves. The wars of virility are without end, since those who learn nothing from history's errors are doomed to repeat them in a cycle of tragedy and farce.'[12]

To explain violence is to explain the male. The reverse is also true, and of far more vital social application. Women may now rule countries at war, or under threat of it, like Golda Meir of Israel, or India's Indira Gandhi: they may go to war (if the episode deserves that name) as Mrs Thatcher did in the Falklands. Women may be capable of great cruelty, even of a reign of terror and institutionalized torture, like that of 'Bloody Mary' Tudor, Queen Mary I of England, during whose short rule (1553–58) more than 300 Protestants were burned at the stake for their refusal to return to the Roman Catholic faith. But women in general do not fight in schoolyards, at football matches or on battlefields. They do not seek out others to beat down and kill: they do not impose their sexual will, heedless of consequence, through force or fear. If there is to be any hope of turning today's tide, we need to understand what goes to make these endless 'wars of virility', the terrible tyranny of the penis. What is the drive, the sexual hunger, the identity crisis, the male passion for power? Passion, inevitably, demands a victim: a hundred thousand, a thousand thousand future victims could be saved if their aggressors could be saved too, before the act of violence which will unite them in one of today's everyday clichés, the blood wedding. By one of the savage ironies in which the twentieth century abounds, Rosa Schulman escaped from Nazi persecution in 1938 only to die half a century later in London at the age of 83, after a hideous rape and battering. Her murderer, James Gillighan, proved to have been in and out of penal and mental institutions all his life. 'Crime must be controlled if the quality of life we all seek is to be attained,' argues William S. Sessions, Director of the US Department of Justice: 'To be controlled, crime must be *understood*.'[13]

If we understood what goes on in the making of the male, could we hope to grasp what is breaking down now in the conventional blueprint for modern masculinity? Could this knowledge shine a light into that dark place where manhood, sex and violence feed into one another, grow, stir, and finally flower in today's hideous outbursts of blood and death? Could it provide the insight so desperately needed into those other contemporary killers, coronary heart disease and ulcers, infidelity and fraud, mass murder, racial hatred and genocide? Into Star Wars, crack, Tiananmen Square?

And into the heart, mind, loves, lusts and real needs of the average normal male?

'He just seemed like any other ordinary regular guy,' said a neighbour of John Wayne Gacy, who planned and executed the serial killings of 33 boys and men in North America over a three-year period in the 1970s.

How does a man get to be an ordinary regular guy?

Where does it all begin?

I SONGS OF INNOCENCE

In every man there lurks an
indestructible kernel of darkness from the
moment of his birth.
Simone de Beauvoir

1 The Primal Eden

Femaleness represents the innate tendency of the foetus. The development of maleness is complex and precarious, a continuing struggle against the basic trend to femaleness.
Lawrence Kohlberg

Of the two lots, the women's lot of perpetual motherhood and the man's lot of perpetual babyhood, I prefer the man's.
George Bernard Shaw

In the beginning was the Mother.
Marilyn French

Every human male is born of a successful fight against his biological destiny: yet that very success destines him to a lifelong struggle. For every adult man, no matter how tall, muscular, hirsute, or well-hung, starts life as a little girl, and continues so throughout the crucial early weeks of life. 'On the biological level, it is now known we all begin existence as a female foetus,' explains Andy Metcalf, author of a study of male sexuality: 'to differentiate the foetus as male, something must be added.'[1] That 'something' is the very essence of maleness, testosterone – the male hormone that also renders men vulnerable all their lives to sex-and-stress-related diseases, in addition to the consequences of their own and other men's aggression.

Yet arguably that very aggression is necessary to ensure the survival of the boy child in the first place, since nature has undoubtedly loaded the dice against his sex. At the moment of conception, every girl is designated 'XX', receiving the same chromosome from each parent. Boys by contrast become 'XY', the 'Y' chromosome coming from the father. The 'X' chromosome, many times larger than the 'Y', carries almost all the genetic programming that the organism will ever receive. Men are therefore from birth not only vulnerable to their own sex-related disorders (cancer of the breast or testicles, enlargement of the prostate, impotence and so on), but they are also more susceptible to stress and general diseases than women are, since their 'Y' chromosome can never give them the protection that women automatically receive from their second 'X'.

This added vulnerability can be seen even before birth. For every 100 female embryos, there are around 130 male; but as the male foetus is far more prone to spontaneous abortion and stillbirth than the female, only 106 of those will ever see the light of day as live births. Even then, nature has not finished with the male. As boy babies are, though usually larger, in general far weaker and less developed than girls (the average girl has, at birth, a maturational lead of four to six weeks over the equivalent boy), they are all too susceptible to the threat of neo-natal complications. Finally, then, when the angel of death has made his last circuit of the lying-in hospitals, delivery rooms and nurseries, only 95 boys survive to every 100 girls.[2] In former times, the male survival rate was even lower, and the extra fragility of boys freely acknowledged. In the reign of Henry VIII the royal physicians were delirious with relief that the much-longed-for, one and only male heir Prince Edward had survived the three days and four nights of his mother Jane Seymour's labour. Even in the late nineteenth century, the midwife who delivered Thomas Hardy tossed the puny boy child aside as 'dead past all rearing' till a faint but persistent mewing from the supposed corpse recalled her to her duties.

This furious early fight for life is an echo of the even earlier fight for maleness, when the embryo has to break away from its primal human state as a female and strike out for the uncharted waters of manhood. Many commentators indeed conclude that the added frailty and vulnerability of boys is due to this enforced divergence from 'the basic human form' of the eternal female. 'In the beginning we are all headed towards femaleness,' comments Dr Stephen Wachtel on the results of his work at the Memorial Sloan-Kettering Cancer Center, New York. 'You can think of maleness as a type of birth defect.' It is only achieved, Wachtel stresses, when the embryonic gonads flood the system with the male hormone testosterone, 'sexing' the brain, and stimulating the clitoris and vagina to develop into penis and scrotum respectively.[3]

Every male therefore begins life 'at a biological disadvantage,' says Dr Ann Oakley of the Thomas Coram Research Unit. 'It certainly appears to be the case that many of the male's troubles are due to the fragility of his biological status as an addition to the basic female ground plan.'[4] For as the flood of testosterone bathes the embryo brain and sets off the sprouting of the genitals, things can go wrong. As a consequence of the complexity of the 'breakaway' process, the vast proportion of hermaphrodites, mutants, and chromosomal freaks are genetically male. In addition, since the 'Y' chromosome is so much smaller than the 'X', and carries virtually no genetic information, the

'Y'-determined male is permanently deprived of the hereditary protection against defect and disease conferred on all women. For this reason, over 100 known serious disorders or biological deficiencies occur only or almost wholly in the male, like haemophilia – 'the curse of the Romanovs' – hypertension, colour blindness, or dyslexia; while during the first year of life, one-third more males than females die from the normal infectious diseases of childhood.

Biology is destiny, male supremacists have assured generations of women. Are men therefore compelled from conception to an endless struggle against the poverty of their genetic endowment ('the inadequate "Y"', 'small and twisted . . . a genetic error', 'a deformed and broken "X"', 'the shape of a comma, the merest remnant, a sad-looking affair' of minimal significance in 'organismal development') armed only with their natural aggression, the male hormone? Does the tiny organism at some level recognize that it is fated to be born into 'the biologically least successful and inferior sex', and respond in the only way it can, by fighting back? Does it find, too, its first, inevitable target in what biologists acknowledge to be 'the natural superiority of women'?[5] Is this, from man's very origins, the secret of the 'kernel of darkness' at his heart?

All women become like their mothers. That is their tragedy. No man does. That is his.
  Oscar Wilde

To some commentators, however, the question of biology is no more than a monkey puzzle. There is no need to resort to genetic inferiority to explain the male's much more fragile gender identity and the problem of aggression. In psychology as well as biology, Andy Metcalf observes, 'for human maleness, something must be added', some new break-away from the female must take place: the break with the mother.

Yet why should a boy need to break away from the one who gives him life? The one being, moreover, whose love is synonymous in every culture with unwavering, unconditional devotion: whose own status is tied up in his existence as the crowning achievement of hers? For traditionally, a mother's status is always higher after the birth of a son. Indeed, even before the birth, folk-lore and proverbial wisdom invariably rate an assumed male above a female: if the child *in utero* seems bigger, stronger, more active, or 'carried higher', it must be a boy. In old wives' tales from China to Peru, boys are said to be born more easily, to cry less at birth, even to give their mothers a better complexion during pregnancy. Even today, surveys show that the boy baby is born to overwhelming preference world-wide. The arrival of a male child is generally a signal for rejoicing everywhere, especially if it is the first, while first-time mothers who have had a boy show a greater sense of achievement and suffer markedly less post-natal depression than do the mothers of girls.[6]

For fathers as well as mothers, the birth of a boy has always been a special delight. Athenian vase paintings from as far back as the fifth century BC proudly portray plump male infants, toddlers playing with their mother, and older boys up to seven years of age, always naked, and always full-frontally displayed to the viewer to show off a lovingly-depicted penis. To the Athenian father, comments Professor Eva Keuls, author of *The Reign of the Phallus*, 'only the male child counted, and his genitals constituted his identity'. The male child thus was assured pride of place in his father's heart and household. The value of the male was brutally reinforced by the treatment of the female – as the playwright Poseidippus recorded in the third century BC: 'Sons are always brought up somehow, even in the poorest families: but even a rich man will expose [i.e. abandon to starve to death] a daughter.'[7]

For thousands of years, human society has recognized and reinforced the life-and-death power of the father. In all that time, however, the real control of the child, from the moment of birth, lay with the mother. She has used it with lover-like abandon, shamelessly glorying in her mastery over the 'little other/lover', in ways that most pro-foundly shape the adult male. Close observation of mothers in many different cultures illustrates the startling degree of favouritism and exaltation with which the little male is treated. A boy, it appears, is more willingly breast-fed than a girl, more readily given the breast when he cries, and weaned later, although he will already be bigger and heavier, and might therefore be thought to need less food than a girl, rather than more. Mothers are also more indulgent of their sons' desires and appetites. A boy is allowed to 'attack the breast', observes psychologist Professor Elena Belotti, his 'guzzling' held up for admir-ation, while a girl will have the breast withdrawn in case she becomes 'too greedy'. Boys are almost invariably given more, permitted more, even fed more than girls: at the age of two months, the male child is breast-fed for about forty-five minutes as against twenty-five for a girl, almost twice as long.[8] Nor is this by any means a thing of the past, or confined to the 'less advanced' societies. Journalist Cassandra Jardine, 'a Nineties mother', reports that her 8 lb 5 oz son was dubbed 'a great greedy boy' by the maternity nurses at a London hospital within hours of his birth.

As with food, so with the other delights of the flesh. The boy child is much more readily allowed to go naked, or loosely clad. He is allowed to explore more freely than a girl, play more adventurously, make messes and get dirty. Most important of all, as an infant he will be permitted to play with his genitals, which will be a source of complimentary jesting, pride, and attention in adults, especially the mother. The mother's worship of what Freud termed her 'little phallus' frequently takes the active form of stroking, petting or playing with the child's genitals herself. 'For centuries in different cultures mothers have been known to soothe their baby sons to sleep by stroking and sucking their penises,' says Dr Robert Wilkins, consultant in child and adolescent psychiatry at the Paxton Family and Young Persons' Unit in Reading. This has the effect of harnessing all his restless energy, focusing it on her, and soothing his aggression, irritability or distress.

To Freud, there was nothing unnatural about this. For him mother love was inescapably sexual, violently emotional, and burdened with all the mother's desires and drives as well as her son's awakening needs. Yet in a passage of strange, almost spiritual exaltation Freud appears to justify the sexuality of a mother's relation to her infant son, and gives her permission for a strong and openly erotic attachment:

A child's intercourse with the one responsible for his care affords him an unending source of sexual excitation and satisfaction from his erotogenic zones ... his mother herself regards him with feelings that are derived from her own sexual life. A mother would probably be horrified if she were made aware that all the marks of affection were rousing the child's sexual instinct and preparing for its future intensity ... However, if the mother understood more of the high importance of the part played by the instincts in the mental life as a whole, she would spare herself any self-reproaches, even after her enlightenment. She is only fulfilling her task in teaching the child to love. After all, he is meant to grow up into a strong and capable person with vigorous sexual needs.[9]

From time immemorial, genital stroking and caressing have been widely practised as a means of stilling and soothing not only the restless baby, but also the fractious toddler or boisterous older boy. Under the harem system of the Middle East, where the male child remained with his mother until the age of ten or twelve, it was considered no more than the due of the future man and monarch that he should be so wooed to sleep, to the accompaniment of a reverential lullaby: 'Sleep, little prince, for tomorrow you wake to be king.' More recently, this semi-hypnotic technique of sedation was the open secret of every skilled *ayah* or *amah*, the native 'treasure' on whom the British memsahib relied so heavily for the care of her children in the days of the Raj. In a West still stumbling through the Judaeo-Christian minefield of sexual sin, guilt and repression, this practice has traditionally been either covert, private and unacknowledged, or heavily penalized. The young Scotswoman May Gray, who became nursemaid to Byron in the late eighteenth century when the little lord was eight, was sacked on the spot three years later when it was discovered that at bedtime 'she came to his bed to play tricks with his person'.[10] But even among the frozen wastes of European denial, Freud had no doubt that genital stimulation occurred both widely and naturally, however unconsciously, since the mother 'is only fulfilling her task in teaching the [boy] to love'. In support of Freud, the French psychoanalyst Dr Christiane Olivier describes an episode from the childhood of a patient, 'Thierry':

> From the time he was two until he was twelve, he would cup his hand around his precious 'thing' to protect it. Against whom or what? Had he any idea? . . . And then there was the trick question asked one day by an uncle who knew a bit about psychology: 'Come on, now: if you're all that afraid they're going to take it away from you, who does it belong to? I thought it was yours?' And up piped Thierry, to the astonishment of everybody, including his mother: *'It's Mummy's.'*[11]

So stroked, so possessed, so adored, is it any wonder that from the moment the dawn of consciousness breaks over his mental horizon, the boy child sees himself as the sun around which all else will revolve? So centralized, so favouritized, so preferred by his mother even to the child of her own sex, his sister, he grows up empowered in a way so natural, so inevitable to him that he never questions how he came by it – indeed he imbibed it with his mother's milk.

And as her mothering has been active, for she is a sexually experienced woman with her own desires and needs and not merely a milch cow, she has centred the source and site of his special power and status in his penis. From his earliest days, the male child learns that his most exquisite and reliable sensations come from this organ. The honouring and pleasuring of the penis, however originally unsought, will always thereafter be intensely desired, as of right expected, and in its absence insistently, inevitably demanded.

Some men talk openly of their memories or fantasies of this primal Eden, when bliss came unbidden and female devotion lapped them in love from one day's end to the next. Miles Johnson, a 33-year-old architect: 'My first memory? A feeling of unbelievable sweetness. I seem to be bathed in light and sweetness, I'm warm and secure and I seem to be the most important thing on earth.' Darren, the ten-year-old son of a Warwickshire farm labourer, has his own version of this, and his own explanation for it. 'We all start as angels, see? Little babies, they come straight from heaven, and you feel like that. Then it goes, and you get, like, ordinary. And it never comes back.'

At the age of 89, 'just an old soldier now, my dear, living on my memories', Brigadier James Faulder has nothing to explain and nothing to hide:

> It was one's nanny of course, in those days a mother never cared for her children, not physically. I can remember Nanny Phillips to this day (Mother always called her 'Phillips', of course, but I called her 'Nanny'), she used to say, 'Bath-time, Master James,' that was always on the dot of six. Then it would be 'Bed-time, Master James,' and I'd say my prayers, have a story from *The Boys' Companion*, dreadful rubbish about boys doing great deeds and so forth, but I loved them. Then it would be 'Very well, Master James, time to put Peter to bed now.' And I would snuggle down in my cot and close my eyes, and she would put out the side-light and slip her hand between the bedclothes and under my night shirt, and stroke me till I went to sleep.

'It was glorious, quite glorious!' concludes the old man. 'Far too damn good for a young boy! These days of course, she'd probably get arrested for it. But it all seemed all right at the time, perfectly natural in fact.'

Danny, aged four, asked by his teacher why he kept rubbing his penis, replied, 'I don't like it when it goes to sleep.' In awakening a boy's penis, the mother or mother figure does not merely awaken the male sense of self, but *locates* it, ensuring that for the rest of his life his penis incorporates his essence and identity: that he *is* his penis. The adored boy-child, worshipped through his sex, is thereby set on the age-old path of phallocentricity, to live a life dictated by the demands of the penis, an existence in which the flaccid, five-inch appendage comes to act as the determinant, barometer and expressive vehicle of all his moods, fears, desires and drives.

Here lies the origin of the reign of the phallus, and also of its deadly tyranny. If the gratification, the empowering of his male sexuality arises without his seeking it, without effort, what man will ever truly feel he should defer his pleasure, bow to another's needs, put someone else unquestioningly before himself? 'Remember that all men would be tyrants if they could,' wrote Abigail Adams in her celebrated plea for women's rights in America. 'I desire you would remember the ladies.'[12] Yet any man who grows up to be such a tyrant may only have the first of his 'ladies' to blame, his all-doting, all-giving, all-forgiving mother.

> The power of men is first a metaphysical assertion of self, an *I am* that exists *a priori*, absolute, no embellishment or apology required, indifferent to denial or challenge . . . This self cannot be eradicated or reduced to nothing. It *is* . . . Male self is entitled to take what it wants to sustain or improve itself, to have anything, to requite any need at any cost . . . This self is the conviction, beyond reason or scrutiny, that there is an equation between what one wants and what one is.
> Andrea Dworkin

But the good mother, as every schoolboy knows, is only half the story. Her love is wonderful, creating a universe in which he is the sun, the moon and the morning star. In the country of her heart she makes him king, and in her assurance lies his power. But then, like every medieval monarch, he has to reckon with the power of the kingmaker. And in that day of reckoning, which may take up a year, a decade, a lifetime, lies the gap between his infant phallic paradise and his brutal adult reality.

For at its best, the mother's love is a continuous reminder of everything the boy must forget if he is ever to be a man, the time of smallness, weakness, and terrifying dependency. 'My hands made your legs what they are,' boast Maori mothers in a traditional chant, referring to the age-old practice of alternately binding their sons' legs to make them 'as stiff as a poker', then releasing them for exercise, display and 'sensuous massage'.[13] This procedure could stand as a central symbol of the essence of motherhood's message: 'Be a man, my son, be a warrior, be strong – but when *I* am ready, not you – and *not yet*.' As Christiane Olivier observes, 'This is the start of the longest but least obvious of the wars against female desire; the place where the boy joins battle in the Oedipal war of the sexes. Against his own mother.'[14]

For the classic Freudian formula makes the little boy not the beneficiary of mother-love, but the prime victim of his mother's 'vigorous sexual needs':

The essence of the female dream is the 'little other' – and the essence of this little other is the phallus. Women become mothers in order to make good their *Penisneid* [penis envy], and the desire of mothers is to go on being mothers ... For women, all other substitutes pale in comparison with the equation 'penis = child'.[15]

Dr Estela V. Welldon, consultant psychotherapist and author of *Mother, Madonna, Whore*, stresses the child's helplessness in the face of this love: 'It is an emotional, physical, social and political *power*. And the mother uses the child's dependency in order to *gain* power or revenge. They can seduce, then neglect the child, one minute gratifying its need, then dropping it.' As a radical psychiatrist, Welldon locates the source of the mother's power less in what she does than in what she is, or rather *has*: 'The uterus has as much power as the penis, but it is an engulfing, smothering power. Thus nurturing is its only form of dominance: it is the way in which the victim turns predator.' The mother's revenge on her son, Welldon suggests, has never been acknowledged, therefore never understood: 'There was such an interest in Oedipus' problems he got a complex named after him, while his mother Jocasta was forgotten!'

'In the beginning,' writes Marilyn French, 'was the Mother.' From the beginning, then, come the boy child's castration fears, his existential terrors and the rage to retaliate, the compulsion not merely to strike back, but to strike *first*. For mothers are too powerful to the tiny helpless boy. His awareness of this begins somewhere between the ages of two and three, and signals the end of the child's 'angel infancy' of unselfconscious bliss. Up to the age of three, boys, like girls, are mother-focused, strongly bonded, and, even more than girls, 'incredibly dependent', comments psychologist Connell Cowan. But while girls can retain and strengthen the bonds with the mother, boys are compelled to separate from all they know and love best, and strike out in pursuit of the remote, intimidating father figure with whom, according to one piece of US research, they may until now have spent as little as twelve minutes a day.[16]

Splitting from the mother, whose 'hands made his legs', her body his body, her mind his mind, is for the boy fraught with stress, pain and loss. The drive towards independence propels him forward, while a powerful hunger for the old warmth coupled with a panic fear of the new dispensation holds him back. To cling to the mother creates anxieties about weakness, engulfment, masculinity itself. To abandon her brings on a terror of that abandonment, of being isolated, unloved and alone. It is the hardest, longest fight of the male's life, a struggle within himself, against himself, in which victory can only be won by defeat.

And he has a powerful, the most powerful, adversary – his mother. How many women freely set their sons free? How many even think of it? How many understand how early it must begin? Perhaps they do: the mother of Ernest Hemingway kept him in ringlets, bloomers, and girls' dresses long after the age of three. As late as puberty, Christiane Olivier records 'mothers who urge their sons to pull out their first facial hairs, the token of the onset of male adulthood'. The violent refusal to respect a son's body or his right to autonomy may even take a far darker form. Michele Elliott, director of the charity Kidscape which campaigns for the safety of children, has documentary evidence of what is incontrovertibly sexual abuse of children, male and female, by their mothers. Such a mother, Olivier argues, will fight to continue her son's dependence and infancy, at whatever cost to him or to herself. The fight indeed becomes her key way of prolonging and intensifying his attachment to her:

> Is it not on account of this desire of the mother's that the boy stays 'little' so much longer than the girl of the same age? Here we see the outward signs of the difficulty in growing up that is experienced by the boy pinioned in the maternal love-trap. Is it not the boy who wets the bed, who soils himself, who in a word, refuses to grow up?

'At this stage in the life of the human being,' Olivier notes, 'we [psychotherapists] see three times as many boys as girls':

> No doubt about it: the anal battle is boys' business – opposition is men's business . . . The boy feels in danger of being sucked back in by the mother and her desire . . . He thinks she is after his sex as well as his excreta. He believes she wants to get it away from him, cut it off, steal his strength . . . panic sets in . . . in the anal stage, the boy plays war. He takes his soldiers out, he invents enemies, he threatens, he kills: he is at war with his mother.[17]

Many men look back from adulthood with painful memories of the destructive power of the mother's love. 'One of the wrongs suffered by boys,' reflected the American writer Lincoln Steffens in his autobiography, 'is that of being *loved* before *loving*. They receive so early and so freely the affection and devotion of their mothers that they do not learn to love; and so when they grow up and become lovers and husbands, they avenge themselves upon their wives and sweethearts.' As an internationally-famous writer and Nobel Prize winner, André Gide similarly found himself in his autobiography struggling to come to terms with his mother's love:

> She had a way of loving me that sometimes almost made me hate her and touched my nerves on the raw . . . she was solely actuated by a desire to protect me from myself, to keep me in leading reins . . . I assisted her in her last moments and when at last her heart ceased to beat, I felt myself sink into an overwhelming abyss of love, sorrow and *liberty*.

The perverse mother, then, is with us and among us far more than we care (or dare) to admit. Naturally enough, she does not admit her perversity, even to herself. When Baudelaire, the legendary *poète maudit* and self-elected 'Imp of the Perverse', collapsed at the age of 45 with tertiary syphilis, his mother made no effort to conceal her triumphant maternalism. 'I shall keep him *like a little child*,' she declared with satisfaction in a phrase eerily foreshadowing Ibsen's later treatment of the same theme in *Ghosts* (1881). It was her finest hour, and it ran and ran. Paralysed, speechless, ravaged by a creeping decay of the cerebellum, Baudelaire endured 'a living death' for seventeen months, as his biographer Claude Pichois records, while still fully conscious of his plight: 'Whenever you looked his way, you found his eyes, intelligent and attentive though darkened by an expression of infinite grief, which those who glimpsed it will never forget.'[18]

Everyone talks about Mummy on the couch.
Christiane Olivier, *Jocasta's Children* (1989)

Win or lose, a man will carry the scars of this battle for life. 'Most if not all the men I meet exhibit some fear of closeness or intimacy with women,' says psychotherapist Tom Ryan. 'But the fear and the wish exist simultaneously. All men who fear women are obsessed with concerns about masculinity. A man's sense of his maleness is always less secure than a woman's experience of her femininity.' The quest for manhood, then, is determined from infancy as an oscillation between these two poles. The endless jar between the lust for freedom and the lust for intimacy form the inveterate yin and yang of the adult male. 'I can't hold it,' confesses John Beavour Halkin, a 33-year-old construction worker from Dallas, Texas, and the veteran/victim of four divorces: 'Sometimes I gotta get out, get on the road, get me some wide open spaces, I need it real bad. Then the first pair of juicy tits I see, I just wanna sink myself in there and never come up to the surface. I can't stay married. I dunno what's wrong with me. I guess I'll grow out of it.' He laughs. But he knows he won't.

These wars of the penis are without end when the battle-scarred warrior is doomed to seek revenge on every new woman for the old injuries inflicted by his mother. In this context the Primal Drama is not 'What Daddy Did' but 'What Baby Wants To Do', that is, both to feed off and to kill the woman, the mother, and to do both at the same time. For Mother can never be forgiven for forcing the boy to renounce his original state of god-like supremacy, his infant bliss; nor for plunging him into the fears and anxieties attendant upon this separation, including the fear that he will never successfully accomplish it; nor for then doing her best to ensure that the separation fails. Countries on opposite sides of the world have a word for it: in Latin South America *mamismo* (the opposite of *machismo*), in Japan *masacon*, 'the mother complex'.

Japanese males may now choose from a number of educational courses devised to combat *masacon*. In serried rows, with ferocious intensity, they absorb lectures on how to extricate oneself with maximum courtesy from the obligation to return to your mother's house each day to eat her food, how to allow your wife to wash your shirts instead of taking them home to mother, how to take a decision without consulting mother first and having to obey her diktat. Against those who are consciously seeking the newer, westernized style of relationship, however, many thousands more are choosing to live with the old ways. Yet East or West, the strains, the demands, the anger will break out, often with terrible results. The mother of the Black Power activist Michael de Freitas ('Michael X') deliberately seduced a white man, a Portuguese trader, to ensure for her son the lightest possible skin. As he grew up, her constant refrain was 'I trouble-trouble to give you good colour, and this what you do to me!' As a boy Michael christened his mother 'Devil Lady', and swore that 'white man-chile make she too big for she boots'. To the neighbours it was obvious 'that one-chile [only child and therefore ill-omened] some day goan kill his mother'. In the event Michael X organized the butchery and burying alive of another woman, who, coincidentally or not, was white.[19]

Sexual murder, perversion and violence constitute the acts of revenge, real or fantasized, that reassure the desperate man-child that he is powerful in himself and therefore safe from invasion, engulfment and attack: that his ever-fragile masculinity is intact. Yet in the endless and self-renewing parabola of his emotional life, as he swings between the twin poles of his compulsion, to be free of woman and to be at one with her, the 'normal' male also stands perpetually condemned to confuse the intense childhood experience of the mother with his desire for other women. Every time he feels attracted to a woman, therefore, even as an adult man, the furious, frightened two-year-old still flourishing vigorously in some dark corner of his psyche begins to scream and cry. 'Man, possessive or what?' demanded a black London DJ of his girlfriend. 'I can't get it on with a chick who's after my dick.' The same message may be heard again and again, even in the cultured accents of Oxbridge or Harvard. 'She made me fall in love with her,' said a rich and successful New York lawyer. 'I wanted to have her – then I wanted to kill the cunt.' This deep psychic confusion is nowhere more evident than in the case of John Edward Farrers, prosecuted at London's Old Bailey in 1988 for the rape of his step-daughter aged eleven, who later gave birth to his child. Farrers, convicted and sentenced to seven and a half years' imprisonment, was said by the defence to have raped the child every time he became angry with his wife. After each occurrence he instructed her, 'Don't tell Mum – we don't want to spoil the happiness of the family.'

'I love thee that I can come into thee,' announces the noble savage of D. H. Lawrence's sexual fantasy, the gamekeeper Mellors, to Lady Chatterley. In the same vein he describes his love-making with his wife:

> She'd sort of tear at me down there, as if it was a beak tearing at me. By God, you'd think a woman's soft down there, like a fig. But I tell you, the old rampers have beaks between their legs, and they tear at you with it till you're sick. Self! Self! Self! all self! They talk about men's selfishness, but I doubt if it can ever touch a woman's blind beakishness, once she's gone that way. Like an old trull![20]

Only this rage, fusing 'woman' with 'mother', empowers the terrified child against the all-powerful female. 'Men have to get away from the mother, then they spend all their lives trying to get back!' comments psychotherapist Adam Jukes. Infant rage comes into play to fuel the break with the mother; but 'the severity of the ego-splitting can be very acute: the process leaves deep fissures in the ego-structure.' Rage then becomes, by some manic connection, the answer to its own problem:

'omnipotent rage is better than to be helpless, terrified and in fear of annihilation.'

The rage to control the uncontrollable (i.e. the female) carries on through life. Denied his own stable core identity, the male is driven to seek stability and impose his autonomy as a way of resolving his ambivalence and the anxiety it engenders, as Dorothy Dinnerstein explains: 'To possess a woman (more precisely, to possess a creature of the kind who later turns out to belong to the category "woman") is every child's dearest wish. When the adult male finds the adult female body ready to respond to him, it reawakens the joy of childhood and the life-giving delight of infancy.' Any check to the female's all-availability evokes 'unbearable childhood anguish':

> The mother-raised woman carries *within herself* the source of the early magical female richness. The male knows that it is always outside him, can get away from him, and therefore to be sure of reliable access to that source, he *must* have exclusive possession of and dominance over a woman.[21]

Adult male sexual possession rests then on the twin pillars of compulsion: first the original, monolithic desire for the ownership of 'the creature called woman', and second, the sense that attachment to a woman is only emotionally bearable, and consistent with maleness and male solidarity, if both she and the feelings she provokes remain under strict, safe control. Rage is invaluable again here to keep woman/mother/lover at bay: she can so easily evoke the unqualified boundless, helpless passion of infancy, insists Dinnerstein: 'she can bring out the soft, wild, naked baby in him.' Quite unavoidably then, adult male heterosexuality will contain strong elements of terror and anger, fantasies of role reversal and revenge against women, and a blanket urge to punish someone, *anyone*, for what mother has done. Stephen Jackson, sentenced in 1987 to three years' youth custody for violent assault, told the jury at his trial in Manchester that his mother had given all her attention to her boyfriend, and left him to 'fight his own battles'. Later, when the first girl he fell in love with left him, he said, 'I decided to get my own back. I pushed her down the stairs and she broke an arm and a leg, and I was pleased about that.' 'I had unspeakable delight in strangling women,' remarked the Italian mass murderer Vincent Verzeni, arrested in 1873, 'experiencing during the act erections and real sexual pleasure, much greater than I experienced while masturbating.' Before his arrest, Verzeni had been a model husband and father, and in particular, quite devoted to his mother.[22]

How much longer will we go on putting up with a situation where men pay us back what they owe to Mother?

    Christiane Olivier

2 The Dawn Chorus

I always have one golden rule for such occasions – I ask myself what Nanny would have expected me to do.

Lord Carrington, former British Foreign Secretary, explaining in January 1983 why he resigned at the time of the Falklands conflict

I do as my father did, and his father before him, and the father of his father, and the first father of our people, who was God. He told us how to live, and his way is right.

Efé proverb of Upper Zaire

Boys will be boys.

World-wide proverb

'She was so deeply embedded in my consciousness that for the first year of school I seem to have believed that each of my teachers was my mother in disguise,' writes the tormented narrator of Philip Roth's novel *Portnoy's Complaint*. 'Of course when she asked me to tell her all about my day at kindergarten, I did so scrupulously. I didn't pretend to understand all the implications of her ubiquity, but that it had to do with finding out the kind of little boy I was when I thought she wasn't around – that was indisputable.'[1] All mothers have, and most retain, this capacity for burying themselves in the depths of their child's psyche, popping up as if by witchcraft when least expected or desired. With her total, indeed to the child quasi-magical powers, the mother has to be deemed the chief architect of the new-born infant's expanding world. But she is by no means the sole ruler of his universe, nor the only labourer in his vineyard. Other voices whisper in his ear, and of these the loudest whisper will always be male. Traditionally the father took little interest in the early years of his infant son. Apart from the unavoidable duty of attendance at the conception, his paternal obligations were largely confined to the ceremonial junketings held to celebrate the birth, and it is only very recently that fathers, in the West at least, have sought to break this pattern of non-involvement. But as the boy grows, so grows too the power of the father, in addition to his sense of responsibility for the man that the boy must become.

At first, though, to the child leaving the breast, this is still very much a world of women. And within it, as countless historical memories and anecdotes make clear, the mother-substitute, nurse or nanny wields a power over the child second only to that of the figure for whom she is deputizing, the mother herself. A loving care-taker will be remembered devotedly throughout her life and beyond. In 1776, as a man of nearly 40, King George III broke off from the pressing anxiety of his rebellious American colonies and his deteriorating mental state to write in his own hand to Lord Bristol, the Master of the Royal Household:

> I have learned that my Laundress Mary Smith died on Monday. She suckled me, and to her great attention my having been reared is *greatly owing*; this ought to make me anxious for the welfare of her children, who by her great imprudence are left destitute of support. I therefore desire you will appoint her youngest daughter Augusta Hicks to succeed her as Laundress.[2]

Similarly in the following century, during the wretched misery of his years at Harrow, Winston Churchill was sustained far more by the letters and visits of his beloved 'Nanny Everest' than by those of his beautiful, brittle mother, Lady Randolph. Everest's death, many years later, not only precipitated one of Churchill's legendary 'Black Dog' depressions, but caused him at the height of his Liberal career as President of the Board of Trade to throw his weight behind 'a structure of pensions and insurance' designed to support 'poor old women'.[3]

Like the mother, however, the mother-substitute has the power to restrain as well as sustain, to deny as well as to reward. 'I have a clear memory of immense irritation with my swaddling clothes,' says Auberon Waugh, 'of fighting to be free, of trying to get out.' And nanny-power was capable of much darker manifestations than this: among a number of troubling tales, Jonathan Gathorne-Hardy, author of *The Rise and Fall of the British Nanny*, cites the example of the nannies who would hold their charges face down over the nursery gas ring, giving them regular doses of potentially brain-damaging coal gas, in order to ensure that the children were drowsy and dimpled with smiles for their mother's arrival at the six o'clock bedside.

Nor are these horrors all a thing of the past. An up-to-date review of all the major studies on child abuse reported in *The Independent* on 23 May 1990 found that in a quarter of all cases involving the abuse of boys, a mother or mother-substitute was responsible. *Independent* journalist Peter Jackson writes bitterly of the nanny who abused his four-year-old son in 1989:

Soon after Beatrix had left our employment as a nanny, we discovered that she had been playing with our son Tom's genitals at bath-time, and poking her finger up his rectum . . . Today, after some episodes of marked 'anti-social behaviour' (which involved stealing and lying), and following consultations with child psychiatrists, Tom seems to be responding well to intensive psychotherapy, and the outlook is good. But his experience seems to have tangled up a normal child's developing notions of truth and lying, right and wrong, trust and betrayal, pleasure and self-control, privacy and open-ness, love and manipulation.[4]

As Jackson honestly records, the nanny had 'an excellent rapport' with the child. She was also 'punctilious about his safety and welfare, and . . . never did or said anything unkind'. Tom himself was 'very fond of her'. The genital activity only came to light when Tom of his own accord asked Beatrix's successor to perform the same actions for him. As soon as he realized that his request had got Beatrix into trouble, Tom changed his story and said he had made it up, poignantly demonstrating the confusion between 'truth and lying, right and wrong', which his father feels to be the most damaging aspect of the case. Beatrix left, to continue, Jackson is sure, working as a nanny. Some mother, somewhere, must be finding her a treasure.

He was the one with the power, the money, the right to read the paper through dinner as my stepmother and I watched him in silence; he was the one with the thirty tailor-made suits, the twenty gleaming pairs of shoes and the starched white dress shirts, the ties from Countess Mara and the two Cadillacs that waited for him in the garage, dripping oil on the concrete in the shape of a black Saturn and its gray blur of moons. It was his power that stupefied me and made me regard my knowledge as nothing more than hired cleverness he might choose to show off at a dinner party ('Ask this young fellow, he reads, he'll know') . . .

My sister was his true son. She could ride a horse and swim a mile and she was as capable of sustained rages as he . . . 'I don't think you should talk about your mother that way, young fellow, she's a fine woman.'

'But, Daddy,' I exclaimed, my voice breaking and

rising up, up the scale into a soprano delirium, 'I *love* my mother.'

'Like. Like,' he said. 'A man likes things. *Girls* love, men *like* . . .'

Edmund White,
A Boy's Own Story (1982)

Even the most noxious of nannies can hardly compete with the power of the paterfamilias rampant, again more likely to be exerted over boys than girls. The dim, distant or absentee father casts a long enough shadow: Jackson Pollock based his life's work on trying to reproduce in paint the patterns made by his long-lost father urinating on stone. In full cry, the domineering father is a beast to be avoided at all costs, since the child's lack of size and strength renders any contest unthinkable. In the world history of brutal, violent fathers, Hermann Kafka was not the worst. But his impact on his son's life was total, and totally destructive. Aggressive, domineering, and determined to make a man of his only surviving son, he tried to teach him how to march, to salute, and to bellow out military songs, with the encouragement of shouted orders, hand-clapping, harsh mimicry and derisive laughter which had a cataclysmic effect on the timid, sensitive boy. At table he would scream at Kafka to learn manners, while himself scraping out his nails, cleaning his ears with a toothpick or picking his nose. The culminating trauma of this brutalizing emergence from infancy occurred in Kafka's fourth year. One night, enraged by the little boy whimpering for water, Kafka *père* burst into the bedroom, plucked him from his bed, and threw him outside on to a balcony where he remained all night.

The effect of this dreadful night, Kafka confessed, never left him: 'Years later I still suffered from the tormenting fantasy that the gigantic man, my father, the supreme authority, could come at night, almost without any grounds, and carry me from my bed to the balcony, and that I was therefore, for him, a complete non-entity.' For Kafka himself, too, the deep fear that he was in essence a non-person was never to be shaken off. 'Everybody made me feel afraid,' he later wrote to a friend, 'afraid of looking-glasses because they reflected an ugliness that seemed inescapable.' From his early teens, he played with ideas of death, nicknaming the street where he lived, 'Suicide Approach'. 'I thought myself pathetic,' he conveyed to his father many years later, 'not only to you, but to the whole world, since for me you were the measure of all things.' Even then, however, as a 36-year-old man, whose memory of the child he had been could still rack him with tears, nightmares and shivering fits, Kafka pulled back from the final indictment of his father's cruelty with an uneasy blend of self-accusation and savage self-irony: 'I'm not going to say I am what I am [i.e. a failure] because of you, but I'm inclined to this exaggeration.'[5]

The shipwreck of Kafka's confidence, as he recorded with clinical precision, had been achieved by the time he was five. It seems almost impossible to overestimate the effect of a boy's earliest experiences, whether consciously recalled or not. Certainly many men recount vivid memories from the time before conscious awareness or recall is supposed to come into operation. Even in his debauched and diseased old age, George Augustus Frederick Hanover, Britain's most notorious Prince of Wales, could remember being presented at the font by his godfather, the Duke of Cumberland (less fondly remembered in Scotland as 'Stinking Billie', the 'Butcher of Culloden'): 'He took me in his arms, an old man dressed in a snuff-coloured suit of clothes down to his knees, and placed me on his knee, where he held me a long time. The enormity of his bulk excited my wonder.'[6] Even more remarkably, Thomas Hardy could recall, so he liked to say, his fraught and well-nigh fatal entry into the world: in the third of the 'In Tenebris' poems he poignantly pictures himself tucked up in his crib in the chimney-corner of the family cottage, 'the smallest and weakest of the folk there, / Weak from my baptism of pain.' Hardy's memoir of his acute infant sensibility contrasts strongly with the family version of affairs: possibly weak from her own baptism of pain, Hardy's mother, Jemima, found her new-born son no better than a 'vegetable', and weeks were to pass before she reconsidered her opinion that she had given birth to a congenital idiot.[7]

'I remember, I remember,' wrote the Victorian poet Thomas Hood:

> The house where I was born,
> The little window where the sun
> Came peeping in at dawn.

Although not all as precocious as the preternaturally gifted Hardy, many men have clear memories of events from very early in their lives. These may be trivial or fleeting: the family dog, a treasured toy, a morsel of cake dunked in tea:

> No sooner had the warm liquid and the crumbs with it, touched my palate than a shudder ran through my whole body. An exquisite pleasure invaded my senses . . . Whence could it have come to me, this all-powerful joy? The taste was that of the little crumb of *madeleine* that on Sunday mornings at Combray my Aunt Leonie used to give me, dipping it first into her cup of real or lime-flower tea.[8]

Proust was not alone in his elephantine power of recall. Inevitably too, any man's remembrance of things past is sharpened by the experience of excitement, frustration, fear or pain. 'My first memory?' says Auberon Waugh, distinguished editor of the *Literary Review*: 'A first memory of violence, being circumcised at the age of three. There were good medical reasons for it, of course. Nevertheless, I remember it vividly – it was very unpleasant!'

I am prepared to fulfil the divine commandment of Ritual Circumcision. Presently my son will be brought into the Covenant of Abraham as it is written in the Torah: 'At eight days shall every male be circumcised unto you for your generations . . . It shall be a token of the covenant between Me and you.'

I appoint the Mohel, here present, to act in my behalf and perform this Ritual. I pray to God that our son will be a pride to his mother and myself, that we may raise him to be learned and righteous and that we may share with him in the fulfilment of his life.

Prayer of Rabbi Chaim Yosef Dovid Asulai

Of all the rites of man, the *bris*, non-medical circumcision, the ritual mutilation of the penis, is one of the most ancient and inexplicable. In Genesis chapter 17, God imposes it upon all the tribe of Abraham, including the 99-year-old patriarch himself, as an exclusive 'token of the covenant' between the Lord God of Israel and his Chosen People the Jews. The ritual, however, antedates even the Ancient of Days: it was widely practised from the dawn of time by the early Egyptians, their Arab neighbours, the Aztecs, the Bantu, the Australian Aboriginals, and various Indonesian peoples including those of Papua, New Guinea. How did it come about, this extraordinary ceremony which both centralizes and celebrates the boy's penis as his badge of manhood and entry to the tribe, while simultaneously reducing it to a bleeding stump? And how does it continue in the modern world? *'Why are we doing this?'* liberal Jewish fathers agonize, before going ahead and fixing up the *bris* as their fathers and grandfathers did before them. Actor Tom Conti takes a jaundiced view of such masculine traditions: 'Men can be such stupid creatures at times.'

To Conti, however, little boys are at the mercy of adults from all sides of the family:

> They are taught that it's manly to be aggressive. They are taught to be competitive at an early age by stupid grandparents who say: 'See if you can run to the end of the room before Johnny.' Seeing little children at each other's throats is the beginning of the end of civilization.

Nor is the threat confined to the senior generation: the power of an older brother can easily equal, if not exceed, that of any parent. Actor Simon Williams recalls the enormous reverence he felt for his older brother, the poet and writer Hugo: 'He was the enchanted, first-born, golden boy. I was overweight and ridiculously short-sighted in my pink National Health glasses, just beaming away. He was God as far as I was concerned and still is. I longed to go to bed at the same time as him. I longed to inherit his trousers, his bicycle, his records.' Hugo too has the clearest memories of this time: 'He was my slave for a year. I've never quite got over it.'⁹ 'Brotherhood' has always represented the highest ideal of relations between men, from Henry V and Agincourt ('We few – we happy few – we band of brothers') to the *Blutbrüderschaft* of the Austrian duelling clubs and Prussian *Junkers*, with their dark fantasies of racial purity and homoerotic dominance. In reality, brothers have unlimited opportunities for degrading and persecuting their younger siblings, and rarely scruple to press home a physical or psychological advantage. In his only half-humorous 'autobiography in fables', *Fredi and Shirl and the Kids*, the American writer Richard M. Ellmann describes an early memory of being suspended out of the window of his family's sixth-floor apartment by 'big brother Bennet':

> Bennet says, IF YOU TELL ANYTHING TO THE FOLKS
> RICHARD I SWEAR I'LL DROP YOU . . .
> CRYBABY RICHARD THE CISSY . . .
> RAT . . .
> LOUSE . . .
> NOSEPICKER
> PRICK
> FUCK YOU I'LL DROP YOU . . .
> I'LL TELL . . .
> NOT IF I DROP YOU. COME ON RICHARD, BE A SPORT . . .
> Everyone likes a good sport.¹⁰

Struggling to establish a separate identity; jostling for dominance; fighting for control, for survival even (Cain and Abel, Jacob and Esau);

it is extraordinary how early the themes of adult life begin to sound among the random notes of boyhood. But then, by the age of four, as Dr John Nicholson points out, the average US male child has watched 3000 hours of television. In Britain, pre-school boy children of the lower socio-economic groupings regularly watch television for an average of 25 hours a week. Their imaginative life accordingly is fed by a two-dimensional fantasy world in which heroes outnumber heroines by three to one, in which women rarely appear except in service roles, and where men are shown as strong, authoritative and in control, always taking charge, always rising to the occasion and proving themselves to be tough, self-sufficient and above all aggressive. The leader of the A-Team may 'love it when a plan comes together'. It never does so in the programme, however, as numerous researchers and parents have remarked, without extensive and protracted violence. In this and a host of similar television productions, violence (as instigated by the bad guys) may be the *problem*: it is also, always (in the hands of the good guys), the only, invariable, *solution*. 'As long as I could remember, I could hardly bear it that I wasn't Superman,' says George Buchanan, a lecturer at Edinburgh University. 'I was longing to be old enough to just blow anyone to kingdom come with my mighty punch. For years I went to sleep every night and dreamed I'd wake up *as him*, huge and powerful, a weapon of destruction!'

As this suggests, from his earliest childhood the young boy weaves a fabric of memories, fantasies, hopes and self-definitions which, as much as the intervention of either mother or father, may help to shape his future and determine his course of action. Rupert Everett dates his decision to become an actor from the day when he was taken to see *Mary Poppins*. 'I was five at the time,' he recalls, 'and after the show was over, I went home totally convinced I was Julie Andrews' son instead of my parents'. I went into a complete fantasy for years about this. From the moment I started fantasizing about Julie Andrews and me, I was always dreaming about being somebody else. As far as I'm concerned, first you have to be a fantasist, then you can channel all that into being an actor.' In a more epic vein, as the son of a Warsaw ghetto family whom he later summed up as 'poor, poor and poor', Schmuel Gelbfisz once saw a great man riding by, followed by a servant who threw out a handful of coins for the starving children. The image of a man too rich to carry his own money launched the young child on the journey he ended as Sam Goldwyn, the man who never learned the meaning of the two words, 'im-possible'.

Sam Goldwyn, he later told a reporter, 'just wanted to be somebody'. This desire has the same root as the *boychik*'s ferocious anger, the fear that the loss of the mother-self makes him a nobody. Some boys are lucky enough, at a remarkably early age, to 'be somebody' and to be recognized as such. When John Milton was fluent in Latin and Greek at the age of three, his father consciously set about ordering the education of a genius. Three was also the age at which Mozart was freely displaying his dazzling virtuosity, and William Blake was meeting angels taking the air on Peckham Rye, and conversing with God in a tree. In some cases, the childhood CVs of great men seem to have suffered a degree of retrospective enhancement – Thomas Hardy claimed to have been found as a child asleep in bed with a coiled snake beside him, a story also told of Hercules, Buddha, and other mighty or mythic males. Another piece of Hardeana designed to establish 'Our Tom's' infant genius, the boast that he could read before he could walk, takes on a different colour in the light of the information that the frail, sickly child, like Charles I and his father James I before him, had reached the age of three before he could stand up without falling over.

Even as an adult unassailable genius, then, laden with years and honours, Hardy could not resist a nervous tinkering with fact and a certain extravagance with the truth, in his determination to lay to rest the small, shivering ghost of the nobody of Higher Bockhampton. How then must the average boy feel? The child who has lost a kingdom and not found a destiny? The poet John Keats, meditating sombrely on 'the burden of the mystery', offered this 'simile of human life' as 'a mansion of many apartments':

The first we step into we call the infant or thoughtless chamber, in which we remain as long as we do not think . . . notwithstanding the doors of the second chamber remain wide open, showing a bright appearance, we care not to hasten to it, but are at length imperceptibly impelled by the awakening of the thinking principle within us – we no sooner get into the second chamber, which I shall call the Chamber of Maiden-Thought, than we become intoxicated with the light and the atmosphere, we see nothing but pleasant wonders, and think of delaying there for ever in delight. However . . . this Chamber of Maiden-Thought becomes gradually darkened, and at the same time on all sides of it many doors are set open – but all dark – all leading to dark passages.[11]

The darkness of uncertainty and the misery of childhood confusion form the theme of many early memories. 'An enormous world was kept dark from us,' says Lord Dacre, formerly Regius Professor of History at Oxford University and authenticator of the notorious faked 'Hitler Diaries'. 'We were forced into ourselves and only allowed to express ourselves in the most conventional manner.' Dacre and his

brother were also kept in the dark about the most frightening event of
their childhood lives:

> We went to children's parties – I hated them. I remember one
> where my father, reluctantly disguised as Father Christmas, went
> up in flames when his cotton wool beard caught fire from a candle.
> He was badly burnt and in hospital for a long time . . . It was never
> admitted that it had happened. What I had seen with my own eyes
> was dismissed as a fantasy. All this was in order to keep up the
> myth of Father Christmas, in which I had ceased to believe
> anyway.[12]

As an act of violence against the child's emotional reality, this story
can be paralleled many times over. Equally damaging in a different way
are the countless, nameless acts of physical violence to which the
growing boy will be subjected, almost from the day of his birth. An
overwhelming mass of research evidence shows that mothers smack
boy children far more than girls, even hitting babies as young as two or
three months old. Expecting to find boys 'more aggressive', they
respond with aggression, with incalculable results. The problem is
exacerbated if the mother is young, poor, single, or otherwise unsupported: seeking causal explanations for the disproportionately high
level of violence in black families, researchers cite statistics showing
that '40.3% of black family units are headed by women, compared
with 11.6% for whites' and that 'more than half (55%) of all black
babies in the United States today are born out of wedlock, mostly to
teenagers'.[13] Maternal violence can also take more bizarre forms of
expression. Henry Miller's memory of his mother must give rise to
doubt that in later life he would ever walk a million miles for one of her
smiles:

> Once she grew a wart on her finger. She said to me, 'Henry!'
> (remember I'm only four years old) 'what should I do?' I said, 'Cut
> it off with the scissors.' The wart! You don't cut off a wart! So she
> got blood poisoning. Two days later she came to me with her hand
> bandaged and she says, 'And you told me to cut it off!' And BANG
> BANG she slaps me. Slaps me! For punishment! For telling her to
> do this! Now how do you like a mother who does that?[14]

With a masterly understatement for which the old goat of the *Tropic of
Capricorn* was not usually celebrated, Miller added, 'I don't have
pleasant memories of talks with her.'

In general, though, the greatest instigators of violence against the male child will be other males. These early years set a pattern not to be broken as little boys, from the time they can toddle, learn violence at the hands of other boys and men. From the onset of social play, at two or two-and-a-half, boys are drawn to other boys, with whom they engage in behaviour that is patently more tribal, more aggressive, more animal than a comparable group of girls. While girls play with each other, co-operating, sharing, passing play materials to and fro and constantly discussing and extending the imaginative basis of the play, boys tend to play side-by-side, ignoring each other, every one engaged in his own project and showing an anxious concern for autonomy against any interference, of child or adult. Engagement with other boys is generally undertaken to prove themselves strong, powerful or more dominant than their peers: aggression, verbal and physical, with mock-fighting and often violent fantasy play ('The soldiers are killing all the space invaders *now*! Bang! Bang! Kill! Kill!'), though ritualized, is a regular event. Dominance is the key issue, say researchers Maccoby and Jacklin, authors of the standard text on sex difference: even the youngest boys make incessant, often desperate bids for dominance, both successful and unsuccessful, in the endless task of maintaining their position in the constantly shifting dominance order.

In the nature of things, though, the threat to the boy from another little boy cannot be too great. The potential for danger lies rather in the generalized atmosphere of violence, of rough, dangerous activity as the mass of boy children, any time after the age of the so-called 'terrible twos', race around 'playing war', in Christiane Olivier's phrase, forcing the less aggressive boys to play along at the risk of being either set upon or left out. When to this general atmosphere of male self-definition through aggression something else is added, the result can be overwhelming. At the age of six, Joseph Kallinger, an abandoned orphan later taken in by a Catholic couple in Philadelphia, had to go into hospital for a hernia operation. When he came home his father Stephen, a poor German immigrant working as a shoemaker, explained what the doctor had done.

'He fixed your hernia . . . but he also fixed . . . your little bird.'
    In the Kallinger home, 'bird' was the euphemism for penis.
    'What's wrong with my little bird?' Joe asked.
    'An evil spirit . . . a demon makes your bird get hard and stick out so you do bad things with it. Then your soul goes to the Devil when you die . . . But you won't have no demon, because your bird will always be small, small, small!'[15]

For the rest of his life Joseph Kallinger, although later becoming the father of four children, was to suffer, like Hemingway and Peter Sutcliffe, violent, overwhelming anxieties about the size and performance of his penis, with recurring episodes of impotence. Like Sutcliffe again, the terror, and the rage against the terror, of being a 'No-Dick' set Kallinger's feet on the trail of the series of hideous sexual murders with which 'the Shoemaker' terrorized a 1960s America drunk on dreams of peace and love.

The aetiology of male violence is rarely so clearly set out as it is in the Kallinger case. Nevertheless, this story throws crucial light on to the mechanism of the construction of violent aggression and the making of the male. Kallinger, like most murderers, was neither unusually tall nor strong (many indeed are below average height, often unusually short, slight or weedy, like Dr Crippen). As a child he was timid, sensitive and artistically gifted, with no 'natural' bent towards cruelty nor any early signs of the killer he was to become. Abandoned by his mother, adopted from a harsh and religious orphanage into the viciously repressive and sadistically punitive Kallinger household, he was subjected to a daily onslaught of abuse about his worthlessness, coupled with a violent introduction to every variety of aggression and pain. As his sanity crumbled, he clung to the only reality he knew, the power of humiliation, fear and suffering above all else.

Violence in the adult male is frequently attributed to their superior muscular strength: men *can* bash women and weaker men, therefore they *do*. The circularity of this argument ignores the fact that boy children under the age of seven regularly engage in aggressive and violent activity, long before they have any physical superiority over girls, and before they have developed the strength or even the balance to make good their aggressive attacks. Nor can the aggression of the young boy be attributed to 'his hormones', least of all to the male hormone testosterone, since no extra hormone infusion takes place at this time: the boy child's body in these years is still remarkably like a girl's, and will remain so until the changes that come with puberty, as yet far off.

Why then does aggression become so marked a feature of boys' activity between the ages of two and three, never thereafter off the agenda, however long they may live? In reality, this question must be reversed: not how do boys become aggressive, but how can they avoid it? From their toys, from the games they are taught, even from the bedtime songs they are sung, they are surrounded by it, bathed in it, till for the majority it becomes the element in which they think, move and have their being. 'Boys will be boys', runs the proverb. To see a group of mothers with their sons, or a father making the first attempts at ball play with a son, is to realize that this is not an observation, but an imperative: boys *must* be boys.

To be male is the opposite of being mother. To be a man, the boy must break away from her, and the further he travels, the greater will be judged the success of his journey. To make the break, however, the boy has to be constantly encouraged, bullied, threatened, thrust forward at every turn and side, and never, never permitted to fall back. An atmosphere of constant aggression, fighting, 'making war' is therefore vital to orchestrate the separation process and keep it moving. Now, as at every stage of their lives, aggression is vital to the survival of males, not because they are stronger, but because *they are thought and feared to be weaker*. Aggression, though widely permitted, supported, or even encouraged by females, is by and large imposed by males: fathers almost invariably show more anxiety about their sons developing a 'real' masculine identity than mothers do. 'You just can't start too early, teaching a boy the things he's going to have to know,' explains 'Cordy' Joe Blacker, a farmer from Bonner Springs, Kansas. 'I'd have little Joe riding out with me tucked in behind my pommel, from he was two. Come three, he'd be riding his own pony. They can never start too young.' The same theory seems to have motivated Anthony Jimerson, of Forest Hills, Texas, who in 1989 gave half a pint of neat bourbon to the five-year-old son of a friend, urging him to drink it 'like a man'. The child died later in hospital.

From the primal sweetness of the infant's Eden to the male world of gangs, games, fear and fighting, is a long, painful journey. The little traveller, however, has no choice but to embark. Some linger longer in the women's world: some also hold on to and value that life, and return to it as often as possible. 'My mum and her mother were the major formative influences in my early life,' says the actor Terence Stamp. 'Even today there is a certain healing quality I miss if denied the company of women for too long.' The demand for healing argues the infliction of a wound: this is Adam's wound, the expulsion from the Garden. For sooner or later, the boy is removed from his mother, and she has no option but to let him go. The agonizingly shy and repressed Cambridge University don and poet A. E. Housman speaks for all the little voyagers on the brink of the next stage:

> I, a stranger and afraid,
> In a world I never made.

There is one important difference in parental behaviour towards boys. Boys are taught, quite early in life, to avoid showing emotions and to refrain from touching and cuddling . . . studies in the University of Wisconsin Primate Laboratory showed that baby monkeys which were prevented from touching other monkeys in childhood (although they could see, hear and smell the others) became violent when adults . . . psychiatrists have found that parents who physically hurt their children had themselves been deprived of physical affection and touching during their childhood . . . a study of other societies found that those which gave their children the most physical affection (by cuddling, by touching, and by letting the child show its emotions) during infancy and childhood had less violence, theft and assaults than societies which treated their children harshly.

Derek Llewellyn-Jones, *Everyman* (1987)

Father! Father! where are you going?
O do not walk so fast.
Speak, Father, to your little boy,
Or else I shall be lost.

Wiliam Blake, 'A Little Boy Lost'

3 Paradise Lost

Alas, regardless of their doom,
  The little victims play!
No sense have they of ills to come,
  Nor care beyond today:
Yet see how all around 'em wait
  The ministers of human fate ...
Ah, tell them, they are men!
> Thomas Gray, 'Ode on a Distant
> Prospect of Eton College'

The bigs hit me, so I hit the smalls –
that's fair.
> Boy who attacked Bertrand Russell
> on his first day at school

At school I was looked on as quite odd because I wanted
to ask, 'Why are we here? Why do we suffer?'
> Jeremy Reed, poet

Fattened and fêted, indulged and adored, the baby boy is truly the man born to be king. Emerging from that infant kingdom is likely therefore always to carry a poignant sense of loss. 'Happy those early days,' wrote the seventeenth-century Royalist and physician Henry Vaughan, 'When I / Shined in my angel-infancy':

When yet I had not walked above
A mile or two from my first Love.

To Vaughan, passionately religious and gifted with mystical flashes which he called his 'bright shoots of everlastingness', this 'first Love' was naturally, inevitably, God. The infant boy, in his world of 'white, celestial thought', was at his closest to this love, this centre – and it was a closeness he could only lose.

For Wordsworth, too, growing up meant the loss of infant purity, the gradual extinction of the divine spark. 'Trailing clouds of glory do we come,' he insisted, 'from God, who is our home.' As manhood looms, it strikes the boy not as the gateway to the freedom of the promised land, but as an intolerable restriction, a life sentence: 'Shades of the prison house begin to close / Upon the growing boy.' However wild and free the 'glad animal' days of boyhood, however intense their 'aching joys' and 'dizzy raptures', every day sees a little loss of the world of gold. To be a man is to be left alone facing the one bleak unanswerable question of life: 'Whither is fled the visionary gleam? / Where is it now, the glory and the dream?'

Nothing in the writing of women can be found to parallel this pervasive masculine sense of loss, a sense not merely of bereavement but of betrayal too. Thomas Gray, recalling his eighteenth-century Eton schooldays, felt with hindsight that the boys sensed with dread the numbering of their days:

> Still as they run they look behind,
> They hear a voice in every wind,
>   And snatch a fearful joy.

Yet there could be no merit in forewarning the 'little victims' of the doom they could neither avert nor avoid:

> Yet ah! why should they know their fate?
> Since sorrow never comes too late,
>   And happiness too swiftly flies.
> Thought would destroy their paradise.
> No more; where ignorance is bliss,
>   'Tis folly to be wise.

For the sons of Adam, as the songs of innocence give way to the songs of experience, there could be only one fate – paradise lost.[1]

Living through the loss, watching day by day as the golden world recedes 'forever and forever on the sight', is an experience no boy passes through without pain. To A. E. Housman, even years afterwards, the ache of dispossession could return with a child-like clarity and intensity:

> That is the land of lost content,
>   I see it shining plain,
> The happy highways where I went,
>   And cannot come again.

Worse still is not loss but violent expulsion, the fate decreed for the male young from time immemorial. For thousands of years, culture, history and tradition have insisted on the removal of the boy child from 'the house of women' and his forcible repatriation to the kingdom of his birthright, the world of men. Everywhere, it seems, the making of boys into men takes this as the first of its objectives, the brutal separation and segregation from all female influence, and the establishing of the vital sexual difference from the all-embracing mother of the early years.

The shock of this change has always been an essential part of the process – some memorable, often violent event marks the boy's break with his infant past, converting a natural transition into a man-made baptism of fire. In classical Athens, the spring festival of the Anthesteria, celebrating the first sampling of the wine harvest of the previous year, was the signal to all male citizens for a three-day debauch. On the second day, boys were allowed to join in the drinking, carousing and play-acting, diverting their fathers with alcoholic antics, either real or assumed. The communal drunkenness, the crudely vulgar, often pornographic satyr plays and the licence for unbridled phallic swagger and display all served as the sharpest possible contrast to the sequestered, indoor lives of the mothers from whom the boys had been taken, and formed a startling initiation and indoctrination into the real world of the Athenian male hitherto hidden from the son.

With segregation comes another essential lesson, that of superiority. Induction into the higher world of the male, by rupturing the relationship with the mother, renegotiates the basis of the relation to all females. In infancy this relation is of the purest, a consuming experience of mutual dominance and desire. As the young child desires the love of the mother with all the force of his ego, so he dominates her through reciprocal love and sexual need. In the world of the fathers, though, dominance comes by right, through might. It is also exerted over all the women in the boy's circle, not simply the first. This too the boy has to learn. His training must now equip him to understand, exploit and uphold a system based not on love but on power, not on parity but on hierarchy. This imperative is neatly encapsulated in an Attic proverb familiar around the Mediterranean for thousands of years before it took root in Corsica – where it was old when the 'Little Corporal', who was later to enshrine it in the Code Napoleon, was young: 'When he is seven, a boy is given a little stick to mind a flock of sheep. When he is fifteen, he gets a bigger stick and looks after cows. When he comes of age, he gets a weapon and bosses women.'

As this suggests, the age at which a boy begins his compulsory manhood training has also proved remarkably consistent through the ages: no such watershed occurs in the lives of girls. From about 1000 BC, every Spartan boy of seven was taken from his mother by a father he hardly knew, and pitched into the all-male world of barracks and training ground. In Rome, from its foundation to its fall, a boy could only remain *in gremio matris* (in the lap of the mother) until the age of seven: then the father assumed total control, personally undertaking or supervising every aspect of the child's education from his initial struggles with the alphabet to his first prostitute. The boy accompanied his father everywhere, to field and forum, to all social, sexual and ceremonial occasions, even to the Senate, where the silence and attentiveness enforced on the small boy, often by savage beatings in advance, were roundly defended for centuries by reactionaries like Cato the Censor as vital to the formation of the Roman character.

In the early modern period, too, seven continued to be the age when infancy was considered over, and the real work of life began. Among the aristocracy of medieval Europe, seven-year-old boys were solemnly shuttled from one noble house to another as they began their training in knighthood by taking service as a page. Lower down the scale their peasant peers began their own apprenticeships, albeit to the humbler crafts of cooper and coper, tailor or tiler, at the same age, or were given their first full flocks to field. This system was not without its difficulties. When the eleven-year-old page Henry Bolingbroke saw his father banished from England by his tyrannical lord, Richard II, he was forced to remain in the house of the banisher. History however has recorded the price later exacted from the deposed king by the unregarded child destined to become Henry IV.

As the dividing line between child and man, the age of seven has continued to exert its strange and unexplained significance into the modern period. Seven was the age at which Hemingway's father presented him with his grandfather's Civil War pistol, and his mother finally agreed to the cutting of his childhood ringlets. Occasionally, too, fate steps in to reinforce the seven-year turning-point, with random yet incalculable effect. Until the age of seven Joseph Goebbels was a happy, healthy, normal boy adored by his mother whose devout Catholic faith he shared. The boy shared too her vision of his future as a priest, especially following an episode when his mother asked him to pray with her for the life of his father, then on the point of death from pneumonia, and after a long night of prayer and intercession the father recovered.

But an attack of osteomyelitis at seven plunged Goebbels into a nightmare of illness, pain and surgery from which he emerged solitary, embittered and marked for life. Clinging to his life plan, he applied to enter a seminary at the age of 14: his rejection then ('My young friend,' said the priest in wonderment, 'you do not believe in God!') confirmed his view that there was 'no justice' in Germany. Instead, he went to university, where he happened to attend a student meeting addressed by an unknown 'Herr Adolf Hitler'. 'The disgrace was ended . . . at that moment I was reborn,' he later wrote.[2]

Even today, most notoriously in England but widely elsewhere in the Anglo-Saxon world too, the practice of sending a boy away from home at the age of seven continues to flourish. Some men undoubtedly cherish fondest memories even of the most dismal of holes. Lord Dacre approvingly recalls his days at 'a very good, spartan school, with cold baths all the year round, in that north-eastern corner facing north into the Firth of Forth.' The legendary St Cyprian's in Sussex, *alma mater* of Cyril Connolly and George Orwell among others, was generally known to have virtually no heating, nauseating food, and the vilest of practices (when one boy was so sickened by the grey, glutinous, coagulated porridge that he vomited into it, he was forced to eat up the whole of the resulting contents of his bowl). Yet old boys leaped to its defence after the circulation of Orwell's bitter memoir, 'Such, Such Were the Joys'.

For most boys, whether their later memories are good or bad, the shock of the ordeal is never to be forgotten. 'That going away is *the worst,*' says writer Colin Thubron. 'Twelve weeks is about as long a time as you can imagine when you are a child.' From the comfort of the familiarity of home the child is plunged, too, into a world of terrifying rigidity, insane ritual and impenetrable jargon ('Shells to the Bursary for battels, Oppidans to Matron before sixters'). The effect of all this bites at the deepest level, and as a result spreads the extraordinary process far beyond the limited numbers of individuals who actually attend these educational institutions. 'The beliefs imprinted by public schools are conduited to all social classes via the professions, the civil service, and the sergeants' mess,' observes health expert Dr Michael O'Donnell. 'They're an abiding influence on English cultural life.' As a medical man, O'Donnell's favourite example is the British preoccupation with the state of their bowels, and their anal humour in general: 'I first encountered Bowel Power at my prep school where, every morning, we passed in line before Matron, who barked at us "*Been?*" Those foolish enough to answer "No" were dosed with a foul-tasting draught, her panacea for everything from a sore throat to a bruised toe.'

Inevitably this experience and the isolation that accompanies it, not to mention some of its darker manifestations, stay with a boy for life. As a very elderly man Lord Hailsham, the former Lord Chancellor of England, can still recall every dreadful detail: 'It was a *terrible* shock – I'd only learned how to put on knickerbockers the day before, and I couldn't tie my tie. We had to get up in the morning to cold baths. And of course the sanitary arrangements were beyond belief – earth closets

– you had a ticket and you had to go in a particular order: I can't tell you how disgusting it was. I was flung into this particular dormitory with thirteen others . . . chilblains in winter because there was no heating and the food *disgusting*.'[3]

Yet the best of cuisine, central heating and all mod. cons. could hardly disguise the true nature of this classic British experience. 'It's something which has remained in my mind, being sent to a middle-class boarding school – horrendous institutions of torture – being ripped away from your beloved family, your mother, at the age of seven,' says film director Hugh Hudson. 'It's kind of early, isn't it?' As the sons of a very British family ('very rigid and very upper-class, British Empire rulers') Rupert Everett and his brother were also automatically 'sent away':

I must say I had a really nice childhood till the age of seven. It's a mad thing to send young children off to school, it's just a stupid tradition that has brainwashed generations of parents. It's completely wrong. It makes you grow up too soon. It makes you come across real unhappiness and rejection too early in life.

My brother was the first to go off. He held on to the back of my parents' car so hard that he grazed his knees as he was dragged along the road.

As for me, I was initially quite excited about going. I had a new suitcase and clothes full of name tags, and at seven, I thought that was great. Then the big day came and we drove off to the school, an old country manor. And as it came into view I suddenly realized what was about to happen and I had a fit of panic.

My first night was horrible. I spent the whole night staring out of the dorm window at a little white house in the distance, which I thought was our house, but which wasn't, of course.

Even after years of boarding school, Everett, ironically later to make his name in Julian Mitchell's definitive public school drama *Another Country* (1984), never reconciled himself to the system: 'I would have done anything to get out, even shoot myself.'[4]

And still it goes on. One new mother recalls leaving her son with anxious instructions not to drink anything after 7 p.m.: 'We'd had a spate of bed-wetting in the weeks leading up to his departure. Among the forms we'd been sent to fill in was one stating that he hadn't wet the bed for the last month. The bed-wetting had started the day we sent the form off.' The first letter, when it arrived, did little to allay concern:

Dear Mr and Mrs Tranter,

I said I would write, so hear you are. I like my new school. My teacher is very nice. I am having fun.

Yours sincerely,

J. Tranter.

'All it communicated was a severing of any bonds that still united us,' commented the mother, *She* journalist Lynn Bushell. 'The "Yours sincerely" was particularly hurtful.'

The young 'J. Tranter' shortly afterwards began to communicate his feelings more directly via a series of reverse charge telephone calls, sometimes as many as three in one afternoon. At half-term, his mother discovered in his desk a 'List of Enemys'. Every boy in the dormitory was on it. 'Give him time,' said the headmaster. 'It's perfectly normal for a boy to take a term to settle in.' In the second term, the boy won the cross-country race. When he writes home now, at least he does not begin 'Dear Mr and Mrs Tranter'. But he hardly ever writes, so it's not a problem. A happy ending, then. And a very British one.

I believed in boarding education until, at the age of 33, I went to Australia and for the first time in my life I met people using day education, and what marvellous family lives they were having! We are born into families. Being pushed off to live with other children is very unlikely to be right. Children are so marvellous, though, they simply settle for what they've got. Then each generation of males comes through to become what society expects of them.

Tim Fisher, headmaster of Bilton Grange
Preparatory School, Rugby

With or without 'the benefits of boarding', as the prep school brochures have it, from seven upwards the boy is forced to accept his severance from the female world. From this point on he is destined to live in a new, strange and often terrifying universe, which many adult men still recall with all the force of childhood's tremors. Even a 'day boy' is at school for a long enough stretch of time to understand perfectly the truth of George Orwell's bitter stabbing recollection: 'Your home might be far from perfect, but at least it was a place ruled by love rather than fear . . . suddenly you were taken out of this warm nest and flung into a world of force and fraud and secrecy, like a goldfish into a tank full of pike.'[5] By a vicious irony, given that the boy is freshly suffering the severance from the one woman who matters in his life, many of the 'pike' will be female. 'It is a disaster that the early training and education of children lies almost exclusively in female hands,' states Christiane Olivier:

> For the boy can find no way out of his castration anxiety, surrounded as he is by all these people who 'haven't got one'. I shall never forget, as long as I live, my son's despairing look when I lifted the hat that the teacher had deliberately pulled down over his face as a mark of shame. There and then I discovered the bottomless pit of humiliation he felt himself pushed into by this creature who 'hadn't got one' . . . his unconscious was like an active volcano.[6]

To the small boy, what can be the logic at work forcing the woman who loves him to give him up to the tyranny of women who don't? The more so as he is now encountering another major difficulty of being male at the same time. As part of the genetic disadvantage of belonging to 'the biologically inferior species', the young male starts his education and the learning process markedly behind the equivalent female on any measurement of verbal reasoning, vocabulary development, rote memory and manual dexterity. Learning to read and write is therefore on average a far greater struggle for the boy than for a girl, and boys have to be referred to remedial centres or reading clinics four times more often than girls.[7] 'Simply holding the pencil and forming a recognizable letter tends to give boys more trouble than girls,' comments Isobel Lefeaux, a primary teacher of many years' experience in Hampstead, London. 'Then when they begin writing, they are usually less fluent, so their stories will be shorter, less interesting, and grammatically less sophisticated than those of the girls. Dyslexia, too – word-blindness – whatever you call this combination of reading and spelling difficulties, this too is a male problem rather than a female one on the whole. 98 per cent of all dyslexics are male, and their problems of processing written language can be very severe, especially at the early stages.'

Some of the world's most acclaimed men have suffered these learning difficulties of childhood to a very marked degree. Albert Einstein could neither read nor write until well past the age of seven, and Winston Churchill has left a poignant memoir of his abortive attempt on the Common Entrance Paper of Harrow School at the age of

12: 'I was found unable to answer a single question on the Latin paper. After two hours of intense brooding, the number of the question, (1), in brackets, a blot, and several smudges were all I was able to produce. Mathematics went the same way. I should have liked to be asked to say what I knew. They always tried to ask what I did not know.'[8]

Churchill was fortunate enough at Harrow to have studied under a humane regime, and therefore escaped the attentions of the slave-driving or sadistic masters who haunt the nightmares of their chosen victims to their dying day. But nothing ever reconciled him to his schooldays. 'I was happy as a child with my toys in the nursery,' he later wrote. 'I have been happier every year since I became a man. But this interlude at school makes a sombre grey patch upon the chart of my journey.'[9] It was 'an unending spell' of misery and monotony, and for Churchill, as for others, one of the worst things about it was the inescapable presence of the other boys. School meant having to endure the initial shock of realizing all that it meant to be male, and subsequently encountering the endless jar of that insistent masculinity against every finer feeling. Historian Dan Irwin recalls his first experience of this:

I'll never forget having to go for the first time into the boys' toilets – I went in, dropped my trousers and they all laughed at me. To this day I avoid male toilets – they're so dirty and smelly, with constant evidence of serious masturbation all around. The last time I had to use one on a motorway there was semen dripping down the walls and a picture of Samantha Fox on the floor. I'm girly, really, I'll go and hide in one of the cubicles any time. I just hate standing in a row, all the men standing side-by-side holding their knobs, they're all really into that as a manly experience.

Embracing the 'manly experience' means learning to identify and reject its opposite. 'By seven, we knew the difference between boys and girls,' says architect Miles Johnson. 'There was masses of willy-showing-off, and jokes about girls being silly and sissy and not as good as us, not in the same world.' For some boys, the fun was not so innocent. 'I hated all that pseudo-sexual stuff at primary school,' says Dan Irwin, 'six- and seven-year-olds going up over the fields and trying to kiss the girls, or making them play really aggressive games. One boy in my class called Martin, he was only seven, he used to play this game called "kiss or kick". He used to take a girl into a shed, and ask her a question. If she got it right he kissed her, if she was wrong he kicked her.' As this suggests, sexual activity in however rudimentary a form can begin much earlier than parents or teachers may be ready to acknowledge, and can be just as harmful in intent, if not in execution, as the adult variety. At one primary school in Birmingham three boys aged between nine and ten were suspended for assessment in the spring of 1990 after they had mounted a mock rape on a nine-year-old girl pupil in the school playground during the afternoon break. Two of the boys, aged nine and ten, held the girl down, while a third, aged nine, rubbed himself against her, simulating intercourse. A number of similar episodes in recent years suggest that, like sexual activity, violence too may be beginning earlier than we think.

Among boys moving up through adolescence, these attitudes of hostility, contempt, or suspicion are progressively reinforced. When 2000 boys in the state of Colorado were asked how they would feel if they woke up one morning and found they were a girl, 'like a bad dream' was one of the few polite and printable responses. While finding yourself in the morning anything other than what you were when you went to sleep undoubtedly has the abstract nightmare quality of Kafka's *Metamorphosis*, it is interesting that these boys could find no redeeming feature in the female. Another recent survey comparing the attitudes of 1000 boys in England, Sweden, America and Australia, revealed a unanimous aversion to females which only differed in degree from country to country, the English boys, perhaps not surprisingly given the history of early sex segregation in this country, coming out the worst.[10]

But the girls, at this stage, still had the power to fight back. 'Oh, those girls, the big bold girls from the end of the street,' rhapsodizes Gwyn Hughes, a trade union official from Tredegar, South Wales, 'they'd come down, swoop down like witches, catch us and kiss us – it was like being raped – and the fear of it was very terrible!' Doubtless to defend the manly sex against the repetition of horrors like these, all cultures, all societies, devote considerable energy, attention and resources to building up the growing boy's body in such a way as to maximize his physical superiority over girls. At birth, nature gives girls certain key advantages over boys. In terms of lung capacity, nervous system, reflex action and other critical attributes, a girl has a maturational lead of four to six weeks over the average boy, a lead maintained and extended throughout the growing period. Through this natural advantage, as widely observed by teachers and parents, girls will regularly walk and talk earlier than boys, will learn to read more easily, will reach puberty ahead of boys, and complete their adult growth while their male equivalent is still suffering the torments of the invasion of the testosterones, with all their attendant miseries of violent growth spurts, unheralded erections, and (yet another primarily sex-determined disorder) technicolour acne.

But the boy, the male, the future husband, father and leader, cannot be allowed to languish in second place. The new-born boy is about 5 per cent heavier than the new-born girl: by the age of twenty, this differential has increased to 20 per cent. Height difference on average between the male and female baby is around 1 per cent: at twenty, the male has increased that tenfold. These differentials, and the gradually widening gap between male and female performance, can be seen in almost every measurable physical activity. At seven years of age, boys have only 10 per cent more muscle than girls: by the age of eighteen, this has become 50 to 60 per cent. Girl babies are born with more efficient lungs than boys: by the age of seven, they have 7 per cent less efficient vital lung capacity than boys: this then becomes 35 per cent less in women than in men. Overall, then, arriving at the gateway of manhood, the eighteen-year-old boy has built up a huge physical advantage over the females of his world, since he is now over 80 per cent stronger than the average girl.[11]

How far nurture simply builds upon nature must remain a matter for debate. Incontrovertibly, however, especially in the western world, the boy child is consistently both given more exercise and allowed more food than his sisters, in a benign circle of self-enhancement whose effect, whether intentional or not, is to exaggerate the sexual dimorphism of nature to the explicit advantage of the male. Among the working peoples of the Third World, in particular, as Dr Ann Oakley has shown, in cultures where all work is shared or where the female role involves portering or heavy lifting and the male does not, there is almost no difference between men and women in adult physique.[12] In races with different cultural imperatives, the Chinese for example, these distinctions all but disappear. But then, the Chinese do not play rugby.

Of course exercise is important, it's essential. It builds the boys up and develops their physique. Then there's the problem of aggression, sports are vital for containing and harnessing that. And it toughens them up – after a rough game or two, they learn how to take a knock. It finds out the leaders, too. You could say it sorts out the men from the boys.
> Dr John Heskett-Smith, former headmaster
> of St John's Preparatory School, London

The battle of Waterloo may well have been won, as the Iron Duke of Wellington was reported as saying, on the playing fields of Eton. But even today, in a world long past the hegemonic belligerence of the European powers or the likelihood of another conventional war, throughout the western world the sports and games of boys are still dictated by antique dreams of dominance through combat which plunge the unwary innocent into a world owing more to Kafka than to Kitchener or Kipling. They are clearly designed, too, to teach, orchestrate and instil aggression rather than minimizing or channelling it. Adult men still recall with a bemused hysteria the violence of their first induction into ball games, whose rationale so frequently is that they contain and proscribe violence. Dan Irwin, still reeling from his first brush with the male urinal, will never forget his first game of rugby:

> The teacher, a big brute called Jones, a former Welsh international – all our fathers thought we were so lucky to have him! – divided us into 'Large-Physique Boys' and 'Small-Physique-No-Talent Boys'. Then the large ones were instructed to target a little one, run at him and 'Take him out!' I'll never forget the look on my poor little sod's face as I ran at him like a madman, then side-stepped at the last minute. Afterwards the whole pitch was littered with little kids crying and screaming, it was like a battlefield. Big Jones strolled over to one of them and said, 'Don't cry, boy, *it's only pain.*'

Do parents know how much and how routinely their sons suffer? 'Of course they do. The fathers do, anyway,' observes the character of Judd in *Another Country*. Pain in fact appears on the school curriculum with a frightening openness and regularity. Learning to endure the daily or weekly 'knocking about' or 'good hiding' is an inescapable part of almost all boys' sports and games, the counter-objective being not to avoid it but to return it with compound interest. Teaching boys to love their suffering, like the birched and bleeding Elizabethan schoolboy forced to kiss the rod, is not merely a by-product but an avowed object of the exercise: to the battered child snivelling on the ground, when he ventured that he did not like rugby because he did not like getting hurt, Big Jones intoned, so Irwin reports, 'It's part of the game! You should enjoy getting hurt, you lie in bed afterwards feeling proud of yourself, feeling up all your aches and pains.'

Nor does the boy's training for manhood restrict itself to the purely ritualized aspects of combat. From the time when the Spartan elders used fanatical fitness training in boxing, wrestling and hand-to-hand unarmed combat to forge the finest army in Greece, possibly in the world, boys have been made to fight, then equipped with weapons and taught how to kill. The less aggressive they were by nature, the stronger the need to make them so. As a young boy who 'detested physical violence', the only one in his junior class to wear glasses ('the mark of the cissy'), US journalist John Walters fell foul of the school bully. Staggering home 'in a torn, frightful condition' he encountered his father, who had only two demands to make: the somewhat over-optimistic 'Did you win?' followed by the menacing 'Did you *quit*?' That same Saturday Walters found himself in a boxing ring, 'flailing away, with Tommy [the coach] and my father standing by'. But the longed-for result happened at last:

> So it went . . . I'd jog home, the bag slung over my back, drifting through the park and enjoying sweet liberation from my troubles. The gym sessions, at first a bitter imposition, became in time a regular part of my life, and I began to like them. I felt myself growing stronger, taller and more confident. Relations with my father improved.[13]

Fathers are invariably heavily involved in their sons' early apprenticeship to violence and pain: they choose, in fact, to 'deliver us to the torturers', as one son angrily expressed it. Teaching the son 'to stand up for himself' blithely occludes any dividing-line between defence and aggression – would the boy need to learn this, if all the other boys were not being taught the same thing? And why do girls not need to learn what should presumably be a basic survival skill of life, when as women they can hardly expect to be immune from men's aggressive and sexual attacks? Above all, what need of his own is the father serving, when the boy's training to protect himself against violent attack and unwanted pain results in a system of sustained and sanctioned attacks, along with the infliction of far greater and more regular pain than if the boy had volunteered for a weekly session with the school bully?

Whatever their motives, fathers are very clear about their duties in this department, as they always have been. The awareness that masculinity, as defined by men, is taught and acquired, not innate, is hardly new: at the turn of the century many American fathers feared that the closing of the frontier, the arrival of the vote and various changes in the workplace, families and schools, were 'feminizing' society. Accordingly the Boy Scouts of America were formed in 1910 to provide a place where boys could learn 'true manliness' from men. So today Timothy Cheung, a 13-year-old Coventry schoolboy, Viscount

Poultney, the 21-year-old heir of the Earl of Lethington, and Ronnie Goldman (58) from London's East End, all report receiving boxing gloves as a present from their fathers at the age of seven, with the insistence that 'you learned how to use them' and 'you learned to look after yourself'. 'All this was strongly against my mother's wishes,' comments Poultney, 'and I must say I found it all pretty horrible, especially at first. Also, I never became any good at it. My older brother could always beat me, so of course he did, though it was always better with the gloves on than with his bare hands.'

The sons of course have no option but to try to follow, impress or resemble this dark god, the father. 'My father was a hopeless alcoholic,' said Hubert Selby Jr, author of *Last Exit to Brooklyn*, 'and I drank every chance I got from my earliest memory. I'd sneak a drink when I was two or three, a sip of someone else's beer, whatever. I never remember when I didn't want to drink. I was so proud of my father because he could work with a hangover. That was my definition of a man and I desperately wanted to be a man.' 'Around the age of eight,' explains psychologist Dr John Nicholson, author of *Men and Women: How Different Are They?*, 'anxieties surface about behaving the "wrong" way. By ten, the boy is firmly locked into doing what peers and parents find acceptable.' From the age of two or three, the boy has become more and more aware of the father as the parent with whom he must eventually identify. Being rejected by the mother, being forced to turn away from her and her world, only makes the hunger for paternal identification and approval the more desperate, the more compelling.

This hunger, this compulsion finds a ready echo in the father's breast. Fathers in general show a far greater anxiety than mothers that their sons should grow up to be 'regular guys', and having missed out on or evaded any close connection in babyhood, they now consciously embark upon manhood manoeuvres in order to exert a shaping influence before it is too late, a concern rarely extended to their daughters. Of all the fathers undertaking compulsory manhood training of their sons, however, one of the most dedicated was Dr Clarence ('Ed') Hemingway. Ed lost no opportunity to take Ernest away from his books or music practice in order to teach him the manly arts of boxing and hunting. A lesser father, let alone a qualified doctor as Hemingway Senior was, might have wondered at the wisdom of boxing instruction, when minute one of lesson one found the young Hemingway flat on the canvas spouting blood, his nose broken in three places and the sight of his left eye permanently impaired. It subsequently emerged that the proprietor of the gym was a keen businessman who used to insist on payment for the full course of tuition in advance, then arrange for the first lesson to be delivered by a former professional prize fighter, a system remarkably efficacious in ensuring that pupils rarely returned for lesson two.

But the devotion of the Hemingways, *père et fils*, to the pains and punishments of machismo knew no bounds, admitted no defeat. In the course of those boxing lessons Hemingway set his lifelong pattern of coming back for more, refusing to call it quits, which only ended with the ruination of his once-splendid body. Nor was the pain only self-inflicted. Hunting was the supreme 'mark of the man'. Ed therefore 'incited Ernest to an endless destruction of fauna', observes Hemingway's biographer Jeffrey Meyers. Hemingway was only six when he locked a sleeping porcupine in the woodshed of the schoolhouse, then returned later to hack it to pieces with an axe. Armed with a gun, he raised his sights to take many more lives, including that of the rare, beautiful and protected blue heron. To a woman who protested, Ed replied furiously, 'Never mind the law, madam – *shoot the birds!*' Indiscriminate slaughter was their religion: 'if it moved,' Meyers says, 'they killed it.'[14]

Hunting, shooting, killing, as sport, exercise or manhood training have lost none of their allure since the days of the Hemingways, despite the fact that both father and son finally found no other target for their guns than the roof of their own mouths. Gun ownership with the implicit right of use (explicit under the US Constitution) feeds not only violence itself, but the climate in which violence may flower. In one of a number of similar incidents in Britain and America over recent years, an eleven-year-old Lancashire boy was remanded by magistrates in Rawtenstall in 1989 accused of murdering his seventy-year-old father, who had been found dead with a single shotgun wound to the chest. And the hunting obsession, like the hunter himself, lurks in ambush and strikes when least expected. In a recent London homicide, a pedestrian, enraged by the behaviour of a motorist at a crossing, reached inside the car for a hunting knife lying there and stabbed the motorist through the heart. No one asked what the dead man, a partner in a firm of respected contract lawyers, was doing with a weapon as vicious as this. Nor are they likely to do so as long as 'Man the Hunter' remains one of the most cherished myths of our racial origins, and the slaughtering of wildlife one of the recommended techniques for making a boy a man.

With its stress on physical prowess, strength and aggression, early manhood training is clearly designed to divorce the boy from all that is female not only in the shape of the mother, but above all from any soft, womanly, human or humane impulses within himself. As such, it often goes painfully against the young boy's tender grain. Given an airgun, the young Winston Churchill duly butchered his first bird, then rushed off to hide in the nursery where he wept himself to sleep that night. As England's war lord Churchill was to preside over more slaughter than Genghis Khan, ruthlessly ordering the blitz of Dresden, for instance. Churchill's boyhood hardening, his apprenticeship of deprivation and distress, with the violent shock of his father's spectacular political fall and ensuing syphilitic madness, may have been unusual. No boy, however, whether subjected to the routine tortures of a patrician childhood or schooled in the working-class 'university of hard knocks', passes through the crucial decade from seven to seventeen without the weekly, even daily drip-feed of sport, exercise and violent physical activity, with their inherently brutalizing lessons in aggression and the infliction of pain.

The Man, in his rough work in the open world, must encounter all peril and trial: to him therefore must be the failure, the offence, the inevitable terror: often he must be wounded or subdued, and *always, always,* hardened.

John Ruskin,
Sesame and Lilies (1865)

II SONGS OF EXPERIENCE

Experience is the name men give to their mistakes.

Oscar Wilde

4   Beating the Bounds

Dolor omnia cogit
[pain will make anyone do anything].
  Seneca

It isn't the fact that you're hurt that counts,
But only – how did you take it?
  Edmund Vance Cook

All for one and one for all!
  Alexandre Dumas,
  The Three Musketeers (1844)

There is no hardening like the routine, unavoidable exposure to 'sporting' knocks and blows. Sport and exercise as manhood training pale, however, in comparison with the long tradition of the infliction of suffering for its own sake. Throughout history it seems to have been considered impossible for a boy to approach adulthood except via a series of ordeals, a regular pathway of pain. In Sparta, fourteen-year-old boys annually underwent the hideous 'Contest of the Whips', a prolonged ordeal by scourging which the boy was expected to withstand in silence until he passed out from pain or loss of blood. A related legend, of the Spartan boy who steadfastly kept a forbidden fox hidden inside his cloak rather than reveal it to his father, though it was gnawing at his vitals, makes the same point: Spartans endured till death. As a fully-armed, highly belligerent city-state whose forces never once stood down from a war footing throughout its thousand-year-history, whose finest flower would repeatedly be called upon to make the final sacrifice as at Thermopylae, where 1100 Spartans held the pass for two days against 100,000 Persians, fighting heroically to the last man, Sparta needed such stoics. The wonder is that the brutalizing of boys through pain has continued to be inflicted long after the faintest of functional physical, military or religious claims could be made for it.

Education systems indeed have for centuries turned on the principle pellucidly expressed by Dickens's Mr Squeers of Dotheboys Hall, that as every boy is an 'incorrigible young scoundrel', when one thrashing is found to do no good, the next must be administered as soon and as strongly as possible, 'to see what good that will do'. The English public school in particular has long flourished in the vigorous tradition that made Nicholas Udall headmaster of Westminster in 1554 after he had been imprisoned for buggering his boy charges while headmaster of Eton. Eton was also the home of the 'Great Beater' Dr Keate, who as headmaster from 1809 onwards once flogged 100 boys of the Lower Sixth in one session.

Despite being only five feet tall, Keate was a man of monstrous strength and Olympic fitness (as his chronicler Jonathan Gathorne-Hardy observes, simply try hitting anything with a walking stick 600 times). But 'six of the best' for 100 boys was nothing to this virtuoso of violence: on his truly great days he often beat the entire fifth and sixth forms together. His prowess was widely admired by parents as triumphing over the deplorable weakness of his predecessor, Dr Heath, who after birching 70 boys (with a possibly ill-advised ten strokes per posterior) had to go to bed for a week with torn ligaments and injury to his muscles. Heath was shown up as pathetically feeble even by the 'enlightened' standards of his own time; even under 'the great' Dr Arnold, the reforming headmaster of Rugby School, 60 strokes of an ash-plant administered to the buttocks of one poor offender were still legal according to the school rules.[1]

Even at preparatory schools for boys between the ages of seven and fourteen, beating was routine, just as in the senior schools: an irony this, as the junior schools had only been devised in the public school reforms of the latter half of the nineteenth century in order to protect the younger boys from the violence and lust of their elders. The experience of Eric Blair, later, as George Orwell, to champion the grievously oppressed with all the passion of one who had been victimized himself, was not untypical. 'Soon after I arrived at St Cyprian's,' he later wrote in the savagely sarcastic memoir 'Such, Such Were the Joys', 'I began wetting my bed.' The headmaster's wife uttered a dire warning. 'Do you know what I am going to do if you wet your bed again?' she demanded. 'I am going to get the Sixth Form to beat you!' In the event, it was the headmaster himself who carried out the beating, with a riding-crop, Orwell bitterly recalled, intoning *You dir-ty lit-tle boy*' in time with the blows. Overheard outside boasting that it hadn't really hurt, Orwell was sent back for more:

This time Sambo [the headmaster] laid on in real earnest. He continued for a length of time that frightened and astonished me – about five minutes it seemed, ending up by breaking the riding crop. The bone handle went flying across the room. 'Look what you've made me do!' he said furiously, holding up the broken crop.

For the first and only time, this beating reduced Orwell to tears; not, he said, because of the pain:

> but because of a deeper grief which is peculiar to childhood and not easy to convey: a sense of desolate loneliness and helplessness, of being locked up not only in a hostile world, but in a world of good and evil where the rules were such that it was not possible for me to keep them.[2]

Orwell's biographer, Bernard Crick, considers that such schools 'commonly institutionalized both manic-depressive and sado-masochistic impulses'. In the light of his later affliction by regular, overwhelming depressions, it is instructive to recall that Winston Churchill suffered for two years at his preparatory school in Ascot the remorseless attentions of a sadistic headmaster whose brutal, incessant floggings 'exceeded in severity anything that would be tolerated in the Reformatories', he later wrote. 'And after all, I was only seven.'[3] Small wonder then that reflecting on his own prep-school experience, the poet Stephen Spender muses, 'They might as well have sent me to a brothel for flagellants.'

It would be comforting to feel that these nineteenth-century horrors were a thing of the past. But it is virtually impossible to talk to a male alive today who has not had some experience of corporal punishment dating back to schooldays, be it only a clip round the ear. 'I hated Downside,' recalls Auberon Waugh, 'for the lack of freedom, the sheer discomfort, the fear of authority, the punishment – I think I held the school record for being beaten fifteen times in one term. Of course it drove the old Adam in, not out. I think I chose to be delinquent in that environment.' The failure of punishment to inculcate any trace of reform has never deterred the kind of teacher whom Ben Jonson pilloried as 'the wisest of your great beaters'. Disc jockey John Peel finds a black humour in the recollection of a contemporary at Shrewsbury School that 'they practically had to wake him up in the night to administer the required number of sound beatings':

> I was beaten in my first term once every three days. It may be hard to believe now, but when I was thirteen, I was rather lovely, and much sought after by older boys, who, if they developed an appetite for you, could have you beaten on a number of pretexts. Several of them have gone on to achieve positions of some eminence in the financial world. I'm sometimes tempted to turn up with a little rouge on my cheeks and say 'I'm ready for you now, my angel,' to some ageing captain of industry.

Corporal punishment is now officially in decline. With the banning of caning from all its state schools in 1987, Britain is at last preparing to catch up with her friends and neighbours in America and Europe where *la vice anglaise*, as flagellation is affectionately known, has never held quite the same attraction. But like Aubrey Beardsley, who remained all his life wedded to the delights first experienced on 'the old school block', some will always refuse to be parted from the pleasure of pain.

My view is that physical punishment is a useful aid to discipline, and in some cases a valuable factor in moulding character. Discipline should not be too soft, otherwise boys grow up weak. I don't believe in putting up with nonsense from the boys. I haven't seen any reason to change my views on corporal punishment.

Nicholas Debenham,
headmaster of St James's School, Queen's Gate,
London, October 1989

Learning violence from their elders and betters, what can boys do but dish it out in turn? Tom Brown was not the only boy whose schooldays were terrorized by bullying. School bullying reaches back into the mists of time, far beyond the archetypal school bully Flashman, the odious tormentor of *Tom Brown's Schooldays*, who interestingly enough has enjoyed a new life as a hero of our times, in the *Flashman* novels of George Macdonald Fraser.

Traditional school rituals, indeed, had little to distinguish them from sheer torture. At Winchester throughout the nineteenth century, in the notorious 'tin gloves' ordeal, a pattern was drawn on the hands of new boys with a red-hot poker until a mass of blisters was raised. Marlborough boys received their burns on their knees, when they had to crawl along the top of a blisteringly hot radiator singing 'Clementine'. Harrow schoolboys suspended new recruits over a stairwell, and tossed them from side to side in a blanket, until one small kill-joy contrived to fall to his death and so put an end to the time-honoured fun.

Every school has always allowed for private initiative in the matter of bullying. As a young man Osbert Sitwell met 'a fine old gentleman' who told him that 'if a boy don't get on at school, it's his own fault. I well remember,' the old man continued, 'when I first went to Eton, the Head Boy called us all together and pointing to a little fellow with a mass of curly red hair, said, "If ever you see that boy, kick him! And if you are too far off to kick him, throw a stone!" He was a fellow called Swinburne. He used to write poetry for a time, I believe, but I don't know what became of him.'[4]

Public and boarding schools arguably constitute a very special case, affecting only a minority of the population, and as such of little consequence to the rest of the world. There is nothing special, however, about the cruelty that those boys can show to one another. On the contrary, few boys, from whatever walk of life, can hope to reach adulthood without some experience of being bullied. Girls in school can be unkind, even vicious, favouring or excluding the lucky or unlucky in many painful ways. But the systematic use of physical violence, of intimidation, ganging up or beating up, and the routine torment of those smaller, weaker or in any way different from themselves, is almost exclusively the province of boys.

Like so much else that darkens or deforms the lives of boys (sexual abuse, for example), the scale of this problem has been widely ignored. Yet its prevalence can hardly be doubted. 'You get it for being Jewish', runs one comprehensive school chant:

> You get it for being black,
> You get it for being chicken,
> You get it for fighting back.
> You get it for being big and fat,
> You get it for being small,
> You get it, you get it, you get it,
> For any damn thing at all.

Like child abuse again, bullying is a 'victimless crime', with the victim rather than the perpetrator being made to feel 'bad', guilty and ashamed. In the nature of things too, the bullied child is usually frantic to avoid naming or exposing the tormentor(s) for fear of further reprisals, or of sanctions from his peer group for breaking the schoolboy code of honour by 'grassing'. This code, absurdly enough, seems to be accepted also by those who should be the boys' first line of defence, the teachers. School authorities everywhere have been culpably slow to acknowledge the existence of bullying, let alone its routine occurrence, especially in economically-deprived or inner-city areas. Yet a 1989 Home Office enquiry into school discipline chaired by Lord Elton, a former Home Office Minister, found that bullying was both widespread in schools and as widely denied by teachers and head teachers. Psychologist Dr Michael Bolton of Sheffield University cites research studies which show that 26 per cent of middle school children had been bullied more than once in the previous term. Michele Elliott, child psychologist and founder of Kidscape, a charity which campaigns for the better protection of children, puts the figure higher: Kidscape surveys suggest that 38 per cent of all pupils suffer some bullying in their school lives, with 5 per cent undergoing prolonged and severe cruelty. In one survey during which Elliott questioned 4000 London children between five and sixteen about their worries, 68 per cent said that they had been bullied at some time. Dr Pat Lister, an educational therapist working on the problem full-time at a London comprehensive, supports Elliott's figures, estimating that the true figure is nearer to three in four.

Girls of course constitute a proportion of these figures, since the separation of victims by sex has not so far been undertaken by researchers into bullying. To professionals in the field, however, there is little doubt that boys constitute by far the majority of both the bulliers and the bullied. 'Of course it's the boys!' says Coventry comprehensive headmaster Michael Middlemass. 'Just look out into the playground! Or come back at four o'clock, see who's clustered round the school gates waiting for someone to pick on. It's always the way.' And unless attitudes like this are changed, it seems it always will be. For schools are not divorced from society, isolated enclaves of protected behaviour and thought. It would be remarkable if bullying in schools today had not picked up on the groundswell of violence in the world outside, and grown accordingly.

And whatever the statistics, the proof of this widespread, silent suffering will only surface in individual examples of trauma, even tragedy. BBC producer Chris Terrill, researching a 1989 BBC-1 television documentary, discovered a case where one boy was so badly beaten that his mother thought he had been run over by a car. Another tormented boy was forced to attend his local hospital psychiatric unit for two years as the school was 'unable' to have him back. His school was also unable to help thirteen-year-old Mark Perry of Oxfordshire, who became the target of a group of bullies because he wore glasses and was good in class. Trying to outrun the gang on his bicycle as he left school one day in 1987, he swerved under a van and was killed. In a similar accident in Birmingham in 1990, fifteen-year-old Daniel Beckett died under a lorry when he tried to escape the traditional end-of-term 'flour and eggs' jape at Tividale Comprehensive School, when boys are allowed to pelt chosen victims. Daniel's mother said that her son, who was quiet, well-mannered, and careful with his clothes, had always been picked on by the older boys, who called him

'Tiny Tears'. 'I had stopped making him go on the last days of term because he was always so frightened,' she said. 'But this time he had to go because he had a maths exam. He was my only child. I don't know how I can go on living without him.'

For the victims of bullying at school, the sentence is not simply one of five or eight years' physical pain and mental anguish: the effects can last far longer. Christopher Snuggs of Abingdon, Oxfordshire, remained the target of the group of boys who had bullied him at school for years after they had all left. Finally he threw himself from a bridge into the river Thames in May 1990. 'He just could not take the hidings any more,' his mother told the inquest. Those who survive find that the after-effects of having been bullied remain with them for life. 'When we advertised for people to take part in the programme,' Terrill says, 'we got a torrent of replies – not just from children, but from adults. The physical wounds heal, the emotional ones don't.'

Most grown men of any age can still name the school bully. Rarely, however, do they get the chance to even the ancient score. As a respectable middle-aged man, Claude Wood of Huddersfield by chance opened his front door one morning in 1989 to an electricity inspector whom he instantly recognized as the man who had tormented him at school 30 years before. In the best *Boy's Own* school story traditions, Wood, although at 5' 4" nearly a foot shorter than his tormentor and suffering from cancer besides, chased his old enemy down the street and 'thumped him on the ear'. The £50 fine for assault he was subsequently required to pay reflects the indulgence of the Yorkshire magistrates to what is normally treated as a much more serious offence.

I just wanted to be one of the lads.
> Darryl Stevenson, convicted of criminal damage and
> grievous bodily harm after football hooliganism in
> Coventry, May 1989

Does any boy ever forget the desire to be 'one of the gang'? The regular infliction of violence, fear and physical punishment upon growing boys creates not merely a culture of pain and aggression, but a *hierarchy*. Confronted with the raw power of those bigger and older than himself, the young boy has no option but to submit. Yet being admitted even to the lowliest place in the gang hierarchy carries with it the implicit promise of rising up through the system: the victim can therefore confidently hope to be empowered in time to inflict the same treatment on others, as soon as he makes any progress up the pecking order. Admission to the dominance structure, however painfully sought, is therefore the first foot on the ladder and the *sine qua non*. However high the price, then, boys will always be found queuing up to pay it.

In any society of boys, membership of the 'in' group, even at the most despised level, is keenly sought and bought at any cost. But with the compulsive, circular logic of cruelty, the group that is to provide protection from fear and pain can only be entered by braving both. Inevitably the ritual of entry involves torment, danger and distress. Would any girl put up with this? 'To get into the gang,' recalled a veteran of World War II of his boyhood days in World War I:

> you had to stand to attention while one of the 'army regulars', as we called the big lads, put live worms down the back of your neck. If you stood still till the last one dropped to the floor through your trouser leg, you were in. If you moved, you were out.[5]

Although gruesome enough for a seven-year-old, this was at least not life-threatening. Older gangs, of boys of ten, twelve and fourteen, imposed progressively harsher and more dangerous demands. 'You had to prove your worth,' recalled another old-timer. Such proof involved, for example, jumping or swinging across a river or canal, when most of the boys, as working-class city kids, could not swim. The boy who passed this ascending series of tests met the final trial of strength in the company of the tough guys who had already made it into the gang:

> The final test was the back-street lamp-post test. The lamp-post had an earthing strap attached to it, and we all held hands in a circle, then the gang leader would touch this metal bracket and an electric shock would whip like a lightning strike through the entire gang.[6]

The greater the danger, the tougher the 'dare', as the American writer Roger Hoffman recalls:

> The secret to diving under a moving freight train and rolling out the other side with all your moving parts attached lies in picking the right spot between the tracks to hit with your back. Ideally, you want soft dirt or pea gravel, clear of glass shards and railroad

spikes that could cause you instinctively, and fatally, to sit up. Today, at 38, I couldn't be threatened or baited enough to attempt that dive. But as a seventh-grader struggling to make the cut in a tough Atlanta grammar school, all it took was a dare.

Hoffman was fighting a losing battle against being the smart kid, bright in class, 'with more As than friends'. The threat of exclusion from the gang if he did not 'dirty up his act' drove him to rise to ever more desperate 'dares': shoplifting, 'sugaring teachers' gas tanks', dropping matches into public mailboxes. The showdown came when the gang leader, a boy failing in school that year, called him out with the freight train challenge. '"A smart guy like you," he said, his smile evaporating, "you could figure it out easy."' It was the worst moment of Hoffman's life. 'I'd just turned twelve. The monkey clawing my back was Teacher's Pet. And I'd been dared.'[7]

Hoffman took the dive, came out the other side, made the grade, and lived to tell the tale. Many do not. The adolescent Winston Churchill, in a foolhardy attempt to leap across a chasm in a 'wild park' on the Bournemouth estate of his aunt, Lady Wimborne, fell 30 feet into a ravine, narrowly escaping death from brain damage, ruptured kidneys, and other injuries severe enough to keep him in bed for a whole year. A century later, ten-year-old Aaron Davies of the Forest of Dean in Gloucestershire suffered 'catastrophic' brain damage which left him quadraplegic, totally incapable, and mute, following an accident with a dumper truck which he was driving with his friend Darren, aged eleven. In the glorious summer of 1990, fourteen-year-old Mark Smeeth drowned in a lake in Farnborough, Hants, after being challenged by friends to swim out to an island in the middle of it.

And boys continue to turn on boys. Every day in the USA, one child is killed with a firearm, and ten others are wounded. 'In the most common type of incident,' reports Washington columnist Charles Bremner, 'a boy between nine and sixteen finds his father's pistol, usually in the bedroom, the place where 47 per cent of weapons are kept, and playfully blasts a younger brother, sister or friend.' The notion of the slaughter as 'playful' is questioned by the Washington Congressional Committee currently taking evidence on guns and children. 'Many of the deaths from these shootings are deliberate,' said one witness. 'Children under fourteen are using guns to settle scores in trivial arguments – like I've heard of someone shooting because someone stepped on their shoes.'[8]

In Asmat [New Guinea], without death there can be no
new life. A young initiate sits for days with the skull of
his enemy at his groin, absorbing through his penis the
essence and strength of the dead man. For this rite, the
men's house is charged with an atmosphere of violence
and exhilaration . . . novices are taken into the jungle
and accused of menstruating while elders push stalks of
sugar cane up their nostrils until they bleed freely . . .
Later, when facial hair appears, the novices attend other
nose-bleeding ceremonies that continue the rites of
manhood. The nasal septum is pierced; so, too, is the
tongue pierced to make the blood flow. The penis-head
is then rubbed with a rough-surfaced leaf, and is cut,
again to allow the blood to flow freely.

> Tobias Schneebaum,
> *Where the Spirits Dwell* (1988)

Per ardua ad astra – whatever its modern inflection (guns, freight
trains, electric shocks), passing through fear, pain and the shadow of
death to attain manhood is as old as human life itself. Rites and
ceremonies of initiation reach back to the dawn of time, and the key to
their meaning is always to be found in the deliberate, ritualized
infliction of violence and the sharing of pain. In tribal initiations,
ordeals imposed upon boys from the age of ten upwards include
stabbing or slashing with hunting sticks or spears, patterning of scar
tissue on body or face (compare the slashed cheeks of the African
Kikuyu warrior with the duelling scars of the Prussian military
academy) and the knocking out of the boy's two front teeth with a
stone. Nor is the pain inflicted purely physical. Among the Ceram
tribes of Indonesia, as French psychoanalyst Elisabeth Badinter notes,
the initiate is taken blindfold from his parents into a dark, secret house
in the depths of the forest. As soon as he disappears within the
precincts, 'a dull chopping sound', bloodcurdling howls and screams,
and blood dripping from swords or spears all signify to the observers
waiting outside that the boy is dead, that 'his head has been cut off, and
that the devil has carried him away to the other world'. Small wonder
then that when the boys return home, after these and other nameless
terrors and torments, they act 'like one totally exhausted after childbirth . . . as if they had forgotten how to walk'.[9] Whatever the function
of these torments (male bonding, group reinforcement or preparation

for war), it is noteworthy that there are no equivalent rites for young females. On the contrary, the celebrations of the menarche by which a young girl is welcomed into adult womanhood generally honour or reward her, for example with small presents or special clothes, while menstrual rituals involve keeping the females concerned as secluded and passive as possible.

Most terrifying, however, are those initiation ceremonies which purport to confer manhood through an attack on the source and site of manhood itself, the penis. For thousands of years the amputation of the foreskin has been widely practised in the magico-mystical belief that it finally detaches the boy from his mother by 'sexing' him as a male. Stripped of the soft folds of 'female' flesh, the 'real' penis can burst forth in all its power and glory, proving the unsexed child to be a man. Necessarily, then, the candidate must be pubertal, and preferably adolescent, to be able to take the all-important stand, and tribes from Ethiopia to Ecuador have for thousands of years bloodied their boys in this excruciating way. Female genital mutilation, the so-called 'female circumcision' or 'infibulation', although a far greater barbarity than the amputation of the foreskin since its genuine equivalent would be the removal of the penis itself, is not required by either Judaism or Islam, and as a consequence is visited upon far fewer females than circumcision is upon males. Only the Jews have traditionally insisted on infant circumcision (Muslims circumcise in early boyhood), as a sign that the 'covenant' so made was with God, not with man or other men.

But the boy can only leave the mother behind by outstripping and so defeating her. For Jung, Bettelheim and others the secret of all initiation rituals lay in 'imitating the role of the mother', 'becoming' the mother, in order to cancel out her power over men. So the initiate passes through the fear, the pain and blood of a symbolic childbirth, by choice, indeed as his first adult choice, in order to be born again not as a child, but as a man and hero. The male establishes his virility by taking over the female's procreative powers, and his strength by choosing to undergo what she cannot avoid. The deep compulsion of this womb-envy accounts for the horrific fate of every boy initiate in the Aranda tribe of Australia:

The ritual surgeon seizes the boy's penis, inserts a long thin bone deep into the urethra, and slashes at the penis again and again with a small piece of flint used as a scalpel. He cuts through the layers of flesh until he reaches the bone, and the penis splits open like a boiled frankfurter.[10]

This hideous ceremony, witnessed by the white settlers, seemed to them unspeakably pointless and cruel, typical 'Abo' savagery. The sophistication of its meaning appears only in Aranda, where the word for 'split penis' derives from the Aboriginal for 'vagina'. In addition, the honorific 'possessor of a vulva' is the title bestowed on all boys who undergo the ordeal. Later rituals also include the regular re-opening of the wound to demonstrate that the initiate could now, like any woman, and better than his mother, *at will*, 'menstruate'.[11]

> Blessed art Thou, O Lord our God, King of the Universe, that Thou hast not made me a woman.
> Daily prayer of Jewish men

No boy, of course, could ever forget an experience like this – one school of anthropological thought indeed contends that the purpose of all painful initiation rituals is to burn into each boy's mind the folk-memory of the key myths and values of the tribe. The only others able to share his experience will be those who have undergone it with him, pain for pain, blood for blood: that group will then be bonded closer than husband and wife, closer than siblings, closer than mother and child. As the boy is violently dissociated from mother, home and family, so he is associated, with equal violence, with the group of other boys who will henceforward be, from rebirth to death, his blood brothers. Such potent group or gang organization has been a key feature of every boy's transition to manhood from primitive tribal society to the present day. 'You had your territory and the other gangs had theirs,' explained a veteran of Harlem street fights, now a youth leader in New York:

> You could never risk your neck outside your street by yourself, without the other guys – man, you'd be shit-scared to do it, crazy even to think of it, you'd be caught, beaten to a pulp, dead. You weren't in a gang, you weren't *nobody*. But to be in was war, just war, you'd never believe the violence, knives, bricks, broken glass. I was so terrified, but I never dared show it, if you showed yourself to be a coward, your life wasn't worth dog-do. No one ever tried to stop the fights, the police just let us get on with it and the people, hell, they used to watch from their windows like a side-show, you know?

Born out of violence, the gang cannot exist without violence. Expelled from the primal warmth of his mother's embrace, turning to the gang for the strength of its solidarity, the boy finds not a comfort structure, but a hierarchy, one which fights others to hold its own position, and fights within itself for the right to lead the fight. 'Growing up, the boys I hung out with fought *all the time*,' recalls Bostonian Kevin O'Marah, a London-based management consultant. 'Looking back, it was pretty violent, and scary with it. You fought just to establish who was tougher, challenging all the time, like a squash ladder. Bodily threat terrifies me, I still have nightmares about it all, but at the time, you just did it.'

'You did it,' recalls Mike McCoy, a London graphic designer of 26, 'because you had no option. And it's no bad training for life as it really is.' Certainly there will not be, for the boy, any future in any male group or society that will not entail challenge and competition, tests and trials of strength. But in a classic double-bind, the gang that tests you, constantly threatening rejection as the price of failure, is also the only support you have, as in the definitive American pre-teen movie *Stand By Me* (1986). Violence, from within or without, simply reinforces the bonds between those involved. 'What the kids in that film were able to find is what I found as a kid,' comments the film's writer and director Rob Reiner, 'that whatever difficulties you had you could always find safety and strength with your friends.' Mike McCoy agrees. 'You had each other against the world, against parents, teachers, girls, other boys, the lot! Really, it was the only solidarity I had.'

The gang is also the primary testing ground of the boy's need to be brave and strong. Today's boy will almost certainly never have to face a wild animal single-handed and lightly armed: he will never have to kill to eat, slaughter other youths in hand-to-hand combat, or defend his woman and her babies to the death. Yet the boyish drive to be tough and terrible has not diminished at all. On the contrary, it is fed and fostered by an endless diet of fantasy figures of phenomenal power and strength. Clint Eastwood and Charles Bronson stalk the screens as the lone avenger who triumphs over countless enemies; Rocky comes up from under against impossible odds; Rambo shoots up a whole nation in single, heroic combat.

These figures express one of the most potent themes in the boy's desire to be a man. 'I don't think you realize how much in his deepest heart a man wants to be a hero,' a 30-year-old social worker told researcher Carol Lee:

I was brought up on it – fantasies of doing incredibly brave things, or of managing in the face of impossible odds – while inside I was a mass of nerves and fear. For me being a boy was like this – the fantasy of being heroic lived with the disappointment of not being. I think upbringing and conditioning do that to us.[12]

This deep, hopeless boyhood desire is shared even by those destined to win their share of fame and fortune, as TV star Jonathan Ross explains: 'I wore glasses, I was skinny, I kept myself to myself. I spent all my time with comics, Batman, Spiderman, The Hulk. I used to particularly like the ones about superheroes with problems. You thought, maybe I could do something heroic too, because I have problems.'

For a few lucky boys, the fantasy of heroism comes true. In 1987 twelve-year-old Ian McLaughlan of Edinburgh rescued his mother and four younger siblings from a burning tenement; in 1989, ten-year-old Mark Combs kept his 84-year-old great-grandfather alive in a Seattle mountain wilderness, feeding him on berries and keeping him warm until help arrived, after the old man had lost their way. For the rest, the heroic rescue only ever happened in boyhood play. American film writer Steve Tesich, author of the classic film of male adolescence, *Breaking Away* (1979), describes a game he played obsessively as a boy in Yugoslavia, with his best friend Slobo in an abandoned truck:

We were flying over the Atlantic . . . engine failure! 'We'll have to bail out!' Slobo would turn and look me in the eye: 'I can't swim,' he'd say. 'Fear not.' I put my hand on his shoulder. 'I'll drag you to shore.' 'Sharks!' he'd cry. But I always saved him . . .

How often have parents, teachers or other adults seen young boys engaged in such adventures and casually dismissed them with the thought, 'They're only playing, they're not doing anything'? On the contrary, they are engaged in the most important activity of their lives. What they are doing is trying to 'be something' in Samuel Goldwyn's phrase: in particular to be that elusive something called a man. Already the imperative is making itself felt, and already the demands of the agenda, however heavy, are plain to every growing boy. By a variety of devices, both legal and illegal (and how many males get through boyhood without so much as scrumping an apple?) and by the constant, incessant, compulsive repetition of them, the boy trains himself to fight off his fears of weakness and failure: to transcend his destructive sense of helplessness and powerlessness. He and his friends convince themselves and each other that they are not puny, small, frail or fearful, not boys at all in fact; not even men, but *supermen*, capable of rising to every challenge, cool and competent under any pressure. The inevitable drawback to this process is that adulthood will always carry then 'the disappointment of not being', as the social worker expressed his lack of heroism to Carol Lee. 'There is a telephone booth in every man's imagination,' says *Cosmopolitan* agony aunt Irma Kurtz. 'He fancies that the moment destiny requires it he can rush in, strip off his city duds, and emerge as Superman, in full possession of astonishing powers.' If only, as Woody Allen says, life were like that.

As boys grow up, then, they prepare themselves, and are prepared, for a life they can never lead. At the same time they fail to prepare for the real world that lies ahead, a world of human interchange and emotional demand, and especially the rich, problematical and complex intercourse between female and male. 'Everything was action,' says Steve Tesich. 'Naturally, not one word concerning the nature of our feelings for one another was ever exchanged.' Naturally? How naturally? Every boy learns to empower himself through this ceaseless struggle for dominance and self-reliance. He has made the break from his mother, and at whatever cost, won entry to the harder world of manhood. He has learned, too, that he can draw strength from the gang, that he is not alone, and an unspoken, unspeakable loyalty to his friends is the price in gratitude he must pay for that. How 'natural' is the result Tesich was himself to discover when his friend was killed in Vietnam. 'I went to his mother's house, and because she was a woman, I tried to tell her how much I loved her son. It was not a good scene. Although I was telling the truth, my words sounded like lies.' How natural is that?

The truth is that the price of manhood training is a virtual de-skilling in every vital area of emotional communication, an education in non-speak. 'It only takes the first nine years of a boy's life to teach him the art of non-speak,' observes psychologist Philip Hodson, 'to socialize him into a person who prefers *doing* to *being*.' The only communication of growing boys is through shared, usually violent or boisterous activity, in itself a process for avoiding speech and the sharing of feelings. Hodson points to an experiment conducted at the University of Colorado on the social development of children at nine years of age, in which twenty pairs of boys and the same number of girls were observed by psychologists as they made each other's acquaintance, explored their surroundings, and began to play. The results were compelling. While the girls hunkered down and immediately started getting to know one another:

In practically every case, the boys ignored each other *as people*. They displayed no personal curiosity. They didn't look in each other's faces. They didn't ask personal questions. They didn't volunteer information about themselves. Conversation was confined to the technical problems of Lego-design. In every essential respect the boys stayed solitary and played by themselves.[13]

The majority of boys will learn in time that there is more fun to be had playing with others than playing with themselves. For the vulnerable few, however, this dissociation from feeling, from shared human warmth, is to have profound and dangerous effects. The boy who fails to find meaning through play, who cannot experience or even approach the urgent ideal of manhood and heroism in any other way, begins, even at the youngest age, to turn to crime and violent activity to fill the void. In a case before a London Crown Court in 1990, the leader of a gang of 'steamers', who attacked Tube train travellers and terrorized them into parting with their money and valuables, was found to be only 14 when he was convicted of robbery, wounding and affray. The true extent of child crime is obscured by national systems of classification – Britain does not even recognize as crime any act committed by a child under the age of ten. Violent assaults, even leading to murder, may be taken or passed off as accidents; equally, child violence is not often sufficiently strong to do any real damage. Yet there is little doubt among specialists that the intention is there, and that it will not simply go away. 'These children are dead inside,' says Dr Shawn Johnson, a New York psychologist specializing in child crime. 'For them to feel alive and important they have to engage in some terrible sadistic activity.'

It is of course a mark of our times that the concept of 'juvenile crime' is fraught with such horror. To Dickens and his contemporaries the acceptance of the male capacity for acts of cruelty and criminality had no lower age limit. A 'murdering young varmint' of fourteen, twelve, or even nine years old was nothing out of the ordinary, and the prison hulks, the convict transport ships and even the gallows saw a regular traffic in boys of ten and eleven. 'It comes as no surprise that boys *can* be violent,' says primary school teacher Isobel Lefeaux. 'But for a society which purports not to accept it, we're doing very little to prevent it.'

To other commentators, child crime is not only increasing in volume and intensity: it is beginning to exhibit many of the extreme, bizarre and sadistic features of adult crime of the present day. A three-year-old London boy, Adam Hennessy, playing in the street in April 1989, was attacked by two other boys of seven and nine who stripped and beat him, then heaped burning rags and papers on his head. A year later, Adam was still receiving plastic surgery and psychotherapy. Such stories can be replicated from all over the world.

In his book *The Cheated*, as he categorizes both perpetrators and victims of today's anomic brutality, the Australian dramatist Louis Nowra has made a collection of such incidents. In New York, two boys aged 12 and 13 held a 73-year-old woman captive for nearly a week, during which they robbed, raped and beat her repeatedly. In Sydney, an eleven-year-old boy was anally assaulted with a penknife by another eleven-year-old. An eight-year-old shot his 79-year-old grandfather to death in Jacksonville, Florida, after warning the old man, 'Don't tell me what to do!' A group of Australian outback boys all under 15 staked another out in the midday sun and tried to whip him to death with a dead snake 'like the Indians used to do'.

Where does it all come from? And how can we check it? Figures from the British National Association for the Care and Resettlement of Offenders show a rising trend in youth violence, with the age of first conviction also dropping: 26 per cent of all known offenders in 1987 were juveniles aged 10–16. Some commentators see child violence as an inevitable response to a society in which a boy may have seen up to 200,000 acts of television violence by the age of 16, including 33,000 murders, and in which multi-problem families are the heaviest TV users. To others, television may malignly shape the form of the sadistic acts, but it does not supply the initial stimulus, whose wellspring lies far deeper in the nature of original sin. 'We are reluctant to acknowledge the roots of violence in the normal male psyche,' writes Ronald Hayman. 'We still like to believe in goodies and baddies, Samaritans and sinners. But thugs, rapists and killers are all too ordinary. The roots of violence are in male sado-masochism; what varies is the way men release their aggression.'[14] What men do, boys copy; what men teach, their sons learn. Until we learn this most obvious of lessons, the sins of the fathers will continue to be visited on their sons.

When you're growing up, that 'Be strong' thing – *it's all propaganda*.
   John Lennon

---

5   Man's Best Friend

Puberty is when Nature says, 'Shake hands with Mr Happy!'
Robin Williams

Adolescence is the birth of the body hairs.
Salvador Dali

Ven der putz shteht, ligt der sechel in drerd [when the prick stands up, the brain lies buried in the ground].
Yiddish proverb

'In adolescence,' said Norman Mailer, 'I only had to say God and I would think of my groin.' Whatever the agenda of his public world, every boy making the home run for manhood has to face one overwhelming imperative of the most private, indeed intimate kind – to be a man, he has to stand up and be counted. Sexual competence and, even more, sexual prowess are central to any concept of masculinity, indeed the key determinant of 'what makes a man a man'. 'The importance of sexual performance dominates the male mind,' says Dr Leonore Tiefer of the Beth Israel Medical Center, New York, 'whether we are discussing the traditional man, the modern man, or even the "new" man':

What so stokes male sexuality that clinicians are impressed by the force of it? Not libido, but rather the curious phenomenon by which sexuality consolidates and confirms gender. In men, gender appears to 'lean' on sexuality, the need for sexual performance is so great; in women, gender identity and self-worth can be consolidated by other means.

For the young beginner, this crucial, inescapable rite of manhood can often seem as bizarre, distasteful and threatening as a masonic initiation ritual, without any of the guaranteed advantages of that induction, as historian Dan Irwin explains: 'You learn where to stick your dick pretty young, that's not the problem. But up until the age of eighteen or so, it's a complete mystery how you get that far, or why you would want to. And why would a girl let you? It seems so gruesome. At my school the bio teacher drivelling on about "love-juice" made us all shudder. We were never taught anything about the human interaction. There's such a lot to learn, it's terribly miserable and confusing. The best thing I ever read about it was a line of Martin Amis: "You feel like a dog on the moon baying at the earth."'

For this adventure, too, the boy is out there all by himself. In every public act, gang solidarity may ensure that he will never walk alone: for this one, however, the only helping hand he can rely on must be his own. And success, as in every other walk of life, will prove elusive. In the long journey from puberty through to the assured adult masculinity of the skilful lover or tender, practised husband, most will travel hopefully, but few arrive. The natural function of human sexuality, the expression of love between a man and a woman, does not automatically follow on from years of adolescent experience in which genital activity, erection and orgasm, take on all the non-sexual loading of the desire for power, control, achievement, peer approval and performance, all the intangibles already so important from the years of pre-adolescent gender training. Significant numbers of men will never outgrow the immature sexuality, the 'lunge and plunge' of the novice years, while even the most mature and sophisticated of men will continue to feel that without his erection and his orgasm, love-making is nothing. For some, like the mass murderer and necrophile Dennis Nilsen, adolescent experiences of the opposite sex, or of their own, serve to forge the last link in a chain whose pathology now takes on its final, fatal form; while even the luckiest youth only survives his rapprochement with the troublesome 'other', woman, through his unquestioning faith in those very factors which will later bedevil his hopes of a genuinely warm and mutual love: the centrality of his desire, his faith in penis power, and the strength of his male will.

When I want to play with a prick, I'll play with my own.
W. C. Fields

To begin with, though, sex is not a two-hander but a game of solitaire. In his celebrated rejoinder to a Hollywood movie mogul's invitation to a round of golf, the tortured Fields speaks for generations of lost boys. The earliest and in some ways always the best of sexual play for every boy is to be found at the end of his arm. Official manhood training has viciously discouraged masturbation, and by insisting on sport, exercise and 'toughening up', treats the whole body as a phallus, teaching the boy to 'be hard', 'stand firm', 'follow through', 'don't weaken, don't give in, don't fail'. Without any formal instruction, however, every boy knows that he can never be a man until, as in every heroic fantasy, the small pink shrimp between his legs turns into a lion and comes roaring out to play.

For the lucky boys this happens, as in all the best *Boy's Own* stories, at one bound: *'Wasn't* it fun in the bath tonight?' quipped Quentin Crisp of his own self-discovery, in a wicked parody of Christopher Robin. 'I was in bed one night when my cock started to feel all warm,' remembers Lawrence Ecclestone, a naval engineer. 'I touched it, it literally jumped up in my hand and, sounds silly, sort of burst into flower. It was one of the best things in my entire life. It was my twelfth birthday – what a birthday present!' The onset of having sex with someone you love very much, in Woody Allen's memorable definition of masturbation, may begin as early as ten, or as late as sixteen. Around twelve, however, is the age that most men recall beginning, including a former champion pitcher for the Dodgers, a Lord Lieutenant of the County of Rutland, and the distinguished editor of the *Literary Review*. Many men, too, recall the first occasion as a moment of special delight. 'The first time I made love, it was with the ground,' says Paco Rabanne, revolutionary dress designer of the 1960s. 'I made a little hole, and when I reached orgasm the earth made some very heady smells – of flowers and rosemary.'

Few boys are lucky enough, on their first sexual occasion, to make the earth move. For some unfortunates, especially in former times, what should have been a source of pride and joy became degraded into something dirty, disgusting, even dangerous. As one Sheffield blade-grinder recalled his turn-of-the-century working-class boyhood:

> When I was thirteen I had a very funny sensation, a slight burning sensation in my little willie. I wondered what was the matter, so I went to the lavvie which was out in the back yard and shared by two families. I touched my willie and it started to spit at me. I looked at the gooey result and felt as sick as a pig and dirty all over. The door opened and my mother came in. She seemed to know automatically what was happening, gave me a clip on the earhole and said, 'Nathan, that'll send thee blind if that does it to thisen too often.'[1]

Blindness, madness, disease: these themes recur with painful frequency in men's memories of adult reactions to their new-found skill.

'You might find some white matter extruding from your private parts, Worsley,' remarked a Marlborough housemaster to the late great journalist and man of letters, 'T.C.'. 'Don't worry about it. It's only a sort of *disease*, like measles.' Throughout the nineteenth century doctors in England and America were convinced beyond reason or doubt that masturbation caused brain rot, moral decay and physical collapse, a conviction which led to a flourishing trade in 'mechanical restraints' ranging from padded gloves and harnesses to spiked penis rings which the hapless offender was forced to wear at night. Until very recently, 'the habit of self-abuse' (for men, though not for women) appeared as a crime on the statute books of the state of Nebraska, USA. Although no longer treated as a sickness, mental, moral or physical, masturbation remains a sin in the teaching of the orthodox Catholic Church, a position reinforced by a recent papal decree.

What is it about the sin of Onan that has for so many centuries driven the fathers of boys to these outbursts of blindness, sickness and insanity? The son's capacity to obtain erection and emission should be the final, all-important proof that he has become that anxiously sought-for thing, a man. Yet in the 'hardening' of the boy into a mini-phallus the patriarchs have been frantic to ensure that they, not he, directed the resulting aim, flow, dissemination, and rate of strike. Masturbation, intoned Baden-Powell in *Rovering to Success* (1922):

> cheats semen of getting its full chance of making up the strong *manly* man you would otherwise be. You are throwing away the seed that has been handed down to you as a trust, instead of keeping it and ripening it for bringing a son to you later on.

No rogering to success for 'Baden's Boys', then.

The strain of this unnatural repression of a completely natural, indeed naturally *uncontrollable* physical activity was in itself enough to produce, if not blindness, neurosis galore. Those lucky enough to live to see their sentence of doom lifted are almost lyrical in their expressions of relief. 'My mother was a very religious woman,' remembers Lord Bath, 'and she wasn't prepared to say much about the facts of life except to say that sometimes little boys did things to themselves which were rather horrible and drove them mad.' Although he had no idea what she was talking about, he recalls suffering the torment of King Lear in the bleak conviction, '*I shall go mad.*' Later the fear was 'that I was the only boy in England who did this terrible thing. But I couldn't stop.' Relief from this torture did not come till over a decade later, when the young lord went up to Oxford:

There was this Bursar, and he used to have all the new boys up at Christ Church, and then he would talk to them. I remember him saying to me, 'Tell me, how often do you masturbate?' I said 'Never!' 'Look,' he said, 'I think you must have misunderstood me. How often do you pass yourself off?' I said, 'Never. Never, sir.' I was so ashamed, you see. I thought it was the worst thing in the world to do. He said, 'Well, you're only the second boy I've spoken to that has come up to this college who's never done that thing.' I can't tell you what a relief it was. I felt that I'm not going to the lunatic asylum, that I'm a normal boy. It was the biggest relief I've ever had in all my life.

Clearly no power of patriarchal terrorism could be enough to prevent boys from doing 'the deed of shame', as one inaptly-named Victorian 'Boy's Handbook' has it. Every older man who had ever been a boy must have known this. Was the object then simply to generate guilt along with every handful of joy? In time every boy would grow up to realize how deeply he had been misled, turned loose in the dark forest of adolescence to wander alone till he stumbled through to manhood with only his rod and staff, as in the 23rd psalm, to be his comfort and guide. Did the boys, or their fathers, ever acknowledge this cruel, monumental fraud? Or was it simply yet another of the ritual ordeals which 'made a man' of an innocent boy?

I believe in the boys and girls, the men and women of tomorrow.
>   The Creed of the Teacher,
>   issued by the Education Council of the USA, 1906

If the rites of gaining entry to the manhood world of erection and orgasm are subject to this degree of phallic loading, how much greater must be the expectations of prowess riding on the parallel rite of passage, gaining entry to a woman? A crucial testing ground for the growing boy, even from the earliest age, lies in the challenge of the opposite sex, the 'women of tomorrow'. Interest in girls, although often coupled with extreme professions of hostility for the sex in general ('*Girls!* Yuk!'), appears at the primary school stage, and few boys, even from the most regimented and repressive of families, will get through childhood without some experience such as this, described with a curious dispassion by George Orwell:

> At five or six, like many children, I had passed through a phase of sexuality. My friends were the plumbers' children up the road, and we used sometimes to play games of a vaguely erotic kind. One was called 'playing at doctors', and I remember getting a faint but definite pleasant thrill from holding a toy trumpet, which was supposed to be a stethoscope, against a little girl's belly . . . After that, as so often happens, all sexual feelings seemed to go out of me for many years.[2]

What can Orwell have meant by that throw-away phrase, 'as so often happens'? For most boys, the reverse seems to be true: that early childhood experimentation both awakens and confirms an interest in sex which simply grows in size and strength as the boy himself does. For the youth who has never known a woman may be a virgin in the technical sense of the term, but his ostensibly pure and undipped wick is in reality an unregenerate wicked willie, wrinkled deep in time, in contradistinction to the female experience: most women only begin masturbating after some sexual experience, be it with a boy or another girl. The apparent male novice approaching a woman for full sexual intercourse some time before his twentieth birthday has in fact had up to a decade of intense phallic activity, either alone with his own penis ('Man's Best Friend') or through and around the penile activity and fantasy of other males. Small wonder, then, that raising the game to make players out of the previously remote and unknown female species induces in many young hopefuls a profound sense of unreality and alienation. This emerges clearly from the widespread use of the term 'It' for sex – 'doing it', 'getting it', 'having it', rather than doing, getting or having *her*.

Yet the urge to perform remains one of the strongest of boyhood desires and drives. Some prodigies translate their natural stirrings into direct action at the earliest possible moment, especially in times past: Genghis Khan, Charles II, Napoleon and Errol Flynn are among many men who claimed, or were believed, to have had full sexual intercourse during their twelfth year. This aping of adult prowess even by beardless boys remains a high imperative and a key mark of status even today.

Precocious sexual experience, however, often against the will of the sexual partner, be it girl, boy, or equally unconsenting animal, is also the distinguishing mark of a number of psychopathological murderers, from Peter Kurten, the mass-murderer who terrorized Düsseldorf in the 1920s, to the American 'college boy killers' of 1924, Leopold and Loeb. In the notorious New York gang rape and sodomization of the woman jogger in Central Park in 1989, most of the assailants were as young as thirteen and fourteen: none was over the age of fifteen. 'By sixteen, we're dealing with career sex criminals here,' commented Judge William Eberhardt of the Criminal Court of the City of New York. US statistics confirm the judge's gloomy pronouncement. In the past five years, FBI figures reveal that arrest for rape by the under-eighteens has risen by 14.6 per cent, for aggravated assault by 18.6 per cent, and for sexual murder, by 22.2 per cent. In the last ten years in America, the arrest rate for boys of thirteen and fourteen accused of rape has doubled. For sexual attacks in this age group, it has soared by 80 per cent, while arrests of twelve-year-olds involved in sexual crimes has leaped by 60 per cent. 'I have been working with these kids for 15 years now,' said Judith Becker, a psychiatrist at Columbia University. 'The age of the perpetrators has been decreasing.' Is this the price society has to pay for the way we live now?

Most, if not all, of these precocious sexual attempts will be fore-doomed to fail. But in a life-long concentration on the penis, if males have learned nothing else they have learned to follow the dictates of their own desire, and to persist until it is satisfied. At fifteen, after three years of informal apprenticeship to the mystery of the orgasm, Wilhelm Reich paid a visit to a brothel in order to advance his studies to the next level, and naturally enough, passed out *summa cum laude*:

> Was it the atmosphere, the clothing, the red light, the provocative nakedness, the smell of the whores? I don't know! It was pure sensual lust; *I* had ceased to be . . . I bit, scratched, thrust, and the girl had quite a time with me! I thought I would have to crawl inside her.[3]

'A man and a woman have one important thing in common at the start of a romance,' comments Irma Kurtz: 'they are both in love with him.'

With so much at stake, it is hardly surprising that for many young men the first experience with a female is usually disappointing, often depressing or distressing, and quite frequently disastrous. Today's young males are having sex with women earlier than ever before in this century. A British survey of 1989 showed that over 50 per cent of all young men had had intercourse by the age of eighteen, and over 75 per cent by the age of twenty, while only a small proportion of their fathers were sexually experienced with women before their mid-twenties.[4] Yet another British study (Sanders, *The Woman Report on Men*) showed that this wider experience did not go hand in hand with greater information or knowledge: only 6 per cent of mothers, and even fewer fathers, had ever talked to their sons on any sexual topic whatsoever. No acknowledgement is made of the young man's often overwhelming emotional or romantic feelings, no attempt to link the physical act with love or tenderness: the beginner, it seems, is almost deliberately kept in the dark.

Predictably, then, the primary urge of the beginner is not love or romance, but pure curiosity. Over half the males in the Sanders survey said that they had no feelings for the girl on their first occasion, but were 'desperate to get going', and 'she was the one who would "do it"'. To the young man hungry for discovery, conquest and validation as a man, refusal by a woman is unacceptable. In a survey of 1000 teenage boys conducted for Planned Parenthood of Chicago in 1989, over 70 per cent gave it as their opinion that it was 'OK to tell a girl you loved her' in order to induce her to have sex, even against her will. Another survey, by Dr Mary Koss of Kent State University, found that 27 per cent of student males admitted to using both physical and emotional force when a woman was unwilling to have sex with them.[5] Other tactics reported by female victims of the dick-that-won't-take-no-for-an-answer include:

● 'My balls hurt, you've got to do something to help me.'

● 'Don't you love me?'

● 'I paid for dinner!'

● 'Are you frigid? Did you have a problem with your father?'

● 'Women say "No" when they really mean "Yes".'

● 'What are you, gay or something?'

● 'If there's a nuclear war tomorrow, you'll die without knowing what sex could really be like.'

● *'Trust me!'*

With attitudes like this, it is hardly surprising that a high proportion of young men report that they gain little enjoyment from their earliest sexual experience; and perhaps not surprising at all that a much higher proportion of young women gain even less.[6] For the men, attraction is often balanced by repulsion: there is a besetting fear of the 'dark continent' of the female genitalia, even a lurking dread of what the Christian Church has for a thousand years called 'the stinking, putrid, private parts of women'. Havelock Ellis only embarked on his great campaign to discover and disseminate the truth about sex after the painful mystifications of his early manhood, when his mother would take him out walking and make him stand beside her while he could hear 'an audible stream falling to the ground'. His sister's comment, 'She was *flirting* with you!' did nothing to dispel Ellis's confusion. In a similar vein John Updike reports, 'The major sexual experience of my childhood was a section of newsreel showing some women wrestling in a pit of mud' – hardly an appropriate preparation for a spectacularly successful sexual debut.

Success, however, seems to be the last thing young men expect on their first occasion: the difficulties, both technical and emotional, seem overwhelming. Seventeen years after his first episode, when he took a 'shopgirl' to a hotel, Kafka could still recall every detail with hideous clarity:

> It was all, before the hotel, charming, exciting and vile; in the hotel it was no different ... I was certainly happy, but this happiness consisted only in my finally having peace from the constant whining of the body, but above all in the whole thing's not being still more vile, still more filthy ... I knew immediately I'd never forget it, and at the same time knew or believed I knew that this vileness and filthiness, apparently quite unnecessary, were necessarily connected inwardly with the whole thing and that it was precisely this vileness and filthiness that had drawn me with such frantic force into this hotel which I would otherwise have used all my strength to avoid.[7]

Like Kafka, many men find that delight leads to disgust, the Shakespearian sense of 'the expense of spirit in a waste of shame'. Loathsome memories of such an experience can be very hard to shake off. 'I wanted to – you know, learn the ropes,' said Philip Maple-Dorham, now an investment banker, 'so I went to a prostitute as soon as I was called up and got to London. It was all quite *unbelievably* vile. I hadn't the faintest idea what I was letting myself in for. It put me off sex for years, almost for life. I feel someone should have warned me what a dangerous – almost delicate – thing the first time is. It can make you or break you.'

Traditionally, the boy did not venture alone and unguided on his first sexual encounter. Throughout history the father or the senior male relative has been closely, often anxiously implicated in his son's emerging manhood, exerting to the full his self-appointed task of delineating the appropriate masculine behaviour. In a show of concern which also carried a calculated sexual insult, the womanizing Philip of Macedon in the fifth century BC hired a celebrated courtesan to initiate his sexually backward adolescent son into the mechanics of heterosexuality, a gesture furiously repudiated by the future Alexander the Great. With the remarkable continuity displayed by manhood training through the ages, this ritual still takes place among modern men, from the British working classes ('It were a knocking shop in South Shields. Me dad said, "It's y'birthday, lad!"') to the international jet set:

> We were on vacation in Buenos Aires at the time. My mother's brothers had business interests there and we always spent a month or two there every winter. It was the older of my two uncles who actually raised the subject and made all the arrangements. But I found out afterwards that my father had given orders for it to take place. No, I didn't enjoy it. She was very beautiful and very skilful, but it was cold, mechanical – almost cruel, you know, to do that to a young boy?

The speaker, now a Florida-based US citizen, would not subject his own son, presently ten years old, to this ritual ordeal of his Latin American boyhood. But if the boy showed no interest in women? 'Then something would have to be done.'

Even when he is free of paternal interference, the novice cocksman may still find himself frighteningly out of control. Michael Scott, a Dorset farm labourer, describes a virtual rape at the hands of one of the cow-girls, a true descendant of Thomas Hardy's bold, merciless 'country copulatives': 'She came at me in the parlour after milking, and made a grab for me right there, and it was all over without me thinking I had anything to do with it.' Nor is it only in the country that women are kissing cousins. Simon Carver, a pupil at a venerable and distinguished tutorial college in Westminster, describes a round-the-table seminar with the history tutor, himself, and the daughter of an Iranian diplomat: 'She was across the table from me, but I wasn't looking at her. We were going great guns on the 1832 Reform Act and suddenly I felt her foot in my bollocks. I literally turned to stone, it was paralysing, terrifying.' Lawyer David Jaglom recalls a 'horror movie scenario' when having successfully pursued a 'very shy, very virginal creature', she turned on him at the moment of truth with the dick-shrivelling demand, 'I want you to give me a nice long slow hard FUCK!' 'Men honestly believe that they want women to come on to them,' comments David. 'But when it happens, it's just a nightmare.'

Not all women are vampires on the first encounter. Some, it seems, are merely corpses. 'She lay there like a dead thing, never moved a muscle.' Versions of this complaint against their first sexual partner were made by many men during the preparation of this book. The anonymous 'she', however, would often have had to be Wonderwoman to work in her own twirl before it was all over. 'I hardly had time to get into her'; 'I came in thirty seconds flat'; 'I never even got her top things off, so I'd got laid without ever seeing a woman's tits'; 'I couldn't wait to get rid of her afterwards'; these and other reminiscences suggest a desperation not simply to 'do it', but to get through it as fast as possible. 'Dipping your wick', 'getting your end in', 'playing your first away fixture', as men recall and talk about it, emerges all too often as another ordeal, another ritual, another scarification in the process of 'becoming a man'.

What drives young men to undertake this great 'leap in the dark', in the eighteenth-century phrase? Not love –

> I did but see her passing by
> Yet will I love her till I die –

first love, almost by definition, is the one you *don't* fuck. The earliest sexual experiences of many men in fact serve to confirm the damaging split between sex and love, between women you fool around with, and women you marry. These are mechanical exercises, not undertaken for the purpose of pleasure, either giving or receiving. Their purpose is twofold: 'to prove to myself I could do it' and 'to have something to boast about to my mates'. Peer-group approval at this stage is in fact far more important than getting a woman's love. Still fresh from the wounds of Jocasta, the young Oedipus inevitably sees woman as his most intimate enemy. Whatever rapprochement may become possible with time, love and maturity, the first approaches are necessarily fearful, adversarial, and violent to both parties. In Philip Hodson's words:

> It takes many years for some men to accept their sexuality and place it in the context of a man–woman relationship. They find it very difficult to dissociate sex from a lust for power *over* a woman in a contest which is essentially *against* other men. There is a frequent stress on quantifiable performance ('eight times . . . eight hours . . . eight women . . . eight towns . . . eighty-eight different positions . . . ') in descriptions redolent of a raid by the SAS. Other men never progress beyond seeing sex as all-action 'genital theft' from the woman, in the sense of stealing an advantage over her, a perfect contradiction in terms.

Aggression therefore lies at the heart of the male–female connection from the outset, shaping and colouring the entire experience as it does every other rite of passage in the making of the male. For how can young men avoid doing to women what both women and men have done to them? Reared under systems of violence, indoctrinated to believe that there is no masculinity without aggression, ground down by those bigger and stronger than themselves, how are they to have any concept of a loving, equal relationship whose mutual object lies in what William Blake called 'the lineaments of gratified desire'?

But then, mutuality of any sort is not the object. Getting laid for the first time is not about learning to be a good lover, husband or partner. Proving sexual competence is a central requirement of masculinity – at this stage, arguably *the* key item of the whole agenda. Genital performance, erection and penetration are therefore quite crucial in establishing any claim to 'be a man', both for the boy concerned and in the eyes of the group. Since the self and the group are the principal reference points of approval, the female concerned can only come off a very poor third in this unholy trinity.

Indeed, prowess in the earliest sexual engagements depends on the young male's ability to get what he wants while giving as little as possible. Any status gained from 'getting one in' is irretrievably lost if he succumbs to any tender feelings of love or surrender, or could be accused of being 'under her thumb'. Like an invading army, therefore, he must conquer then decamp, occupy but never fraternize. In the time-honoured tradition exalting profligacy in men and sexual restraint in women, he gains by her loss. His manhood spurs can only be won by taking from her, as Jungian analyst Robert A. Johnson explains in his discussion of masculine development in the light of the myth of Parsifal and the Knights of the Round Table:

> The boy gets masculine virility by overcoming some great obstacle . . . in a contest that requires from him courage and risk, and in this way he takes on the power of the Red Knight for himself. Generally such a victory consists in winning something in the face of opposition . . . Unfortunately, his winning isn't any good unless somebody else loses . . . he's got to win, be top man. Boys will struggle fiercely for this; it is a matter of life and death for them.[8]

As this suggests, women are not the only victims of the young male urge to make himself bigger by diminishing another. On the threshold of adulthood, Philip Hodson states, 'boys are well into the important business of finding their place in the masculine pecking order. They fight, bully, cajole and browbeat their weaker brethren. Emotionally, they learn the happy knack of making themselves feel better by making others feel worse.' The resulting damage is not only experienced by those on the receiving end but also by the young men themselves: 'by the time men reach manhood, they are regular specialists in "non-speak" about important emotional issues.' In the happy assumption that it is a mark of manhood to be emotionally invulnerable, they suffer themselves to become emotionally crippled, taking pride in their ability to 'put up and shut up', and thus avoid showing or sharing any of their intimate inner life. 'Men do not communicate,' agrees writer Colin Dunne. 'Indeed, at this point in our evolution I don't think men are quite ready yet to take on feelings.'

Yet the young man who repudiates intimacy and dependence can only increase his emotional hunger. To Robert Johnson, 'most men find it all so difficult, so painful, so incomprehensible, that they immediately repress it . . . it's terrifying to approach that hunger in ourselves.' When the young man can neither acknowledge nor feed his need for love and warmth through the act of sex, he suffers a critical loss, since sex is one of the only two forms of physical contact sanctioned for the male of the species. Yet the other, the violent and unloving impact of contact sports, coming as it always does in a boy's life before he experiences the clash of bodies in a sexual context, inevitably pre-forms both expectation and event. For how can the boy who for years has won one set of spurs for aggressive ball-play, hard tackling, or rate of strike, switch at a stroke to the tender lover that is every woman's fantasy, if not her right?

What is it with you fucking girls all of a sudden? . . . They'll talk to me, they'll agree to go out with me, they'll eat with me, they'll drink with me, they'll neck with me, they'll even agree to get into the same bed with me. But will they fuck me? Oh no, not them. Not them – *oh* no. (Who the fuck are they anyway, that they won't do that?)
> Martin Amis,
> *Success* (1978)

I got off with women because I could not get on with them.
> Ian Fleming

Arguably, the boy who is left to discover his own sexuality, however hedged about with fears and constraints, is the lucky one. In reality the story is all too often far grimmer than this. 'What a disconcerting picture of male sexuality many boys have as they move through adolescence,' notes Deirdre Sanders, editor of *Woman* magazine, in her survey of male sexuality: 'Strange men who hang around waste ground, and shift their seat in the cinema wanting to touch them: a resounding silence at home on the urgent difficulties they are experiencing and their desires to touch themselves . . . Yet adults think, the boys are alright: it's our daughters we have to worry about . . . Boys are abused by parents, grandparents, aunts, uncles, older brothers, sisters and cousins, and rarely, if ever, seem to confide in anyone.'[9]

Almost every male has his own boyhood story of the strange man in the cinema. 'He was always there, every Saturday morning, and he'd offer you sweets to slide his hand up your trouser leg,' Miles Johnson recalled of his Cardiff boyhood. Much harder to deal with was the groping hand which wandered your way not from a stranger, but from a teacher, parent, or family friend. Boyhood traumas uncovered among men from Britain, Australia and America during the preparation of this book, almost never previously revealed to anyone, include the following:

- at seven, being bathed by 'Uncle', an old friend of the family, who played with the boy's penis and his own throughout.

- at nine, being forced by 'a big boy with a penknife', the son of neighbours, to stroke, lick and suck his penis to orgasm.

- at ten, an older sister's sixteen-year-old boyfriend enforcing anal sex, and presenting a model car afterwards.

- at eleven, being lured into a relationship of mutual masturbation with a 30-year-old teacher.

- at twelve, father explaining 'the facts of life' – boys relieve themselves and avoid 'the corruption of masturbation' by using each other's back passages. Boys didn't tell their mums about it. Practical demonstration offered and only by a (pubic) hair escaped.

- at thirteen, forced to be altar boy by devout Catholic mother. Subsequently forced on a regular basis to take part in 'midnight mass' by the priest, who favoured *soixante-neuf* in full vestments behind the altar.

'In 75 per cent of sexual abuse cases reported to the police,' observes Dr Arnon Bentovim, consultant psychiatrist at the Great Ormond Street

Hospital for Children, 'the offender is known to the child and is often a close member of the family. The abuser often uses secrecy, threats and fear. Children are afraid to tell because they think they are somehow responsible.'

Of sexual offenders against boys, many of the most determined and persistent are to be found in the so-called 'caring professions' which allow, indeed facilitate, unlimited access to their target. It seems likely that the scale of sexual activity by teachers against their pupils has never been recognized. Boys enjoying 'the benefits of boarding' are particularly at risk: incidents of sexual abuse occur in around 75 per cent of boarding schools, a London conference on child sex rings and institutionalized sex was told in December 1989. 'Paedophiles will manoeuvre themselves into situations where they come into contact with potential victims,' said Detective Chief Inspector Roger Gaspar, the Metropolitan police officer who broke a 15-strong London sex ring in 1987. Valerie Howarth, executive director of the charity Childline, also told the conference that the incidence of abuse in boarding schools is 'very high':

When there is abuse, I believe teachers do know about it but don't say anything. I have also been shocked by the reaction of some parents who say it is par for the course of growing up, that the boys will get over it. That is the feeling of people who have gone through the public school system themselves. They say: 'It makes a man of you.'

'Day boys', however, will not necessarily be safe from the attentions of the practised pervert. Michael Grufferty, a deputy headmaster in County Durham, was convicted in 1990 of offences of indecent assault against junior boys in his care which stretched back for almost ten years. Similarly Philip Batten, a 43-year-old teacher from Reigate, was jailed in 1989 for indecently assaulting a fifteen-year-old pupil after getting a group of boys drunk, and showing them pornographic videos. Batten's actions were described by his defence counsel as 'a moment of inexplicable madness', ruining, as in the oft-heard formula, a blameless career in teaching. 'All that means is that we never caught up with them before,' said a senior police officer.

Inevitably, teachers are not the only offenders. A 1990 police operation against a child sex ring in Liverpool during which at least eight children between six and eighteen were taken into care, netted company directors, an education authority official, and several preachers. The scale of the problem is 'awesome', says Commander Richard Monk, head of Scotland Yard's Obscene Publications Branch which finds itself increasingly dealing with paedophilic material. And it is growing. The Department of Health Survey of Children and Young Persons on Child Protection Registers for 1988 shows an unprecedented number of victims added to the list in that year. While the survey covers girls as well as boys, the scale of operation against boys, even by other boys, is only just beginning to come to light. Young boys who abuse other boys were mainly victims of abuse themselves, and need special help, says Dr Judith Trowell, a consultant psychiatrist at London's Tavistock Clinic: 'We must intervene quickly, helping boys, mainly from ten up, to change their behaviour, or more fundamentally their fantasies. Once adults, with an established abusing pattern, the task is so much harder.'

The task, however, has never been more urgent. Child sexual abuse, according to 1988 NSPCC figures, is rising by over 20 per cent a year, and the number of all children registered as victims has more than doubled since 1984. 'It is the perfect crime,' says Commander Monk, 'because the children never tell. It is committed by driven men, who are now about the biggest group of re-offenders in the criminal justice system.' Boys and girls alike will be subject to the feelings of guilt, shame and implication by which sexual abusers keep their victims in thrall. Only boys, however, are regularly exposed to adult males in group situations like team sports and Boy Scouts, a Leicestershire branch of which recently told a judge at the 1990 Crown Court trial of one of its helpers for having videos showing boys between eight and fourteen engaged in homosexual acts, that it had 'encountered no problems with his involvement in the Scout movement'. And only boys are subject to the early manhood training now drilling a boy to believe that he must no longer share his feelings and experiences with his mother, or anyone else. Marry that with the insistence that a boy must stand on his own feet, put it together with the rampant and rapacious sexuality of the older male, and what you have is nothing less than a buggers' charter. How many boys have been forced to offer their silence, tears, pain, penises, anuses, to serve the myth of the manliness of man, and to protect the male prerogative of their abuser? How many will continue to do so before we acknowledge the scale of this appalling offence?

From seven to seventeen, then, the boy learns to be a man. Cast out from his infant world of gold, expelled, divorced and abandoned by his first and most devoted love, he exchanges that sublime intimacy for the stunting and blunting gang world of constant action, incessant competition, hierarchical jostling and concomitant insecurity. The emotional hunger thus created will never afterwards by truly fed, the restless searching anxiety never totally allayed or stilled. Alone in the brave new world of men, a stranger and afraid, what can the boy hang on to? What becomes his emotional centre, his chief instrument of expression, his mute confidant, unfailing comfort and friend? What but his other self, his real self – his penis?

From earliest adolescence, in confirmation and continuation of the first lessons of mother love, the boy learns that his penis is both the only reliable source of pleasure and the site of his personal power. From this discovery stems the fatal association of non-sexual attributes (power, achievement, even peer approval in the notorious boyhood dick-measuring and wank contests) with genital activity, erection and orgasm. A hard penis means manhood, control, and the bursting bliss of release. Dominance and desire, the ruling passions of infant and adult male alike, come together in the first erection.

And with the first erection, the boy becomes a man. Awakened, an innocent no longer, he can make daily demonstration of the simple masculine equation, penis = power = self. He has earned this reward, having passed through many ordeals, trodden many pathways of pain, to achieve it. And in the classic masculine pattern of moving the goalposts as soon as the goal looks like becoming readily attainable, he is then told that his one-off, jerk-off penis-power is not enough. Getting it up may be the first mark of manhood. The real test however lies in getting it *in*.

In where? The precondition of becoming a man, the first condition of early manhood training, is withdrawal from the world of women. Segregation is founded on superiority: contempt must follow. 'Women have very little idea how much men hate them,' observed Germaine Greer. The adolescent boy knows very well how much he hates girls: YUK! His gang has performed for him the vital work of switching his primary allegiance from the single female to the group male. Now, at the point of maximum separation, he must try to retrace those tracks, switch the points. At the moment when he is most alienated from the world of women he must try to get back, quite literally, in touch. Having pulled back from all and everything that means, suggests, feels, or smells like woman in order to 'be a man', the only way he can prove the success of the transition is by crossing back, by re-entering that world, by entering *her*.

He knows she is out there waiting, the woman who will take his penis, 'break', in the familiar but painfully suggestive phrase, 'his duck'. The prospect is appalling, terrifying. 'I could hardly think of anything else for *three years*,' says Sam Jefferson, Rhode Island lawyer. 'And on top of everything else at that time – oh boy, I can't believe I didn't go crazy.' Trembling on the brink of manhood, frantic for his first woman, damned if he does, damned if he doesn't, the boy is also wrestling with a powerful cocktail of other needs, imperatives and drives. Transcendence: he must make himself powerful and free. Emotional impoverishment: the deliberate blunting of his skills of empathy and communication. Compulsory violence: pain as achievement, and no achievement without pain. Penis power: the central power, the only power, which is, demands, must be, must have, *now*.

All these are elements and constituents of every normal male. They are also the key psychological features of every psychopathic killer. How and why, then, does 'normal' manhood training come so close to the clinical profile of the abnormally cruel and insane? How does the rite of passage echo so closely the making not of a man, but of what we choose to call a monster? What cruelty continues to inflict on every little boy fresh from the arms of his mother these hateful and self-hating rituals of manhood? Above all, as the youth, desperate to 'measure up' in his own mind if not in hers, makes his first approaches to the dangerous female, what has he to say to her? Where does he even begin?

Sadism is not a name finally given to a practice as old as Eros; it is a massive cultural fact which appears precisely at the end of the eighteenth century, and which constitutes one of the greatest conversions of Western imagination: unreason transformed into delirium of the heart, madness of desire, the insane dialogue of love and death in the limitless presumption of appetite.
Michel Foucault

---

6 Majority Rule

I have always disliked being a man. The whole idea of
manhood in America is pitiful . . . Even the expression
'Be a man!' strikes me as insulting and abusive. It
means: Be stupid, be unfeeling, obedient and soldierly,
and stop thinking. Man means 'manly' – how can one
think about men without considering the terrible
ambition of manliness. And yet it is part of every man's
life.
> Paul Theroux,
> 'The Male Myth'

The atrocious crime of being a young man I shall
neither attempt to palliate nor deny.
> William Pitt the Younger

'When I became a man,' wrote Saint Paul, 'I put away childish things.'
This statement has thundered down the generations as the perfect
model of how it should be done. What seem to have gone unremarked,
however, are the great sage's key omissions: he fails to reveal to the
waiting world just *how*, and he is similarly silent on the moment
when, the process is achieved. Looking back, too, from the achieved
status of assured manhood, Paul makes no mention of the various
hurdles still to be surmounted, the last rites of boyhood to be observed
and transcended, whose success or failure will determine now a life
well lived, or the confirmation of a future darkened with frustration,
violence and crime. This lack of instruction may account for the
difficulty experienced by most of the male sex in following in the
footsteps of the apostle. 'Becoming a man' for the majority of men is no
blinding light on the road to Damascus, but rather an anxious uphill
hike through hostile terrain in a thick fog. 'Putting away childish
things' sounds a lot easier than it is – for the young male struggling
through the process of leaving boyhood for maturity, hanging on is a lot
more common than letting go. 'You're as old as you think you are,' says
England cricketer Ian Botham, *'and I'm sixteen and a half.'*

Historically, traditional patterns strongly supported the boy in
transition or determined the metaphysical moment at which he
'became a man'. Initiation rituals, barmitzvah celebrations and their

like, all made a public statement that the boy had undergone a decisive change in status, and welcomed him to the exclusive club of the adult males. In Rome, the seventeen-year-old boy was formally admitted to manhood via a torch-lit procession to the Senate, followed by a religious ceremony and sacrifice, and a great feast for which his father spared no expense. On this day the boy formally doffed the short tunic of childhood and was invested with his first *toga virilis*, the semi-circle of fine white wool which, however itchy in hot weather, draughty in cold, and tricky to manage at all times (especially in moments of passion or urgent personal need), nevertheless made the wearer a man in the eyes of all. For the twentieth-century male, getting out of short pants into the first flannels or cavalry twills lacked a very great deal in comparison and today, when even the youngest boy may wear long trousers if his mother so decides, the modern equivalent cannot be found.

For us, with no clear cultural rites of passage, the achievement of masculine status is inherently problematic, confused and conflict-ridden. Today's youth too often finds himself waiting for a climacteric that never comes, as the Yugoslav-born American writer Steve Tesich explains:

> Everyone told me that when I turned sixteen some great internal change would occur. I truly expected the lights to go down on my former life and come up again on a new enchanting one. Nothing happened.
>
> They lied again when I turned eighteen. There were rumours that I was now a 'man'. I noticed no difference, but pretended to have all the rumored symptoms of manhood. Even though these mythical milestones, these rituals of passage, were not working for me, I still clung to the belief that they should, and I lied and said they were.
>
> My twenty-first birthday was the last birthday I celebrated. The rituals weren't working and I was tired of pretending I was changing. I was merely growing – adding on rooms for all the kids who were still me to live in.

The boy is left, then, to face this key stage alone, for during the decade in which every foundation stone for his future life must be laid, he has nothing but silence and disinformation for company.

The imperatives, though, are well-worn from endless swapping around between young men, like the street-trade in marbles of former times: 'looking after yourself', 'getting ahead', 'staying cool', 'none of that girl stuff', 'being "the Man"', 'fighting your corner', and 'not taking nothing from nobody', the flurry of negatives there underlining the crucial importance of the fight not to be 'put down'. Violence and dominance continue to rule the agenda of the young man in the same way that they shaped his life as a boy. The difference now is that the threat and challenge of other boys is much more serious – 'at seventeen or eighteen, you can *kill* someone,' recalls Kevin O'Marah – while the adult world of older males has by no means finished with its rising young. The need then for transcendence, for the action, ritual or system that will obliterate all softness, weakness, pain, or fear of pain in favour of infallible power and superhuman strength, is now greater than ever.

The official agenda by which a young male 'makes something of himself' looks harmless enough. To become a 'real man' in every sense of that unreal phrase, to position himself for fulfilment as a husband, father, citizen of his community and success in his chosen walk of life, he must undertake three inescapable tasks, like the folk heroes of former times – he has to get out of the ruck, into a job, and into a marriage. Unofficially, though, he has to compete with other young men and against himself to achieve all this, while the older men stand by to ensure that no one escapes what they suffered in their turn, and to take an undisguised satisfaction in any setback or failure. 'Now you know you don't know everything,' was one father's response when his son, a newly graduated physicist, could not find a job. In a similar vein, a boss firing Harvey Rabinowitz, now a Santa Monica lawyer, from the job he needed to put himself through college, opined, 'You're gonna thank me for this, kid. I guess you'll look back on it as the most formative experience of your life.'

Additionally these emotional trials take place against a background of unrelenting physical anxiety. Adulthood brings the moment when every man has to accept that he is what nature has made him, and rarely does this seem good enough. Men of all ages, cultures, occupations and sizes freely confess that manhood brought no escape from the adolescent angst about 'measuring up'. The testosterone invasion of the body which produces puberty is normally completed between the ages of twelve and seventeen. By eighteen, puberty's pay-offs in the form of the deeper voice, the treasured growth spurt and the man-sized penis are complete. Now the newly-fledged male has to learn to adapt to the rhythms of his testosterone cycle: research at Stanford University has shown that men, like women, have a regular hormone cycle which consistently links with mood, emotion and depression. As this male cycle has been one of the best-kept secrets of the universe – not until the 1980s did it occur to scientists even to investigate the possibility that men, like women, could suffer from 'the time of the month' – young males frequently find themselves being pressurized to 'play the man' when their natural instincts are urging them in quite the opposite direction.

The Stanford research also explodes another widespread and potent myth, that the male hormone testosterone somehow causes, even excuses, male aggression. On the contrary, the researchers say, when large quantities of testosterone are coursing round the body, only a minority of men experience any feelings of aggression. The rest experience sadness, sinking even to deep depression, while a lucky minority get happy/sexy and 'feel the sap rising'.[1] For most men, then, 'becoming a man' in the biological sense of the term does *not* produce a strengthening flood of male 'brain chemicals' but a genuine anxiety: now the man he is to be has burst from the husk of the boy, will he be a good enough specimen of manhood?

For some unfortunates, the biological bonanza – pumpkin into prince in five easy stages of sprouting body hair, burgeoning genitals, outsize Adam's apple, longer limbs and more muscle mass – is destined to be nothing but a cruel joke. As the vast majority of freaks and sports of nature are male, this is the final stage at which their physical deficiencies have to be acknowledged as beyond assistance or cure. For others, though, the surgical and technological advances of modern medicine, together with today's much greater understanding of genetic processes, can offer the kind of transformation which to the victim of one of Mother Nature's little pranks is nothing short of miraculous. At nineteen, Austrian Ladies' skiing champion Erika Shinegger took a routine sex test to enable her to compete in the 1968 Winter Olympics. Confidently expecting a gold medal on the basis of training runs that had already made her the world downhill skiing champion, Erika instead was pulled out of the team and flown hastily back to Innsbruck when the tests revealed, in the words of the Olympic biologist, that 'whatever he calls himself, there is a man skiing in the Austrian ladies' team'.[2]

'Erika' proved to have been mis-sexed at birth through the combination of a hidden, unseparated penis and undescended testicles. Six months of microsurgery re-fashioned his external genitals and released his testicles from their long imprisonment inside his abdomen. Restored to manhood, Erik underwent his delayed puberty, and without benefit of hormone treatment found that his voice broke, and he had to begin to shave. As a man, Erik Shinegger went on to marry and to father a daughter. He still remembers, however, as his biggest thrill his first visit to a men's lavatory: 'I thought "Now I can really pee, I'm so glad!"'

Walk tall,
Look the world right in the eye,
Walk tall . . .
                US popular song, Don Wayne

Erik's delight in finding himself a fully-equipped, sexually active male in place of a non-menstruating, flat-chested freak of a girl can hardly be imagined. For most normal men, however, early manhood is accompanied by a series of agonies about personal size that can most aptly be summarized under the heading, *'Is this it?'* Adult male height is in fact apparent at a very early age: it is not generally realized, as growth tables from the Great Ormond Street Hospital for Children confirm, that the growing boy has made *one half* of his full growth by the time of his second birthday. Throughout primary and secondary education, any school pie chart consistently shows the same boys clustered in the top percentile for height and rate of growth. Only rarely will a break for the top be made by any of the 'shorthouses', as small boys were euphemistically known in the East End of London, and many taller boys know the Alice in Wonderland nightmare of being a child trapped in an uncontrollably-expanding gigantic frame: the comedian John Cleese was 6' 1" by the age of twelve.

Few miseries, however, can compare with those of the young man who, after years of waiting and hoping, has to accept that in a world where the tall man is king, he will always be the royal dwarf. In every society known to man, height brings dominance, success, approval and esteem: detailed and well-documented research shows that even in completely irrelevant circumstances, given two men to choose between, men and women alike will consciously or unconsciously prefer the taller. When two lecturers deliver an identical lecture, for instance, the taller will invariably be rated 'more intelligent'. If there are two paper applications for a job, both with identical qualifications, and the board is casually told that one applicant is 5' 6" and the other 6 foot, the six-footer gets it. Taller men are born, it seems, to dominate and win: graduates in Britain and the US who are over 6' 2" in height have on average salaries at least 12½ per cent higher than other men. And in the entire history of the Presidency of the US, only Jimmy Carter has ever beaten a taller man to the White House.[3]

The sheer fatuity of the bulk principle of power was exposed as early as AD 235, when the Roman legions on the Rhine made Verus Maximus, an illiterate Thracian peasant, Emperor of Rome because of his great size. A handful of pint-sized despots, from Napoleon to Stalin, have also demonstrated that inches are not everything. For Joe Average, however, unsupported by power, pomp, or lifts in his shoes, who cannot be Willy Shoemaker, Paul Simon or Dudley Moore, it matters. 'I've gone through life as "Rich the Tich",' says Richie Bachman, a Boston wages clerk, 'and I haven't got used to it. You could say I've learned to live with it. But I still dream I'm going to wake up one day and find I'm six foot, not five.'

Every man carries his ego at the tip of his penis.
    Jane Deknatel Newmark,
    Hollywood film producer

If inches matter on the male spine or lower limbs, nowhere are they more important than on what James Joyce evocatively dubbed 'the middle leg'. This fear of inadequacy goes back to the earliest childhood experiences, as Freud explains:

> They notice the penis of a brother or playmate, strikingly visible and of large proportions, at once recognize it as the superior counterpart of their own small and inconspicuous organ, and from that time forward fall a victim to envy of the penis.[4]

Perversely enough, having had this crucial insight, Freud went on to apply it to girls, not boys. But as Woody Allen observed in his celebrated 'disagreement with Freud', and as the world is beginning to acknowledge, you don't have to be a woman to suffer from penis envy. When would girls, especially in Freud's historical period, ever have had a chance to 'notice' these mythical mighty male members flashing round their heads? Men, however, begin at an early age on the lifelong habit of surreptitious cock-watching. In public lavatories, swimming baths, gyms, even at the ballet, they will always, in the word of car salesman John Ford, compulsively 'check out the opposition':

> I'll be honest, my penis has never been as big as I'd like it to be. Don't get me wrong, I never get any complaints! But when I was a kid I'd look at these huge great hairy things the older boys had, and eat my heart out for one of them. As I was growing up I worried constantly that mine wasn't growing big enough. I still like to

keep an eye on other ones whenever I can, just to make sure I'm within the normal variable.

At this stage of their lives most young men will have up to ten years' experience behind them of regular masturbation, with its equally regular reassurance of successful erection and emission: as one television executive put it, 'it's so good to know that your cock works'. Many men too have by now had at least one successful engagement with another individual, be it boy or girl, successful at least in the sense that penetration or mutual stimulation and orgasm were achieved. Yet the adolescent anxiety about 'measuring up' persists even in the face of satisfactory experience. Pleasuring yourself, pleasuring another, are not the criteria that count. What counts is being able to 'shape up' in the eyes of other men. And from that scrutiny there seems to be little escape.

For the normal male, adult response to the sight of another man's penis seems to be a knee-jerk (or rather middle-leg-jerk) compulsion to look, linger, evaluate for size and circumference, make the inevitable comparison and then, if at all possible, enjoy a good gloat. Journalist Adrian Dannatt visited a nudist camp which offered an astonishing range of variations on a theme:

> There was a tubby little man whose low-slung belly could not conceal a fabulous endowment that dangled near the dimpled knee. There was a well-built young boy, all toned and muscled, who seemed to have missed the point. Perhaps he practised some sort of yoga inversion technique.
>
> Now men are notoriously sensitive concerning such matters. However often they are fed the lie that 'It doesn't make any difference to a woman', they carry on, quite rightly, knowing it does. Certainly if I owned one of the strange, retracted versions I saw on display, a recalcitrant, shy little thing, a nouvelle cuisine portion of garnished mollusc, I would not be sitting, legs akimbo, in a Day-Glo armchair, eating chips. I would be at home in a darkened bedroom, battling with the weights and measures.[5]

Errol Flynn, Hollywood gossip ran, had a penis so long he had to wear it strapped to his leg. Yeah! And when Virginia Rappe died after the notorious party at Fatty Arbuckle's when a violent rape destroyed her internal sex organs, it was no champagne bottle that ruptured her spleen, but the mighty organ of the 300-pound comedian himself! Every gang, every locker-room is alive with the same compulsive, competitive buzz of interest in other men's penises, usually disguised as male humour: if one man is publicly honoured with the title of 'Ten-inch Trevor', another is sure to be humiliated with the nickname 'Chipolata'. However often men are 'fed the lie' that the size of a penis makes no difference to a woman, 'they carry on, quite rightly,' says Adrian Dannatt, 'knowing it does'. What is this but an extension, as it were, into adult life, of the boy child's earliest penis envy? In other words, how can men ever believe that women care so little about king-sized cocks when they care so passionately for and about them themselves?

In reality it may well not be the pride and the passion of the penis rampant that strikes a woman's attention, but the sheer absurdity of the whole thing, as Esther Vilar reveals:

A male erection appears so grotesque to a woman the first time she hears about it that she can hardly believe it exists. The moment she realizes, however, that it can be produced by the slightest degree of provocation, and that it is not necessarily even that of a naked woman – a film or a photograph might do – then she will never cease to be amazed. It is, after all, a reflex action, rather like hitting someone on the knee. Probably no theory ever evolved by man has been as absurd as Freud's theory of penis envy. To a woman the male penis and scrotum appear superfluous in a man's otherwise neatly constructed body. It seems incredible to her that a man cannot withdraw his penis after use and make it disappear, like the aerial on a portable radio. Not even in her deepest unconscious would she ever wish to possess a thing like a penis.[6]

Vilar's mocking mystification could be paralleled a thousand times in the writings of other women. But who cares? What price women's opinion when the true story of male sexuality is the love affair between one man and his dong? Man and penis: those whom God hath joined together, indeed at the very root, let no woman put asunder. And logically enough, their warmest feelings and strongest sense of solidarity are reserved for those who share their passion for the penis: other men. Society, Freud insisted, is rooted in male homosexual love, sublimated into teams, organizations and group ties. Women, by their very nature oppositional, inevitably threaten the precarious erection of masculine sexual identity, a threat to which male society responds by strengthening the bonds, tightening every rope that makes a man a guy.

Yet when the whole of the vast dark continent of adult male sexuality is reduced to the pin-point of the penis, the loser is not woman but the man himself. Admittedly the rage and purity of the male faith in penis-power mean that in sex, too many men make love to themselves. The ideal female partner of all too many a male fantasy is no more than an urgent, adoring orifice that turns into a pizza immediately afterwards, as the joke has it. Her orgasms are only necessary as a reassurance for him of his prowess, and in the teeth of all evidence to the contrary (Masters and Johnson, Shere Hite), he refuses to use tongue, lips, teeth, touch, to produce it, but relies on his naïve faith, no, his demand, that penile thrusting alone must bring it about. Woman is the victim, too, of the widespread young male belief that if she 'really loves him', his 'girl' will do anything for him, *and will enjoy it*, even to the point of obligingly producing her own orgasm during oral sex through the uncontrollable heady delights of all the strenuous sucking and licking necessary to produce his.

For most women, though, faking another orgasm here or there is no big deal. Women know too that while a heterosexual man believes that she 'belongs to' his erection, in reality his erection is always, both literally and metaphorically, in female hands, since it cannot happen in a vacuum. The concentration on the penis, however, cuts men off from their partners, their feelings, and their potential for mature erotic pleasure. The purpose of the act becomes display, as the peacock penis spreads its tail and crows. 'Even in bed, I pose,' confessed the poet Thom Gunn; recalling one such poseur Irma Kurtz wrote, 'in bed, only his penis was present'. Yet the dick-driven male eventually loses his grip on that reality too, his close contact with his root. From the days of Casanova, compulsive cocksmen have recorded the schizophrenia of this separation as their overworked organ begins to take on a life of its own, even a special name or title denoting its separate existence, becoming 'the beast below', 'Nimrod' (the 'mighty hunter' of the Bible), or 'the master of ceremonies'. Lord Rochester favoured 'the Rector of the females', D. H. Lawrence 'John Thomas', while in a flood of similar cod 'Ockerisms' Barry Humphries offers 'the one-eyed trouser-snake', the modern English version taking the strine, so to speak, of the nineteenth-century Oxford undergraduates' classical joke name for the penis, 'Polyphemus'.

Yet though only a one-eyed Cyclops, and no match for the Greeks to boot, Polyphemus was both a king and a giant. Even the most apparently offensive of nicknames for the penis ('arse-splitter', 'cunt-catcher', 'kidney-kisser') are in fact acts of homage, boasting, and wishful aggrandizement. The penis, in short (even if it is not a short penis), is never big enough by itself, as the film critic Richard Dyer comments with some amusement:

Penises are only little things (even big ones) without much staying power, pretty if you can learn to see them like that, but not magical or mysterious or powerful in themselves – not objectively full of real power.[7]

Loaded with 'magic and mystery', treated as the source, site and symbol of the potency of the male, the penis cannot stand up to its own PR. Throughout history, however, the frailty of the organ has only intensified the frenzy of the myth-making. Prehistoric man lovingly fashioned outsize penises of bone and clay as offerings to the Great Mother, a touching tribute to the strength of men's belief that whatever they hold dear, women must too. The notion of the super-penis – larger than life, rock-hard, infallible – thus pre-dates human civilization and formal conceptualization. This profound wishful longing, the remodelling of unsatisfactory reality into flattering fantasy, in fact comes from the time of 'magic thought', before men's minds could connect cause and effect, or grasp the inevitability of constraint upon the penis with its boundless appetite and will.

And so it is today. A hundred thousand years of human existence, ten, twenty, forty thousand years of social organization, five thousand years of civilization and a millennium of the most phenomenal intellectual, scientific and technological progress ever known, have done nothing to root out the deep, irrational, masculine faith in penis-power. Yet the real organ can never live up to its symbolic equivalent, the phallus. For the phallus never fails. It is the Teflon erection, smooth, shining, indestructible. It makes a boy a man, and a man a king: it strikes awe and fear into the heart of female and foe alike. It *is* power, and it *conveys* power like a blessing on the whole man.

The truth, however, could not be more diametrically opposed to this phallus-in-wonderland scenario. Far from being potent with magic, strong and free, the penis needs all the help it can get. For all but the youngest of men, the penis in search of an erection demands consider-able stimulation, mental, physical and manual (questioned as to his foreplay techniques, one man interviewed for this book replied, 'I say, "Give us a hand here."'). For the young male, the penis is even more uncontrollable, as erections come and go unwilled: young males are in fact the heaviest consumers of pornographic magazines like *Playboy*, *Penthouse*, *Mayfair* and *Knave*. Blind to paradox, those who unselfcon-sciously bang on about men's 'natural urges' and 'inevitable desires' see no contradiction in the fact that it so often takes massive, multi-million-pound industries and all the machinery of boots, basques, suspender belts and black lace to produce what is trumpeted as so 'natural' and 'inevitable', to leg up the middle leg. And as he strains, groans, gasps, frowns and flails in the desperate struggle to make the penis do the work of his limitless fantasy and unjustifiable desire, how often does the young male ever stop to ask himself if a man should be so dominated by a small piece of meat, in the endless, vicious male cycle of dominance and desire?

I had often looked at my penis and thought, 'You moron.'
> Paul Theroux,
> *My Secret History* (1989)

Woman is on heat, and wants to be fucked.
> Baudelaire

The man who could invent the push-button penis, with finger-tip control and lifetime guarantee of erection at will and success and satisfaction every time, would not only make a fortune – he would also be the greatest benefactor of distressed humanity since Sir Alexander Fleming. In his absence, every male works on the penis he has been given as best he can. For the young male, the principal means of 'measuring up', as indicated in journalist Adrian Dannatt's response to another man's 'shy little penis' ('I'd be at home, battling with the weights and measures'), is via sport and physical activity. The frenzied body-building, lifting weights and pumping iron undertaken by so many young men is yet another instance of male will overriding unacceptable reality, since they all know that the penis is not a muscle, and cannot be 'built'. At this stage, though, and for many years to come, sport is a key ritual of adult masculinity, since it serves so many other purposes, all the more important for being unspoken, unacknowledged, indeed unconscious. Among numerous men who subsequently won fame in other fields, the following all began and distinguished themselves as sportsmen: Burt Reynolds (American football), Jimmy Savile (wrestling), Errol Flynn (boxing), Bob Hope (boxing), Colin Moynihan (rowing and boxing), Dr Benjamin Spock (rowing) and Johnny Mathis (athletics).

At the simplest level, a sport or physical activity is usually under-taken from a desire to enhance body image: not simply to become better looking, but to change the body's shape. 'Popular wisdom has it,' says Professor Michael Kimmel, co-author of *Men and Masculinity*, 'that women are uniquely preoccupied with their bodies, expending tremendous energies in fitting them into normative models of femininity, while men see themselves as just about perfect.' Research under the direction of Dr Marc Mishkind at Yale University, however, clearly shows that young men suffer all the same anxieties about appearance as women do: that they are desperate to be 'the right shape' and that they consider the 'handsome hunk', the classic muscular mesomorph, to be *the* masculine ideal in the eyes of other men. There is also a widespread belief among men that the 'hunk' is the masculine type *par excellence* in the eyes of women, again a poignant and powerful indication of how far men prefer to believe what they want to believe, rather than a truth which challenges their reality: research consistently shows that women prefer gentle hands to broad shoulders, and kind eyes to bulging biceps, valuing sensitivity over toughness/ virility/machismo (i.e. insensitivity) in every research programme ever devised.

But of course, the sportsman straining for excellence, the body-builder pumping iron, is not doing it for a woman. 'Muscular meso-morphism equates with physical potency,' says Kimmel. 'The body image, potency and masculinity are all bound up.' Building up the aura of infallible strength, endurance and unchallengeable power ('They don't mess with you if you look tough!') in fact does for the body image what the young man cannot do for his penis. Sportsmen like Chicago Bears linebacker William Perry, known as 'the Refrigerator', actors like Arnold Schwarzenegger and Sylvester Stallone, in effect each becomes a public phallus, huge, rock-hard, gleaming and veined with blood. And as the phallus first stirred and came to life in the primeval swamps of the male imagination, so males above all are uniquely alert to its siren call and baleful power. Becoming an athlete, body-builder or 'jock' is therefore a clear and overt statement of manhood and male potency, and the clearest possible message to other men.

'Except for war,' said Robert Kennedy, 'there is nothing in American life, nothing, which trains a boy better for life than football.' Throughout the western world, thousands, millions even, are follow-ing his words. 'Football is tremendous, the most intriguing form of competition there is,' said US management consultant Kevin O'Marah, 'and above all, it's a metaphor for life':

> They coached us that way all along, it's like life, it's like America, it *is* life. It's a combination of team work and individual behaviour, it involves competition, strategy, planning, time

limits, boundaries, rules. Even the football is oblong and bounces funny, so there's a legitimate element of luck or chance, just like life, but you can overcome that by working hard enough, being good enough. Winning too – in football that's always clear, and you learn to develop your own sense of well, *I* won, even if the team didn't.

Separated as they are at this stage from long-term, close and loving relations with women, young men also find in sporting activity a legitimate outlet for passionate emotions both of love and hate. It says much for the ritual deprivations visited upon the young male that what he is not allowed to discuss with his mother or sister, the unfolding of his emotional world, the youth is expected to share satisfactorily with the whole of a baseball or rugby team. In flight from the all-consuming female, the young man readily finds what Kimmel calls 'a psychologically safe place' in the tribalism of sport, where physical contact with other penis-possessors is sanctioned, where emotional investment is welcomed, but where all this is governed by extremely rigid and predetermined rules.

Yet since the male body in this context *becomes* a penis, in sport 'you're only ever as good as your last performance'. As with the most demanding of mistresses, the stress is all on prowess, achievement, 'how did you make out?' In this endless circle of proving and proving again, even without the ultimate certainty of defeat by age, sport becomes 'a structure of failure'. The individual either frequently or eventually fails his own self-imposed standard, in competition with himself. The majority fail in competition with each other; they have to, so that the few may be supremely triumphant. Above all, sport and physical prowess, far from being a solution to the youth's fears of weakness and loneliness and the problems of masculinity, in fact serve to reinforce the original problem, as Professor Michael Messner of the University of Southern California Program for the Study of Men and Women in Society explains:

The athlete's sense of identity established through sports is insecure and problematic *not* simply because of the high probability of failure, but because *success itself* in the sports world *amplifies* many of the most ambivalent and destructive traits of traditional masculinity. Within this hierarchical world, to survive and avoid being pushed off the ever-narrowing pyramid of success, the athlete must develop a high goal-oriented personality that encourages him to use his body as a tool, a machine, or even a weapon to defeat an objectified opponent. He is likely to have difficulty with establishing intimate and lasting friendships with other males because of low self-disclosure, homophobia and cut-throat competition. And he is likely to view his public image as a 'success' as far more basic and fundamental than any of his interpersonal relationships.

With its heavy stress on the values of traditional masculinity, its exclusion of women, and its inherent inability to offer warm and intimate relations with other men, sport must be counted as a primary rite of male deformation, and as an anti-preparation, even an aversion therapy, for warm and equal male–female relations for the whole of the rest of a man's life. A former England international, once assured of anonymity, looked back in anger on his days as 'one of the boys':

They're all scoring the whole time, taking the piss, stupid jokes, totally detrimental humour. Then they're slapping each other on the back, looking friendly, and you realize, this is the nearest they'll ever get to closeness. It's all physical – 'Good tackle, mate!' Whereas when you see a group of women, they really care about one another, they ask questions and really want to know the answers!

I think I knew this early on. We were doing a training session at school, doing a shuttle game. I was standing on the dead ball line and one of the younger kids ran by me. He was very dark, pretty in a womanly sort of way, with bum-fluff on his cheeks and a chubby face. The coach suddenly leered at me and said, 'Cor, Jason's got a nice arse on him, I wouldn't mind if my missus had an arse like that.' Then he gave that particular laugh that men give and you know something dirty has just happened. God, the world of men can be fucking horrific sometimes!

Yet in a touching illustration of the fact that men who are not given what they love learn to love what they are given, many men look back on their youthful sporting days as the apotheosis of their manhood. 'It was fantastic!' recalls financier Robert Straker-Jackson, a former Oxford rugby Blue. 'Getting out there, running the ball, a good hard game – that's what life's all about really, isn't it?' Learning to see 'the game' as 'what life's all about' in place of life itself with its infinitely greater challenge, richness and complexity, is one of the reasons that men remain boys, unable to 'put away childish things'. For how could any man be expected to 'put away' the thing that commands his primary love and allegiance after his repudiation by the world of women? How can he reject this brave new world with its promise of making him all things bright and beautiful in the eyes of other men? The purity of a young man's passion for 'the game' can light up the rest of his life, either as player or spectator, by its fierce glow. The group and its physical activities, the team and the games played together, take on an intensity of adoration all the greater for being divorced from any human subject. As a grown man looking back on his baseball days from the apparently safe harbour of early middle age ('I was *thirty-six years old!*') Lee Eisenberg still tapped straight into one of the most powerful and overriding emotional realities of his entire existence:

> When I say that baseball is a game whose essence is time, I'm referring to nothing less grandiose than *life time*. For at the end of the day, when the lights go on, baseball is that thing we picked up along the way that we carried with us longer than any other. And I include religion, the love of a good woman, and just about any hobby you can think of.
>
> Baseball gets into our vitals. Its colours, heroes and rituals take root in our innards when we are boys. We carry them into adolescence, repress them through puberty, keep them on ice through early manhood, then thaw them out and keep them alive and flourishing until the day when we are tucked up under a blanket of real grass. Everything else in our lives comes and goes. Baseball endures. Baseball was a better love than my first love. It is an older friend than my oldest friend. This is one goddam beautiful game.[8]

And then it's over. You don't know which way to go. Your light has been turned out. You miss the roar of the crowd. Once you've heard it, you can't get away from it. There's an empty feeling – you feel everything you ever wanted is gone. All of a sudden you wake up, you're 29, 35 you know, and the one thing that has been your life is gone. It's gone.

Retired professional footballer
Marvin Upshaw

Once schooldays are over, of course, participation in sport is no longer compulsory. Nothing obliges the seven-stone weakling to take part in physical activity – but he must be sure to find some other way to avoid getting sand kicked in his face. For what cannot be dodged by the newly-fledged young male is the compulsion to establish, to demonstrate, and so continually to test his manhood if not through this, then through another form of excessive activity all too frequently involving violence, danger or death.

The intimate, Freud would say erotic, connection between man and machine is widely known, not least to advertisers, who have built some of their most successful campaigns on its premises. The sinister side of this symbiosis is also widely publicized. Any newspaper in any country yields a daily crop of the sombre stories of its kiss of death: JAIL FOR DOUBLE DEATH JOYRIDER or YOUTH IN FATAL CRASH KILLS SEVEN. In a typical incident, and far from the worst of its kind, two eighteen-year-old youths were clinging to the roof of a car travelling at high speed through the villages of Oxfordshire in January 1990 when the car overturned, crushing them both to death. Carl Droughton, of Runcorn, Cheshire, was sixteen in June 1990 when he crashed the car he was driving, killing himself, and inflicting severe head injuries on his seventeen-year-old passenger. British statistics for the period 1988–9 show that almost six times more men than women died behind the wheel of a car that year, a staggering figure even allowing for the comparatively greater number of male drivers. For motorcycles, in highly industrialized and Third World countries alike, the figures are even worse: in Britain, for example, over 90 per cent of 1989's fatal motorcycle casualties were males between the ages of 16 and 30.

The irresistible, death-dealing machine does not even have to be driveable, it appears, to exert its fatal fascination over the young male. Seven US servicemen died in separate incidents in Britain in 1989, when vending machines fell on top of them. Witnesses reported seeing the men rocking the 800-pound machines in order to trigger the release mechanism and so obtain a free drink. 'It seems to me that there is a threat to the public here,' commented the London coroner Dr Douglas Chamberlain, recommending that vending machines should henceforward be secured to the wall to ensure public safety. What public is he talking about? Is it conceivable that a young woman, even if she had the muscular strength, would risk her life for a free 7-UP? And why has no government, no figure of authority, no campaigner, no parent, ever tried to stop the senseless slaughter on the roads? Are we so wedded to the myth that boys must 'prove themselves' that we allow them to throw away the lives they might have had as men?

'If one is to be a man,' proclaimed Norman Mailer, 'almost any kind of unconventional action often takes disproportionate courage. Society makes enormous demands on the courage of men.' Mailer's 'hipster huckster metaphysical argy-bargy', in Ian Penman's phrase, has been openly derided by Alfred Kazin: 'His idea of courage has only to do with aggressiveness – nothing else. That's not courage – there's no will needed. The will is not to do it.'[9] It is a will that most young men lack – or rather are never allowed to opt for. On the contrary, beneath the overarching injunction to 'be a man' are specific imperatives demanding the most extreme exertion of self for successful resolution: every young man has to 'prove himself' (to his parents, to his peers, to his boss, to the woman he will marry) and he has to keep on renewing this 'proof' until the day he dies.

But 'prove himself' what? Why is he unacceptable as he is? Behind the inexorable demand of masculinity that its young acolytes must manifest it or demonstrate it in this way lies the blank, unquestioned assumption that he is not good enough in himself. There is a presumption of inadequacy – almost of insubstantiality – in the raw material of boyhood, which cannot but strike at the core of his confidence. Is it for this reason that some young men, in extreme cases, are driven to ever more bizarre acts of self-validation or self-definition? 'Death Wish' was the name given to one young man by his friends because of his 'dangerous and foolhardy behaviour', reported the January 1990 edition of *Medicine, Science and the Law*. Since adolescence, one of his favourite tricks had been smashing beer mugs against his head. He died at the age of 23 while attempting to swallow a pool ball for a wager. Was he trying to 'prove himself'?

And who is demanding the proof? Teachers? Parents? In January 1990, William Church, aged 17, 'obsessed with gaining entrance to Trinity College, Cambridge', hanged himself with a bicycle security chain, 'because he could not face the thought of failing his exams', as a Norfolk inquest recorded. Or does the pressure come from peers? Tony Tucker, also 17, knew that new recruits to the Typolac paint factory where he worked in Skelmersdale, Lancashire, in 1987, had to undergo a 'jocular initiation ceremony' in which they were pinioned to the floor while paint thinner was poured over their penises. 'The thinners would give the sensation of coldness to their private parts, and then a sensation of heat, which would give a stinging discomfort,' said William Waldron QC at the later trial of the ringleaders. 'It happened to all young starters, and Tony was willing to submit to the ceremony.' What Tony could not have been willing to accept was the subsequent 'jocular' by-play with lighted matches which led to a fireball explosion and his death three weeks later from burns covering over 80 per cent of his body. What did that 'prove' to anyone?

Such incidents, whenever they occur, are invariably dismissed as 'tragic accidents'. They are not accidents. On the contrary, each and every one of them is predetermined by a set of decisions, social values and demands contingent upon masculinity wider than anyone is prepared to take responsibility for. Until the elements of manhood training and the definition of 'what it takes to be a man' are overhauled and revised, these 'accidents' will continue to happen.

And we shall all be the losers. Young men think, believe, know that they are immortal. Older people know differently, and know too that the young of any country are its most precious reserve. When the million young Englishmen died in World War I and the countless millions of Russians in World War II, for every young man lost there were three other losers: his mother; the woman he might have married; and the country he could have enriched. There is some justification at least for the death of the finest flower of manhood in wartime. There is none whatsoever in time of peace.

Because the majority of young men make a safe, successful transition to adulthood, are we to care nothing for those who do not? How can we approach these questions of bravado, irresponsibility, over-reaching, without a closer examination of what the victim-losers were reaching out for, what agenda they are following, and what distant drum-beat so dictates all their steps that these random yet fated acts of violence and self-violence can happen, and continue to happen? Until then, some young men will be perpetually doomed to the fate of all those who, as the Greeks used to say, the gods truly loved.

> If any question why we died,
> Tell them – because our fathers lied.
> Rudyard Kipling

III MAN AND SUPERMAN

Beware of the pursuit of the Superhuman:
it leads to an indiscriminate contempt for
the Human.
George Bernard Shaw

7   Ecce Homo

To be a man, as popular music and mythology have it, is to be 'king of
the town, cock of the walk, top of the heap'. Few men, however, grow
up to enjoy the grandiose unchallenged status implicitly promised in
this conventional formulation. Their reality can be the very opposite,
an existence fragmented by heavy, often conflicting demands, and
compartmentalized into work, home and family as the only way of
staying sane.

For much is expected of the adult male – too much, in many cases.
He has to carve out a career and through it make his mark on the world;
he has to form and ideally to sustain a marriage; he has to win bread
and to provide, year in, year out, for those he calls his own. Contem-
plating this crowded agenda, any man might be forgiven for sharing the
feeling behind Bertrand Russell's celebrated pronouncement on the
Ten Commandments, that they should carry the instruction, 'Only six
to be attempted'.

And all these actions the adult male must carry out with clarity,
conviction, power. He who hesitates is lost; who shows weakness is
despised; who fails will be thrown to the jackals. The authority of
manhood, therefore, is not a mantle that descends by right, but is won
through a series of painful struggles against the brute force of circumstances, against the poverty of man's emotional training, but most of
all against other men. Work, for instance, is a prime site of adult
manhood significance – yet how many men ever make it easy for
another man to enter the world of work? Companies, occupations,
professions jealously guard their entrée, and consistently convey the

silent message, 'make your own way up the mountain'. And even once within these charmed circles there is no relief. Every structure, every institution of the world of the adult male, with its hierarchies, methods of competition and elimination, and inexorable system of rewards and punishments, faithfully reproduces the system in which as a boy he was brought up, learning to endure what he now cannot live without, the rites of man.

For as boyhood and youth set up the structures and inculcate obedience to them, so now adult manhood brings the right to be on the giving, not the receiving end. Handled as they have been, what can men do but pass it on down the line in their turn? After a young lifetime spent at the bottom of the heap, now they have risen to the top they know from experience the way things are done. Yet adult male things are never done as easily as men like to think they are, or as manhood demands that they pretend that they are. Work, marriage, fatherhood, all these are built on a complex and interlocking set of expectations and tensions in which hopes of personal fulfilment, happiness and success are at war with other equally integral themes of dominance, power and possession.

None of these inherent strains in the manhood agenda is ever stated or made plain. On the contrary, the young man is consistently told that if he can only begin, 'get his foot in the door' or 'on the first rung of the ladder', the rest will follow. He will of course begin: first with a job, since he must, in the classic phrase, 'make a living'. Then he must take a wife, and with her the Pandora's box of the eternal female. From there it is only one small, often almost unnoticed step into the biggest challenge of all, the assumption of fatherhood and the power of the patriarch. In all these worlds, of work, marriage and fatherhood, he will be playing by the rules he has been given, the rules of men. And the rest will certainly follow.

I went to work in a warehouse and I'd only been there a couple of days when a load of the young blokes got me in a corner and started to pull my trousers down. They got my cock out and greased it and massaged it, then they put horseshit on it and rubbed it in. It was horrible, the most horrible shock really. But you accepted it, and when the next new lad came along, you were there doing it with the rest of them.

Ted Harrison,
London factory owner

'Work is a mountain, and from the time you know anything, you know you've got to roll your boulder up it,' says London University sociologist Max Milkin. Some men are lucky enough to find their mountain range at an early age and to know from the outset where their futures lie. 'I was sixteen when I first got to know Wordsworth and saw poetry in every stream, poetry in everything,' says Sir Stephen Spender. Men as diverse as Orson Welles, J. D. Salinger, Bobby Fischer and many others were equally fortunate in seeing clearly as boys the road they would tread as men. Nor does a man have to be a genius to see his road ahead, broad and clear. Michael Murphy, now a Catholic priest, then a student at Trinity College, Dublin, recalls the onset of his religious vocation with rueful humour: 'A gang of us went to see Audrey Hepburn and Peter Finch in *The Nun's Story*. I came out weeping, telling everyone, "I want to be a nun!"'

Even those subsequently accounted geniuses do not always find the choice of career path easy or painless. At seventeen, Winston Churchill was the despair of all around him. 'He rather resembles a naughty little sandy-haired bulldog,' his grandmother Jerome wrote to his grandfather, 'and seems *backward* except for complicated games with toy soldiers.' Lord Randolph, at his wits' end over a son who was too dull to coast through Oxford, too dull even to be put to the law, seized on this glimmer of interest and enrolled his son in the army. 'The toy soldiers turned the current of my life,' Churchill later remarked.[1] Nor is the young man allowed to make his own unaided choice. 'My mother wanted me to be a fiddler or a rabbi,' says Saul Bellow. 'I had my choice between playing dinner music or presiding over a synagogue.' Maternal ambition plays a substantial though often negative part in the career decisions of many men. 'I am sure I am not a success in the eyes of my mother,' observed leading psychiatrist Professor Anthony Clare. 'She would have liked me to be either Pope of Rome, or President of Ireland or something!'

Overweening maternal ambition is of course the stock of every comedian from Menander to Steve Martin. What is not so widely acknowledged is the limitless ambition that afflicts every young man, if only in fantasy. Quizzing eighteen-year-old Americans about the work they would like to do, Studs Terkel found that the majority of them wanted to be 'something from *Dallas* or *Dynasty*'. Above all they wanted to be in the position of 'J. R.', the head of *Dallas*'s 'Ewing Oil', because 'he kicks butts'. 'Their values come from TV commercials,' commented Terkel in disgust.[2]

Even without dreams of power and untold wealth, young men have to be ambitious for work, or else find themselves another equally potent source of validation in the eyes of 'real men'. For work remains the primary definer of adult manhood, and the simple social question 'What do you do?' conceals within it the far more loaded demand, 'Tell me what you're trying to be.' For as Lois Wyse, President of Wyse Advertising, New York, points out, 'A man is his job, while a woman is herself.' A woman's cycle gives her constant bodily reminders of her femaleness: men have to manufacture their maleness and its routines. Sex may be given, but the appropriate psychic identity is not. Work offers the obvious benefits of money, security and status. But above and beyond, especially in the infinite plasticity of late adolescence, it offers the definition of a prescribed role and hence the comfort of certainty in an uncertain world.

A job or occupation is also essential in adult manhood as something to take refuge in or hide behind. 'If you can say "I'm a naval engineer",' says Lawrence Ecclestone, 'you can talk about what you *do*, you don't have to talk about yourself.' The longer a man works, the more established he becomes, the more impenetrable the disguise: bankers or lawyers, house-painters or taxi-drivers are never seen *as men*. The choice of a life career, then, although superficially guided by interests and abilities, will also be determined by the urge to develop as good a 'cover' as possible. Nor is the choice of occupation purely defensive, as Dustin Hoffman indicated in his reflections on what he learned about manhood after exploring womanhood during the making of *Tootsie* (1982):

> One of the things about being a man in this society is giving away as little as possible. Part of manhood is not to be taken advantage of. Poker is the classic masculine sport where the whole thing is bluff and knowing where someone's vulnerability is, so you can attack and try to take something away from them.[3]

With so much riding on getting a job and making a success of it, it is hardly surprising that some beginners will undergo the tortures of Hades in order to make their mark. Twenty-seven-year-old Marco Pierre White, one of Britain's most successful chefs and the youngest ever to win a Michelin star, is typical of those who, in one métier or another, create their own hell:

> Any chef who says he does it for love is a fucking liar. At the end of the day it's all about money. I don't enjoy it, having to kill myself six days a week to pay the bank. But if you don't cut the mustard you're finished at the end of the day. If you've got no money you can't do anything; you're a prisoner of society. At the end of the day it's just another job. It's all sweat and toil and dirt: it's fucking misery!

In his determination not to be 'a prisoner of society', White has made himself a prisoner of his fashionable London restaurant, Harvey's, where he works at a frenzied pace from eight o'clock every morning till two or three a.m. the next day. Locked into his own system of verbal and emotional violence, self-punishment and pain, he naturally visits it on those who work for him: 'Fucking wake up! What a dickhead! What a plonker! Next time you're out! D'you understand? OUT!' In another flurry of unselfconscious phallic terrorism, the maestro defends his handling of the sous-chefs who chop, grind, whisk, slice and slave for him in his hell's kitchen:

> You know what makes the food good at Harvey's? It's the bollockings! If I didn't bollock them, they'd send any shit out. The more I give a boy a bollocking the more I respect him and the more I care for his talent. When I say 'Fucking move your arse, baby!', if any boy answered me back, I'd sack him instantly.[4]

Dicks, arses, bollocks, plonkers and fucking – what an extraordinarily highly sexualized world of work men both create and inflict on one another. The kitchen of a great chef may be, quite literally, a hothouse. But the same deep drive to humiliate beginners, to instil feelings of weakness and vulnerability if they are not there already ('You've got to break them down before you can build them up!'), and the ever-present homo-erotic tension mark out a wide variety of occupations, especially if they are manual, physically demanding, or all-male. 'Even though I am 27 years old, it's important for the other men to treat me like a very young lad,' says production-line worker Andy Weissman. 'Sometimes they get real mad and start calling me the worst thing they can imagine, and that is a cunt. They're always competing and grading themselves, and using women to grade each other. The lowest grade is to be like a woman. I guess this was the first time I became aware how important it was for men to use feelings about women to prove to each other that *they* were OK.'

The more overtly 'masculine' the job becomes, the higher the level of sexual tension, macho posing and phallic swagger. Jim Stoddard joined an oil rig off Los Angeles after an upper-middle-class college-educated background because he wanted to 'feel like a *man*'. Plunged straight into full production, his only training the hysterical screaming, barked orders or deliberate misinformation of the older men, he soon learned 'the humiliation that underlies that pride':

> The experience of the veteran roughneck is his most prized possession, the only thing that separates him from inexperienced

'worms' like me. And so basically simple skills begin to seem like magical potencies, their learning an ordeal of pain and mystery. These are the rites of manhood, never to be explained, only endured.

'Manhood' in this context also meant an obsessional insistence, jokey but menacing, on phallic power and supremacy, especially on the implied *droit de seigneur* of the dominant males over any younger man's body. On his first night aboard the rig, Stoddard was subjected to 'vicious kidding about anal rape', and told he would be 'cracked open like a shotgun' if he bent over in the shower to pick up a bar of soap. Later he learned he had narrowly escaped 'the classic treatment for breaking out a new hand: having the dope brush shoved up his asshole. Dope is a foul, greasy sealant used on pipe threads; it stings, and is almost impossible to wash off.' Waiting in vain to experience 'that warm glow of shared masculinity', Stoddard learned instead that 'whatever all oilmen share, it is not a camaraderie of mutual defence. It is an appreciation of their ability to "screw" each other.' This 'screwing' of men by men takes place all the time, perfectly illustrating that machismo, in whatever form, has nothing to do with appealing to women, but promises a higher form of sexual dominance over other men. Stoddard, battling with secret fears about the gay tendencies in his own sexuality, was amazed by the incessant joking insistence upon homosexual humour coupled with the 'roughnecks'' conviction that whoever else was a 'sissy', *they* were not 'queer':

Most joking between men is at best a friendly way of keeping each other in shape for the really hostile encounters, when every emotional hole is an opening for mental rape. Anal sadism and the competitive dynamic to make the other guy into the 'woman' are at the core of this type of humour.
    A: Hey, wasn't that you in my sack last night?
    B: Naw, couldn't have been. I'm tied down every night, asshole down, for protection from you.
    A: You better, waving that sweet ass of yours around like you do.
    B: Now I know you been telling people you sucked my dick, but you don't have to lie. I mean telling them it tastes like a lemon and all . . .
    And so on, with no relief in sight.[5]

The world of the roughnecks, as they would be the first to boast, is its own very special kind of hell. But it is hard to think of any profession or occupation whose entry is controlled by men, where the new recruit is not subjected to some painful or punishing ritual of acceptance or rejection by the self-appointed gate-keepers. Social class, wealth or prestige offer little defence: the humiliations visited on an engineering apprentice in the north of England will be comparable to the ordeals undergone by would-be fraternity members of the Ivy League colleges of America: till the day he died, Tennessee Williams never forgot the vicious 'paddlings' he received at the hands of the Alpha Tau Omega leaders of his university, so 'spine-breaking' he could hardly crawl back to his dormitory afterwards.

At twenty-five, thirty-five, forty, grown men are still visiting hell upon themselves and their families, subordinating all other concerns in the endless struggle to pass accountancy exams and bar finals, to obtain medical or surgical qualifications or to get a PhD. All are systems in which, like sport, many must compete in vain in order to enhance the glory of those who win; they are 'structures of failure' devised to honour through the pain of the losers the potency of the winner, the valorized male. Inescapably then, either winning or losing, either suffering the trauma of rejection and failure or the confirmation of success, will equally confirm in novice males all the elements which make men dysfunctional in later life: the ritual infliction of emotional and physical violence, the denial of weakness and the search for transcendence, the centrality of the penis as the ultimate standard and *sine qua non*, and the unshakeable, fantastic faith in penis-power as the answer to everything.

Now my father was musing within himself about the hardships of matrimony, as my mother broke silence. –

'My brother Toby,' quoth she, 'is going to be married to Mrs Wadman.'

'Then he will never,' quoth my father, 'be able to lie *diagonally* in his bed again.'

Laurence Sterne,
Tristram Shandy (1760)

Marriage is the only war where one sleeps with the enemy.

Mexican proverb

Why do men get married? Thomas Hardy married because he went on a trip to Cornwall looking for a romantic adventure in the old fairy kingdom of the region he knew as 'Lyonesse', and bumped into a woman dangerously on the verge of old maidhood and looking for a man. Baden-Powell, founder of the Boy Scout movement, married because his mother told him to. The truth is that men marry because they have no alternative – or rather, because the alternatives available are unacceptable to them. Marriage is compulsory because it is a crucial test of a man's ability to establish himself in the eyes of other men. Getting a wife, forming the essential unit that will provide the basis for a family, is a central way for a man to prove he is a *Mensch*.

In most cultures, too, getting married has always been a primary social obligation. Marriage is a positive duty incumbent upon every Jewish male, for instance, and every refusenik is judged to have diminished the glory of God. Sages and scholars were expected to marry just as much as more worldly men, and the idea of voluntary bachelorhood or celibacy was unthinkable – 'just as well talk of a voluntary leper,' comments Jewish historian Chaim Bermant. These obligations persist in many parts of the world even today. Dr Srinivas Kamineni, a 26-year-old London anaesthetist facing an arranged marriage with an Indian bride due to be brought to Britain, killed himself in March 1989 by connecting a fatal intravenous drip to his own arm. To his fiancée he wrote that the marriage would have dishonoured her; to the police, 'if resuscitation attempted and proves successful, litigation for assault will follow'.[6] To Charles Murray, author of *Losing Ground: American Social Policy 1950–1980* and guru of the New Right, there is nothing unreasonable about society's imposition of compulsory marriage and fatherhood:

> Men who do not support families find other ways to prove that they are men, which tend to take various destructive forms . . . through the centuries young males are essentially barbarians for whom marriage – meaning not just the wedding vows but the act of taking responsibility for a wife and children – is an indispensable civilizing force. [Without marriage] too many of them remain barbarians.[7]

To ensure that the young man does not suffer for his compliance, every society has traditionally endowed a husband with a very great deal of power within the marriage. As recently as the last century English husbands beat, sold or imprisoned their wives at will. In 1848 a Mrs Dawson applied for a divorce from her adulterous husband, who had for years flogged her with a horsewhip and brutalized her with a metal-spiked hairbrush. Her petition was refused: her husband was within his rights. Moreover, observed the judge, it was not in the public interest for the rights of the husband to be undermined by the action of one discontented wife. A husband's rights extended over others too. Among a large number of similar newspaper advertisements in eighteenth- and nineteenth-century America, one John Wilson of South Carolina in October of 1865 ordered any man, woman or child to turn over his runaway wife to the authorities, and prohibited any individual from offering her food, water, shelter or credit, 'on pain of prosecution'.[8]

The power of husbands over wives, both physical and mental, was explicitly defended in their time by Rousseau, Hegel, Kant, Knox, Calvin, Luther and Freud. With champions like these, and enshrined in law codes from Hammurabi to Napoleon, it is hardly surprising that these rights (or wrongs) have survived with impressive vigour into the modern period. At the age of 114, for instance, Mrs Carrie White of Florida was at last deemed sane enough in 1990 to leave the asylum to which her husband committed her in 1909. Although she had no history of mental illness, Mrs White suffered hallucinations and delusions during an attack of typhoid fever after childbirth. Three weeks later, her husband had her certified as a lunatic, a judgement which went unchallenged until the nonagenarian was 'rediscovered' in 1984. As recently as May 1990 a young American woman, Donna Carroll, aged 28, was convicted on a criminal charge of adultery brought by her ex-husband in the state of Wisconsin. Mrs Carroll's ordeal began when her husband and father-in-law, after a bitter divorce and custody battle which ended in her favour, decided to 'exercise their rights' over an affair she had when the marriage was breaking down. Over one-third of the states of America still have such legislation on their statute books, 'for the protection of marriage and the family'. Similarly in England in 1987 former mental nurse Dave Brady had his pregnant wife committed to a mental hospital under a compulsory detention order following a family row. 'He said he wanted me out of the way to get a bit of peace and quiet,' says Fiona. It was almost two weeks before she saw a psychiatrist, who told her, 'You haven't got a mental problem, you've got a marital one.'

There is in unhappy marriage a power of misery which surpasses all the sorrows of the world.
Disraeli

'I wish I were married,' wrote Lord Byron, bored with romantic conquest, to Lady Melbourne in 1814. 'I don't care about beauty, nor *subsequent* virtue, nor much about fortune. But I should like – let me see – liveliness, gentleness, cleanliness, something of comeliness, and my own firstborn – was ever man more moderate?' Yet, married the next year to a wife who united all these qualities and more, and adored him besides, Byron could endure neither it, nor her. Raging, he cursed church, parson and wedding-bells as they drove away from the ceremony and demanded of his wife if she presumed to sleep in the same bed with him, since he hated sleeping with any woman. Greatly daring, the little bride elected to do so, and spent all night listening to her husband's tears, groans and screams of 'My God! God! *I am in Hell!*' In such a dreadful lottery, possibly more fortunate was the bride whose groom made no pretence of observing any romantic or even conventional niceties, like the eighteenth-century Princess Caroline of Brunswick: her Prince of Wales arrived at the altar stinking drunk, 'looking like death and full of confusion', and once within the bridal chamber toppled head-first into the grate, where he collapsed insensible, and where his bride left him.[9]

Byron and the Prince Regent were at least under the compulsion to perform a dynastic duty for which they had been trained from birth. Today's young man, with no particular reason to marry one woman rather than any other, can still experience the horror, the claustrophobia, of the life sentence of close confinement with an unloved partner whose every word and deed is a searing reminder of the gap between expectation and actuality. 'I loved her with a grand passion,' confessed poet and critic A. Alvarez in his poignant account of the failure of his first marriage, 'or I thought I did: like my idols Frieda and Lawrence.' As he brought his bride tea and toast on the day after their wedding, he pictured the dialogue: '"And so good morrow to our waking souls . . ." "It was the lark, the herald of the morn . . ." She bit into her toast and said "You didn't cut off the crusts." It's the wrong script, I thought in panic.'[10]

Has any writer, male or female, done justice to the burden of misery men can carry in marriage? Historically, expectations were lower, the distance within marriage greater (well-born couples never slept together, for instance, a custom observed by members of the British royal family even today), and even among working-class families, although living conditions may have been more cramped, the experience of day-to-day roles was widely separated. Marriages themselves were shorter, too: between accident and child-bearing, infection, privation and disease, the average Renaissance marriage lasted no more than eight years. Today's husband is conditioned to expect

Dream Girl, Wonder Woman and Supermum all rolled into one, and her charms are supposed to hold him in thrall for the next 40 or 50 years. 'Married love never lasts,' observed the pathetic, abused wife of the Prince of Wales, Caroline of Brunswick, after a marriage that more than lived up to the grisly promise of her ill-auspiced wedding night, 'dat is not in de nature.' H. G. Wells agreed. 'A day arrives in every marriage when the lovers must face each other,' he wrote, 'disillusioned, stripped of the last shreds of excitement, undisguisedly themselves.' Facing that moment, argues film actress Glenn Close, is far harder for men than for women. 'Men have always been at the mercy of women, and still are,' she said of her screen roles in *Fatal Attraction* and *Dangerous Liaisons*: 'We are emotionally and spiritually stronger than men, and more ruthless: men are more vulnerable.'[11]

And marriage as a *machine à deux* seems almost designed to exploit a man's vulnerabilities. He is supposed to be the head of the household, the breadwinner, the 'Mester'/*Meister*/Master in almost any tongue: in reality he may well find himself living in a house which has been dictated by circumstances not choice, where every item of furniture, every cushion or curtain, has been paid for by him, but selected by someone else. He marries in the joyous hope of unlimited, unfettered sex: in almost every marriage husbands report sexual rejection, cold or cruel responses to sexual overtures, and even years of sexual humiliation. 'The Iron Curtain', as one husband called it, can come down as soon as the golden ring is on the bride's finger. One husband reported whisking his bride off to a beautiful hotel, where he had arranged the ultimate candlelit dinner for two, followed by a romantic hour of dancing cheek to cheek. As they arrived at the door of the bridal suite the bride turned to face him, and placing a restraining hand on his chest, said 'We've had a wonderful evening – let's not spoil it.'

Is it any wonder then that men, as they are repeatedly assured in contemporary psycho-speak, 'fear intimacy'? 'When your wife is your passion-killer, you really need to throw momma from the train,' said one independent television producer. Film critic Richard Dyer has written at length about 'the female derision about the patriarchal overestimation of the penis'.[12] The whole process of becoming masculine, from the still-to-be-created masculinity of the little boy to the Head-of-the-Household authority of the paterfamilias, is endangered by the female. At a stroke, however virginal, ignorant, crass or clumsy she may be, her very existence has the power to throw her man back to the profound, primeval, blissful time of 'angel infancy', when he was her centre, her focus, her *raison d'être* – a nostalgic evocation all the stronger for calling up her too implicit threat to his masculinity, her desire to possess, to dominate and to destroy.

For nothing creates as much conflict in a man as being drawn to a woman. Her body, her love, her care, her way with flowers, food or words (one man described falling in love with his ideal Jewish mate when she observed 'there's no smoke without salmon'), draw him like the fire on the hearth. At the same time, memories of the primal dependency on the woman of all-power, the first mother, fill him with terror of weakness, of engulfment. His manhood has been built on his ability to leave his mother, to detach himself from her and her ways, and cleave to the clear, if distant image of the father and the way men behave. Just as a girl empowers herself through affiliation to the female, so a boy only achieves personal power through separation and autonomy. And what is marriage or 'intimacy' but an admission, however far down the road, of that primitive, savage need, that hunger which to feed is to die?

> She's my woman
> I'm her man
>
> I'm her eggs and bacon
> She's my frying pan
>
> I'm her lot
> She's all I've got
> – like water to a drowning man
> R. D. Laing

Or, of course, to kill. 'Men do kill women,' observes Victoria Sackville-West casually in her novel *All Passion Spent* (1931). In the close combat zone of marriage, for many men violence and destruction are the only logical, indeed richly merited response to the provocation that is woman. Like love, married hate takes many forms. Even before the spectacular divorce in which he branded his young wife an alcoholic, a druggie, an adulteress, a part-time hooker, a slut and a bad mother, Hubert Pulitzer, heir to the Pulitzer publishing fortune, had shown his radical dissatisfaction with his wife as she was: taking her to a plastic surgeon, he had inspected, selected and handled the range of silicone breast implants available for a fuller bosom before ordering, 'We'll have this one.'

Men have destroyed women verbally, financially, emotionally and sexually, often in the frenzy of rage that allows no pity and no pause. When Londoner John Tate's estranged wife blocked the sale of their home, he took a chainsaw and removed the inner floors of the house before smashing all the windows of the remaining shell. In Scotland, reported the *Daily Telegraph* on 9 March 1989, a company director abducted his estranged wife, and bound, drugged and raped her after she rejected his pleas for a reconciliation. Such incidents, and worse, can be replicated many times over in the pages of any newspaper. For all these men, love, rejection and frustration formed a lethal cocktail with the challenge to their rights of power and possession, themes that can never be absent even in the most loving or liberal of unions. 'I'm just an ordinary man,' a wife-murderer told Anna Ford. 'All I wanted from life was a nice home, a family and a steady job':

My wife was two-timing me. I just blew my top and that was it. I stuck my knife in her. I treasured her. The judge says, 'You put your wife on a pedestal. You shouldn't put your wife on a pedestal.' Well, if you can't put your wife on a pedestal, who can you put on a pedestal? I'm a person who's got morals and principles.[13]

In 1989, according to the *US Department of Justice Report to the Nation*, 90 per cent of all crimes in America committed against married partners or former married partners were committed by men. In Britain in the same year a survey carried out by the Polytechnic of North London for the Hammersmith and Fulham Council made the following findings. Of the women in this borough, by no means the worst or most deprived in London:

- 48 per cent had been attacked or threatened by their partners in their own homes.

- 30 per cent had been assaulted at least once.

- 13 per cent had been threatened with death.

- 13 per cent had been raped.

- 10 per cent had been attacked with a weapon.

'[Marriage] is an honourable estate,' says the English Book of Common Prayer, 'ordained for the mutual society, help, and comfort that the one ought to have of the other.' But as long as men and violence go together like peaches and cream, for all too many couples this comfortable formula will remain just that, a hollow phrase.

I felt a warm personal hatred for the Pope. We had all of us tried. We didn't need him or anyone else to tell us that divorce was wrong and cruel and heart-breaking. He should try marriage.

Andrew Brown,
religious affairs correspondent,
The Independent

Not every marriage is doomed to resemble a cross between a gladiatorial contest and a perpetual Siberia. Many endure and flourish as a social arrangement which has little to do with the happiness and fulfilment of man and wife as a couple. The separation of the role of husband from that of father has a long history. 'Never trust a wife,' runs the Chinese proverb, 'though she has given you ten sons.' Today's men too draw a distinction between these twin pillars of achieved manhood status. 'As a father, I'd give myself eight points,' confesses film star Michael Douglas; 'as a husband, five.' For some, there can be no doubt where their priority lies. 'The best reason for marriage is to have children,' says Pakistan Test cricketer, international playboy and legendary matrimonial escapee Imran Khan. 'Of course I wanted a family,' agrees Auberon Waugh. 'That's what we're on this earth to do – otherwise life is entirely selfish.' The 'maternal instinct' has been widely debated throughout the ages. Less well attested in recent years, but no less real, is the desire of very many men to father a child before they die.

For some, this springs from a primal and avowed longing which mirrors the supposed penis-envy of women, and with far more reason. 'There's a lot about being a woman that I've always felt robbed about,' says Dustin Hoffman. 'I can't carry children; I can't bear children; I can't breastfeed. When it comes to all that, I've always felt like a stage-hand.' In any sequel to *Tootsie*, Hoffman concluded, he would insist on giving birth. Hoffman's feelings are echoed by actor Lewis Collins, in a declaration far removed from his *Who Dares Wins* professional he-man image:

I would love to have children. I'd be a good daddy, everybody says so. But you can't buy them at Harrods. If it were possible for a man to bear a child I think I would do it. I'd even consider saying to someone, can you give me a baby please? Whenever I think deeply about it I get a bit broody. If you don't have children it's almost as if you haven't lived, you haven't fulfilled your entire purpose of being.

In this approach, common to many of today's young men, modern fatherhood shows an interesting return to a much older attitude. Historically, fatherhood was the only parenting role of any weight or significance. Fathers like the celebrated seventeenth-century American Puritan Cotton Mather, or the eighteenth-century British statesman Lord Chesterfield, unquestioningly assumed full responsibility for their sons' and daughters' physical, mental and moral growth, and the role of the mother in all this was negligible. To the child, the father was god of its universe: he supervised its studies, punished its transgressions, guided it into an occupation, and controlled its choice in marriage, the whole panoply of paternal power backed up by a battery of financial, legal and religious sanctions.

Over time, the paterfamilias ever present in households of all classes as governor, overseer and even demi-god gave way to the radical change in work patterns which removed men from the bosom of their dependants and demanded their attendance elsewhere. In the twentieth century, to be a good father has meant a man's being away from his family for most of the time, driven by the inexorable demand of 'breadwinning'. Geographical separation entails emotional distancing too. Professor Michael Kimmel points out: 'The father was kicked upstairs, as they say in industry, and was made chairman of the board. As such he did not lose all his power – he still had to be consulted on important decisions – but his wife emerged as the executive director or manager of the enterprise called the family.'[14] It is this cold and unappealing model of fatherhood which is currently under strenuous revision.

Fathers should be neither seen nor heard – that is the only proper basis for family life.
  Oscar Wilde

'What's the point of having a baby if you never get involved?' demands *Magnum* star Tom Selleck, in one casual remark overthrowing the age-old assumption that a father's responsibility to his infant offspring ends at the moment of conception. Today's model father accompanies his wife to her ante-natal classes, remains with her through the birth, baths the baby, does not shrink from his share of the nappies, and takes the kids to the park every Saturday where, side-by-side with all the other participant dads, he demonstrates the skills of twentieth-century fathering. 'All I've done since Hannah was born is stare at her,' continued Selleck of his new-born baby daughter. 'I'm very much involved in taking care of her. I mean, Jillie is breastfeeding and I make sure I watch.' Selleck is only one of a number of modern doting dads. Mel Gibson takes his six offspring with him wherever he goes, cheerfully accepting the resulting educational discontinuity as the price for being 'not so much a family, more of a tribe'; boxer Frank Bruno broke down and cried on British television during a link-up with his little daughters, aged six and two; and Bruce Willis has turned his Hollywood home into a fortress since the birth of his daughter Rumer: 'I'm so scared of some nut stealing my baby.' It all seems a long way away from the classic model of Victorian middle-class parenthood, when the father, absent in the city all week, occasionally even needed Nanny or the governess to remind him of his various children's names.

Yet according to psychologist Charlie Lewis, author of one of the few studies of modern fatherhood, *Becoming a Father* (1986), the 'new father' is more apparent than real, and fathering itself has changed little over many years. The classic 'Sunday-in-the-park' fathers, Lewis contends, 'are only there to avoid peeling the potatoes for Sunday lunch: they sit reading the papers and just let the kids get on with it.' Even the much-vaunted value of the presence of the father-to-be at the birth of his child is now coming under scrutiny. Dr Michel Odent, French pioneer of the active birth movement, feels the husband's presence may do as much harm as good: 'Traditionally women at birth were always assisted by other women, and there were very good reasons for this. If a man is sensitive to his wife, he doesn't inhibit her. But too often he insists on breathing with her, telling her what to do next, controlling her. And from my observations of the participation of these men, it seems that sexual desire afterwards can be severely reduced.' London advertising executive Barry Spender wholeheartedly agrees: 'I'll never forget the screams. And the blood, the pulp – it was totally horrible. I still feel like shit about ganging up with the doctor and refusing to let her have any pain relief. I was so determined that our childbirth was going to be "natural". When she came home, I couldn't even look at her for nearly six months. That hardly mattered though – the last thing she wanted was to have anything to do with me.'

And however enthusiastically some men play at nappy-changing in the early days of fatherhood, the drive to compete and win in the eyes of the world together with the tyranny of their new-found breadwinner role, means that most men do not even consider sacrificing career success 'to spend more time with their families', in the classic political formula of British Cabinet resignations. 'It just doesn't make financial sense,' says Barry Spender. 'And besides, I love my work, I couldn't stand giving that up. To get to the top of the pile means I've got to go all out now. Of course that means I don't see as much of the children as I'd like. But hopefully I'm building them a good life for the future.'

As this shows, the traditional idea of adult male success, 'what makes a man a man', is hostile to both concept and practice of anything like 'the new fatherhood'. And without the young father's full, active and prolonged participation, fatherhood itself reverts all too readily to its traditional form, which for millennia has meant not love, hardly even pride, but power and possession. The vigour of these age-old preoccupations can be seen in the timeless struggles for custody and control like that fought by the actor Peter O'Toole through the courts of England and America over his only son Lorcan. It emerges too in the terrible and strictly twentieth-century conflicts over frozen sperm, fertilized eggs, embryos and foetuses. Canadian Jean-Guy Tremblay took his former girlfriend Chantal Daigle to court over her decision to have an abortion when she found herself pregnant after the relationship ended. Told at the Supreme Court emergency hearing that the 23-weeks-pregnant Daigle had gone ahead anyway, Tremblay announced, *'she just killed my child.'*

The feminist challenge to the power of the father, as shown in acts like this, is very new. Yet that power, however strenuously exercised, rarely brought with it any warmth, closeness or love. It did not even guarantee responsibility: Rousseau, who stressed that 'he who cannot fulfil the duties of a father has no right to become one', in fact abandoned all five of his own children. Today, when most of the former structures of patriarchal power have broken down but have yet to be replaced by any agreed alternative, the modern father is all too frequently caught in a two-way bind: good intentions towards the new-born scrap of humanity fail to withstand the daily, monthly, yearly pressure to 'get on', 'get ahead', or finally to 'crack it', and career imperatives grind the 'new fatherhood' into the dust.

'Fathers,' wrote Margaret Mead, 'are a biological necessity, but a social accident.' Denied a new agenda, out of time with the old, modern fatherhood can become an accident waiting to happen. Overstretched, alienated, dispossessed, the unhappy husband and father takes refuge in his work and becomes even more a stranger in the promised land. When the father is little more than a boy himself, the stage is set for intolerable conflict. Overburdened young mothers resort to nicotine or alcohol, become depressed, and as a last resort allow their children to go into care. Young fathers, all too often, reach for the first weapon they ever had, and the solution which has served them well on every occasion before in their lives as single men: violence. Paul Durst, aged twenty, was convicted at Norwich Crown Court in 1990 of pouring boiling water over the leg of his six-week-old son, 'because he would not stop crying'. The resultant scalding was so severe that the baby's leg had to be amputated. Durst told the court, 'I am sorry for what has happened to my son.' In the same year twenty-one-year-old Peter Ellis of Nottingham killed his son because the seven-month-old baby would not stop crying. Ellis told the police that the steroids he was taking for body-building made him aggressive, and that he wanted to sleep after drinking ten pints of beer. The last thing he remembered after battering and punching his son and throwing him into a cupboard, were the baby's 'soft weeps' from behind the closed doors before he died.

The prime site of male violence, its cradle and crucible, has always been the family. Given the claustrophobia of the nuclear unit as refined by conditions of twentieth-century existence, and the intensity of the passions it both generates and banks down, the wonder is not that some men become violent to their wives and children, but that many thousands more do not.

> At forty-five,
> What next, what next?
> At every corner,
> I meet my Father,
> My age, still alive.
> Robert Lowell

8   Plato's Club

There are only two times in this world when I am happy
and selfless and pure. One is when I jack-off on paper,
and the other when I empty all the fretfulness of desire
onto a male body.
> Tennessee Williams

Drinks are served by Geba Kahn, first mess sergeant,
who has been serving there since 1910 . . . The visitor
asks Geba Kahn what the British officers used to do
here in the evenings half a century ago.
  'Play bridge, sir,' says Geba Kahn.
  'Oh, tell him what else,' one of the Pakistani officers
says.
  'Sodomy, sir,' Geba Kahn replies.
> Jonathan Gathorne-Hardy,
> *The Public School Phenomenon* (1977)

He said that all they that loved not tobacco and boys
were fools.
> Thomas Kyd's evidence against
> Christopher Marlowe under torture, May 1593

Even for the serious career achiever, the man of power and glory
favoured by fortune with a loving wife, 2.1 fine children and a lifestyle
that is the envy of all who know him, the price of manhood is high. To
the vast majority of his fellow men struggling less successfully further
down the tree, the toll exacted at every stage of the route can become
too much to pay. For a significant proportion of adult men, however,
undertaking the burdens of wife and family in addition to those of life
itself would simply be an impossible addition to the problem of
establishing themselves as men. Under no circumstances can it be part
of the solution to that problem, as it is for the majority. In western
cultures at least, most gay men know before they reach the age of
maturity that the ad-man's dream of the 'normal' way of life is not for
them.

Like sexual experience itself, homosexuality seems to dawn on boys
earlier than is generally accepted. At seven, the crucial turning-point

for the onset of manhood training, Tennessee Williams was nick-named 'Miss Nancy' by his abusive, alcoholic father. Male prostitutes are frequently 'on the meat rack' or 'on the Dilly' by the age of ten. Nor does a boy have to have been seduced or perverted to have such early intimations of the nature of his sexuality, as one homosexual adult explains:

> I often try to think back to when I first knew I was gay . . . I was about ten years old and was at the Boys and Girls Exhibition at Olympia. I don't know why, but suddenly I looked up at the ceiling and it was very dark with just a few spotlights in it, and I felt I was in outer space. Then the thought suddenly came to me, you are homosexual. I'm not sure I knew what the word meant at the time, but I knew I behaved in a way that other people found unsatisfactory.[1]

'By the age of sixteen,' says John, a salesman in his forties, 'I *knew* I was gay. And I knew that was it, for the rest of my life.'

Every year, all over the world, thousands, even hundreds of thousands of young men are making the same acknowledgement. Yet even in an age apparently obsessed with surveys and polls, no accurate figures of the adult male homosexual population can be found. To date, the USA is the only country that has considered it either important or worthy of any attention to try to determine the true numbers of its gay men. The work of Kinsey in the 1940s, when his data produced the suggestion that 13 per cent of US males were either primarily or exclusively homosexual, ensured that all-American manhood could never be the same again. Equally controversially, Kinsey also found that 40 per cent of American men had had some overt homosexual experience after puberty, however fleeting its nature.

Despite contemporary outrage – to the late Senator McCarthy homosexuality was and always would be 'this great, evil, anti-American vice' – no one in his time succeeded in undermining Kinsey's data or his conclusions. And, for fairly obvious reasons, no subsequent work has seriously challenged it either. The accurate establishing of homosexual preference depends entirely on truthful, subjective reporting. Yet in a society where heterosexuality is virtually compulsory and where severe penalties can befall the open gay, how honest can a man afford to be – even with himself? Hollywood heroes like Rudolph Valentino, Rock Hudson and James Dean are not the only men whose lives, careers and entire stock in trade depend on keeping up a lifelong successful pretence of 'normal', 'healthy' manhood. And where, on the 'gay–straight' axis, does 'normality' lie? If it is true, as

Kinsey found, that as many as 40 per cent of post-pubertal males are committing homosexual acts, then to enjoy the love or physical closeness of both men and women is probably much more 'normal' than most of us would be comfortable with admitting. Arguably it takes the fame, prestige, money, unassailable status and just plain cussedness of a Marlon Brando openly to admit bisexuality, and to live with the consequences.

For the consequences can be both cruel and irreversible. Homosexuality remains a crime, punishable with savage, often sadistic penalties, in Mexico, Cuba, the Soviet Union, Singapore, the Republic of Ireland, some states of Australia, half of the USA, and everywhere that Islamic law prevails. In the USSR, for instance, Article 121 of the Russian penal code provides for five years in a labour camp for consenting adults, eight if a minor is involved. Like sexual offenders almost everywhere, gay men in such prisons can find themselves punished twice over, once by the barbarity of their surroundings and again by the victimization they almost invariably encounter from fellow-inmates and guards alike. In China, implication in a homosexual act attracts 'political re-education', which the victim may not survive. Even in the supposedly and self-consciously more enlightened West, neither the concept nor the practice of 'gay rights' has made any real headway outside the major metropolitan or urban centres – it would take a brave man to come out in Nether Wallop, or Appleton, Wisconsin – and no known gay has yet made the headway in public or political life recently achieved by women and blacks, or even by members of much smaller and more despised groups like extreme nationalist or right-wing alignments. On the contrary, the regular recurrence of scandals like that surrounding US Congressman Barney Frank in 1989, when Frank was thrust into national notoriety for his involvement with a rent boy operating a call-boy ring, shows how little the general public is ready to tolerate any homosexual activity other than a pale and discreet imitation of respectable heterosexual pairing.

Subject to these threats, fears and tensions, few homosexual men attain maturity without a good deal of confusion, doubt and distress. All males, in all cultures, 'learn' heterosexual masculinity as an integral part of growing up. Acknowledging or even glimpsing their gay orientation therefore involves them in a painful redefinition of their own masculinity, indeed their inner self. For Tennessee Williams the open admission of his sexual nature at the late age of 29 had been preceded by a series of 'almost psychotic' episodes of which the following, occurring during a tour of Europe when he was sixteen, was typical:

Abruptly it occurred to me that the process of thought was a terrifyingly complex mystery of human life.

I found myself walking faster and faster as if trying to outpace this idea . . . I began to sweat and my heart began to accelerate, and by the time I reached the Hotel Rochambeau where our party was staying, I was a trembling, sweat-drenched wreck of a boy.

At least a month of the tour was enveloped for me by this phobia about the processes of thought, and the phobia grew and grew until I think I was within a hairsbreadth of going quite mad from it.[2]

Even in a society more open and less hostile than Williams's repressive world of half a century ago, it is very hard for the young homosexual to avoid the negative aspects attributed to his sexual orientation. 'Normal' masculinity, explains Professor Michael Kimmel, as inculcated in virtually every home, grade school, sporting association or summer camp, insists that the boy split off from and despise first the troublesome female (both his mother and the feminine in his own nature) and next, anything that 'doesn't measure up', is less than male. Chief of these is the homosexual, or any hint of it: 'Homophobia is thus a vital component of heterosexual masculinity.' Gay men therefore must necessarily internalize some at least of the hatred of homosexuality with which they have been brought up. Many can only cope by pretending to be straight, and by sticking to this until they can endure it no longer. 'Gay men can often only drop "the male role" when it has become clearly dysfunctional for them,' says Kimmel. 'Until then, they will always be "martyrs for the masculine ideal".'

I've used the word homosexual rather than gay because I've never regarded it as a very gay thing to be gay. I think you have more problems and if I could have changed it, I think I would. But it's like being Jewish. You're landed with it, and there's not much you can do.
    Rabbi Lionel Blue

'I tried at one point,' confesses the popular media personality Lionel Blue of his own homosexual odyssey, 'to let the body rip.' A major part of the difficulty of being a homosexual man is the widespread perception of the entire group as predatory, sexually voracious, promiscuous, and faithless. Constance Wilde wrote furiously of Oscar's 'filthy, vile, disgusting, *insane* life' when a less homophobic judgement might have found it indiscreet and self-indulgent, but little more so than that of many heterosexual men of his age and class. Certainly Wilde exemplified the preference of many adult male homosexuals for a variety of partners: Tennessee Williams's avowed aim throughout his thirties and forties (perhaps to make up for the dry gulch of his twenties) was to end up in bed with a new partner at least once in every twenty-four hours. Yet this desire for novelty, this compulsive quest for conquest, this satyriasis even, is not confined to the homosexual male. It has been a characteristic of masculine dominance behaviour from the first of the Chinese emperors to John F. Kennedy, and has achieved mythic status in the legends surrounding Don Juan, Casanova, Errol Flynn. The heterosexual cocksman, however, becomes a hero: the homosexual, as Wilde was to discover, his polar opposite, a pervert, criminal, outcast, or 'son of Cain'.

Faced with the ever-present and savage rigidity of the official masculine party line, even those who are genuinely heroes by any other standard can find that this aspect of their lives may poison all the rest. With or without the romanticization of his exploits as 'the Prince of Arabia', T. E. Lawrence was distinguished for a number of exceptional attitudes and acts, not least in the eyes of the Arabs whose freedom from Turkish tyranny he helped to secure. Yet even before the trauma of his rape at Turkish hands, he had suffered from an intermittently paralysing doubt and self-disgust: afterwards, possessed with a fury to humiliate himself among the ranks of the 'common' soldiers and airmen, he saw no future other than in masochistic self-denigration. 'I long for people to look down on me and despise me,' he wrote. 'I want to dirty myself outwardly so that my person may properly reflect the dirtiness which it conceals.'[3]

Lawrence's life, a long calvary of self-denial, torment and self-hatred, came to a fittingly ambiguous end with the still unexplained and fatal motorcycle crash in 1935. His story, though extreme, strikes a chord which sounds with varying degrees of intensity through the lives of many homosexual men. 'Show me a happy homosexual,' cries Michael, a character in *The Boys in the Band*, the gay drama and surprise Broadway hit of the early 1980s, 'and I'll show you a gay corpse.' In the same vein J. R. Ackerley, an intimate of E. M. Forster's male coterie for over 40 years, was tormented by the conviction that he was not a 'real man'. Ackerley's father had displayed a dauntingly aggressive heterosexuality, keeping two wives and families to satisfy his desires, and his brother met a hero's death in action at the Battle of the Somme. Measured against these two standard manhood indices, Ackerley felt himself all his life to be a pitiful apology for a male.

Even today the stranglehold of traditional masculinity, the tyranny of the compulsion to 'measure up', makes too many lives miserable. James, a very successful London lawyer, now 34, looks back in anger on the last twenty years:

I am a male, fully male as I see it, with all the normal male attitudes and appetites – I love good food and wine, I enjoy listening to music, and the idea of England winning the Test series does to me exactly what it does to any other man. I'm a responsible member of society, I pay my taxes, in fact I pay so much I often think I'm keeping the bloody Treasury afloat! I'm also in a stable relationship. I've been with Richard for seven years, during which two of my partners have divorced and countless friends' hetero relationships have foundered. Yet I'm constantly aware that in all their eyes I'm not a real man, and *they are*. Since I knew I was gay, since I was fourteen that was, I've been fighting that. It's taken a long time for me to feel that they're wrong. And it's cost me more than I can say. I still get angry whenever I let myself think about it. It's got to change, it's changing now. But it's too slow for me.

As a child I was taught that homosexuality was a sin. When I became a medical student it was a perversion. When I became a houseman, it was a deviation. By the time I had been appointed a consultant, it had become a variation. Now it's an alternative lifestyle. By the time I retire it will have become compulsory!
   Dr John Gallwey,
   consultant specialist on AIDS

In any attempt to suggest that modern homosexuals are suffering from the continued imposition of an antiquated and inhumane agenda of official masculinity, it is salutary to recall just how recent, historically speaking, the hostility to male homosexuality is. From the dawn of Greek language, thought and literature in the eighth century BC, the love of men was integral both to the concept and the practice of Greek maleness. As such it permeated every aspect of Greek life from the highest to the lowest. To Plato, homosexual love and desire were the starting-point for his metaphysics, as expressing the soul's search for divine beauty and its one perfect partner; to the poet Straton, a beautiful boy was no more than 'a smashing bit of homework' whose principal function was to unbend the mind for poetic composition.

This easy juxtaposition of male love and lust, together with a totally unproblematic acceptance of homosexuality, shine through in every surviving anecdote or piece of evidence from the era of classical Greek civilization. Plutarch recalls a certain Theron who, challenged for the love of a beautiful boy, chopped off his thumb and dared his rival to do the same; Xenophon writes of intervening to save both men when one of his bravest officers had offered his own life to rescue a 'hyacinthine' youth he saw being led to execution one day; and neither gesture seems to have been considered excessive or strange. Yet the countless acts of romantic love, devotion and heroism are constantly offset by a joyful relish of the crudest physical realities and a no-holds-barred approach to other men's amours: the infatuated Theron was advised by the poet and philosopher Maleager to 'leave off squeezing hairy arses', while according to the satiric poet Eubolos, the Greek heroes of the war against Troy took ten years to finish the campaign because they couldn't leave each other alone, until in the end they 'all went home with arses wider than the gates of the city they took'.

Yet even within the apparently relaxed and accommodating framework of the practices of the Greeks, the themes and structures of the expression of sexual feeling by men for men offer some suggestive similarities with the forms of heterosexuality which have been considered standard throughout the ages. In the belief of the Greeks, male lovers fell into two very distinct categories, the *eromenos*, or desired boy, and the *erastes*, his adult male lover. It was taken for granted that no male would both accept penetration and seek to penetrate another at the same stage of his life. In boyhood he was sought or bought, the passive object of any older man's attention, intermittently admired for his 'rosy bum' or 'a pair of thighs that even old men twitch for', but accorded little more status or fine feeling than a piece of furniture, and sometimes even less, as this sally from Aristophanes' *Knights* makes clear: 'Here's a folding stool for you, sir, and a boy to carry it – and if you feel like it, sir, make a folding stool of him too!'

To be a man, in Greek eyes, was to be the opposite of this. 'The arrival of the beard,' says the philosopher Dion, 'liberates the boy from the tyranny of *eros*.' For *eros* was never a reciprocal relationship, the mutual sharing of sexual delight: it referred exclusively to the right of the adult male Greek citizen to 'make trial of' (*peiran*) any boy he fancied. Pursuing a boy, indeed many boys, was something all men were expected to do, and the 'meat or game' available at the prime hunting sites (the gymnasium, the bath-house, the athletics track where the boys competed naked) was eagerly discussed. The chosen boy was expected to be available at all times – one writer boasts of taking a victor of the *pancration*, a ferocious blend of boxing, wrestling and all-in combat, 'when he was dripping in blood'.

As this suggests, the major element of any boy's attractiveness lay in his passivity and receptiveness. Good looks were important – Greek lovers lyrically hymn the 'slender waist', 'virginal eyes' and 'hyacinth locks' of the boys they desired – and passions, however brief, could run high: any man 'heated with male fire' could never thereafter bear 'the pale food of women', insisted Plutarch, while to Anacreon the quest was so important that every boy of the moment became 'the charioteer of my soul'. But the stress was entirely upon the feelings and desires of the adult male: the boy, like so many others around him in the Greek world, women, slaves and foreigners, for instance, was no more than an undeveloped and hence inherently inferior being, ordained by the gods to serve the needs of heroes and men.

Immaturity, therefore, was the key to boyish beauty. Love lyrics harp insistently on the boys' pale, smooth, hairless bodies, and there is no pubic hair shown in any of the countless vase paintings of homosexual youths. In marked contrast to later, particularly twentieth-century ideas of what makes a man desirable, the small, delicate penis was much admired. The ideal beloved was not effeminate – the most prized boys were usually champions of the gymnasium, or victors in javelin, discus or running events. But they were very young, since the essence of their appeal was pre-pubertal. Given that boys in Mediterranean countries tend to arrive at puberty at any time from the age of ten onwards, on average around two years earlier than those of more northern latitudes, Greek men therefore started chasing boys whose youth, in almost every later culture, would brand their seducers as phedophiles.

Choosing a small, youthful or undeveloped partner ensures that the disposition of power, emotional, sexual and financial, stays very firmly in adult male hands. To take, as all Greek men did, a succession of young boys, each to be discarded when his attractions waned, makes a very clear statement of their unimportance and demonstrates the supremacy of the man's sexual needs and imperatives above all. This centralizing of the adult penis and the sanctity of its demands reached such a pitch in the life of the Greek city-states as to attain the level of a religious cult. Enshrined and worshipped as the phallos, its human frailty negated by monumental representations in wood, marble or stone, the penis dominated almost every aspect of Greek life. At the theatre, satyrs and centaurs equipped with outsize and terrifying genitalia were a constant reminder of men's wish-fulfilling penile fantasies, while the auditorium itself was dominated by stage penises, huge and erect, placed about the playing area. At home a herm (a square stone pillar surmounted by a head of Hermes and adorned halfway down with carved genitals, penis erect) stood at every front door. Phallos-sticks were used in song and dance, phallos-birds are a constant motif in Greek art, phallos-stones, of every size except small, were erected in any likely location. The penis even had its own theology: Priapus was the god of (in?) the erect penis, while Phalles, whose cult was particularly strong among young men, was the god of tireless, indeed ruthless sexual activity.

Inevitably this glorification of the penis and the urgent insistence on the tyranny of the rights of man led to an equally insistent downgrading of anything which was not man. The degradation of women among the Greeks, their far greater risk of death at their fathers' hands by exposure at birth, their denial of education, their deprivation of the stimulus of company and free association, their virtual incarceration in the *gyneum* or women's quarters are well known. Much less familiar is the way this contempt of women was used against men. Any man who was not continuously active and successful in relations with both women and boys was subject to taunts of effeminacy. Any youth who failed to throw off the passive 'female' role in homosexual activity as soon as his beard came was a particular object of public scorn, and adult male prostitutes who 'flogged their arses round the market-place', as Aristophanes describes it, were held to have forfeited their right to consideration as responsible citizens or even grown men. Any cuckolded husband, whose own manhood rights of property and possession over his wife had been violated at this most basic level, had the right to revenge himself on his rival by attacking and debasing the other's manhood in return. Consequently every adulterer caught in the act had to submit to having his pubic hair singed off and a radish forced up his anus by the outraged husband. Women trimmed their pubic hair in this way, men never: consequently the offender's punishment lay in being feminized both front and rear, frontally by being treated as a woman, in the rear by being reduced to the passive role and being forced to accept penetration as women and boys were, but never real men. For a male, even a young one, the association with anything female was bitterly resented as the worst possible insult. When the sixth-century tyrant-king Periandros of Ambrakai said to his youth in a drunken upsurge of coarse humour 'Aren't you pregnant yet? I've fucked you enough times!' the boy killed him.

Integral then to the themes and practices of Greek homosexuality was the acceptance of male domination and the right to inflict pain and humiliation, or at least to enforce submission, on those lower down the scale of adult manhood. Young men could only progress up the hierarchy and shake off the taint of womanishness by learning how to inflict what previously they had had to endure, by becoming predators where before they had been prey. The same assumptions dominated the homosexual codes of ancient Rome, China and Islam. When Julius Caesar embarked on his legendary affair with Nicomedes, King of Bithynia in 81–80 BC, the relationship itself was nothing: what hurt his reputation and hung round his neck till he died was the widely-reported rumour that Caesar had played the passive role as Nicomedes' 'wife'. In the early Arab world, despite a few mild murmurings against homosexuality in the Qur'an, overt homosexual activity was not considered incompatible with the highest religious, legal or moral standards or the most respected social position: the revered holy man of the sixth century, Ibn al-Farra', a teacher of the Qur'an in Almeira, took a boy who had refused his advances to court, where the judge ruled that the youth must submit to the master, a triumph lovingly celebrated in lyric verse by the victorious old goat:

> Then the *Qadi* [judge] indicated to the flowers
>   that they were to be taken,
> And to the mouth that it should be tasted,
> And when the beloved saw him on my side
> He abandoned his resistance and I enfolded him.
> I continued reproaching him for his long unkindness
> And he said, 'May God forgive a past mistake!'[4]

> Sodomy, fellatio, cunnilingus, pederasty,
> Father, why do these words sound so nasty?
> Masturbation can be fun,
> Join the orgy everyone.
> *Hair* (1968)

The great downturn in the estimation of homosexuals, and with it their standing and fortunes in the world, began around the twelfth century with the emergence of the modern world and in particular with the consolidation of the great religions of Christianity, Judaism and Islam as international institutions regulating not merely religious worship but social activity, all legal and financial affairs, even thought. Before this, the patriarchs of all faiths seem to have adopted the attitude expressed by Mark Antony in a letter to Octavius Caesar, 'Can it matter where or in whom you stick it?'[5] An eighth-century ordinance of Pope Gregory III decreed a penance of one year for homosexual acts between males, three for any priest who went hunting; similarly in the early eleventh century, penances codified by Bishop Burchard of Worms imposed eighty days of prayer and fourteen years of fasting for one offence of adultery by a married man, while habitual anal homosexual activity between men only merited forty days and twelve years respectively.

From the twelfth century onwards the rise of Christian intolerance, both religious and national, caught homosexuals along with Moors, Jews, Turks and all other infidels in its ever-widening net. This conflation of the sexual with the religious emerges clearly in the term 'bougre' (English 'bugger') which originally described the adherents of the Bogomil heresy, first noticed in Bulgaria in the tenth century. Between about 1150 and 1350 then, homosexuality changed from being a personal predilection viewed with humour or charity to a vicious and deadly sin crying out for the harshest penalties. Homosexuality itself inevitably persisted, and individuals, especially those of wealth, power or high birth, continued publicly to flaunt their preferences or amours: Richard I of England, 'the Lionheart', had an open and passionate affair with King Philip of France, when the two young kings 'lived, ate and slept together, and the one loved the other as his own so that the world marvelled at the love between them', as a contemporary chronicler recorded. Similarly Edward II a century later loved Piers Gaveston without concealment from the age of ten, and remained steadfastly faithful to him despite having to marry and father a son to secure the succession. But Edward's love cost Gaveston his life; and the unspeakable horror of Edward's death, by a red-hot poker inserted into his anus, in itself proclaims a primitive, sadistic and retributive urge to make the punishment fit the crime.

This unquestioning, unhesitating enforcement of the tyranny of 'normal' sexuality has continued to the present day. In the New England of the Founding Fathers, homosexuality was punishable by death just as it had been in the old country. Even after the death penalty was revoked, from the sixteenth to the nineteenth century in England men convicted of homosexual acts were invariably pilloried so viciously that any conviction constituted an unofficial death sentence since they so frequently died of their injuries. Less than a hundred years ago the sentence of the judge, Mr Justice Wills, at the trial of Oscar Wilde in 1895 perfectly encapsulates the view of all right-thinking Englishmen of his day:

Oscar Wilde and Alfred Taylor, the crime of which you have been convicted is so bad that one has to put a stern restraint upon one's self to prevent one's self from describing . . . the sentiments which must rise to the breast of every man of honour who has heard the details of these two terrible trials [and] the horrible charges brought home to both of you. It is no use for me to address you. People who do these things must be dead to all sense of shame and one cannot hope to produce any effect upon them. It is the worst case I have ever tried. That you, Taylor, kept a kind of male brothel it is impossible to doubt. And that you, Wilde, have been the centre of a circle of extensive corruption of the most hideous kind among young men, it is equally impossible to doubt.

I shall under such circumstances be expected to pass the severest sentence that the law allows. In my judgement it is totally inadequate for such a case as this. The sentence of the Court is that each of you be imprisoned and kept to hard labour for two years.[6]

Staggering as if he had been struck, Wilde passed from the court to his death, social, professional, financial and ultimately physical. Nor was he to be the last of the homosexual victims of what Macaulay had dubbed 'the British public in one of its periodic fits of morality'.

We were as men who through a fen
    Of filthy darkness grope:
We did not dare to breathe a prayer,
    Or to give our anguish scope:
Something was dead in each of us
    And what was dead was hope.

For Man's grim Justice goes its way,
    And will not swerve aside:
It slays the weak, it slays the strong,
    It has a deadly stride:
With iron heel it slays the strong,
    The monstrous parricide!

Oscar Wilde,
'The Ballad of Reading Gaol'

For Oscar Wilde his homosexuality was, at least in part, like so much else in his life and work, a public gesture, a conspicuous and deliberate protest against the hypocrisy, complacency and mediocrity of his own day. Almost a century after Wilde's death, homosexuality may still be the only resort for the cultural refusenik who cannot or will not conform to the conventional masculine agenda: who has passed through all the manhood rites without wanting to adopt them as his personal rights. It can hardly be accidental, for instance, that Sydney, Australia, 'where men are men and sheep are nervous' as local humour has it, and San Francisco, USA, where the final frontier meets and dissolves into the dream factory, have a higher proportion of homosexual to heterosexual men than anywhere else in the world. Inevitably homosexuals, like any other minority group, persecuted or otherwise, will be drawn to settle among like-minded people. The growth of such colonies however does not answer the question of why they arose in the first place. To the young Tennessee Williams the homosexual was potentially 'homo emancipatus', the only human type which might be completely free of dishonesty, perversion, and the compulsion to play the crippling roles of happy husband and fond father. The 'free man' of Williams's philosophical and sexual fantasy finds its beau ideal in Stanley Kowalski, hero of Williams's masterpiece A Streetcar Named Desire: part noble savage, exalted above the common herd, unspoiled and untouched, part 'brute beast' blindly following his instincts in the 'pure animal joy' of his nature, Stanley is both above and below the life of his time, out of it on every level. Only through contact with such men, Williams wrote wistfully, could a man hope to break out of his 'little cave of consciousness' and find 'the moment of grace when a word, a gesture, raps out a code message on the walls of the prison': then, and only then, 'sometimes – there's God – so quickly'.

Yet by one of those painful paradoxes which govern all sexuality from straight to gay and back again, homosexual men are dominated by almost all the same cultural norms, standards and ideals of sexual behaviour and sexual attraction as those governing their heterosexual brothers. 'I met a young guy at a party the other day,' says Andrew, a barrister's clerk. 'He was banging on about how he wanted to be bronzed and hunky to impress girls. I wanted to tell him I wanted to be like that too – to impress boys!' No man, it seems, can easily escape the desire to impress with size, strength, manliness. 'No, I'm not a queen, I can't stand all that queeny stuff,' says Jason, a male model. 'Big and butch, that's my look. Outdoor, bronzed, "Marlboro country" – I'm in the solarium week in, week out, all the year round.' Even the self-confessed 'queens', though constantly reminded of their lower place in the homosexual hierarchy through taunts like 'size queen' or 'coon queen' (the Japanese writer Yukio Mishima, who committed *seppuku*, or ritual suicide [*hara-kiri* in the western corruption], was a 'suicide queen') will nevertheless compete among themselves, constantly jostling to establish a pecking order. 'I like sex, I like lots of it,' confides Tom, a television actor. 'And I usually get what I want. I like cruising, and I'm good at it. Not like *her* [indicating an elderly actor across the BBC bar]. She's too old to cruise successfully any more. Never had all that much to offer anyway, from what I've been told. You have to know what you're doing, it's a skill. Most of them haven't got it.'

All homosexuals, whether consciously or not, are, at some level, in refusal of patriarchal norms. Yet as there is no life outside patriarchy, no form of organization, whether social, emotional or occupational, in which a man can take refuge from the dictates and structures of conventional manhood, a degree of conflict seems quite unavoidable. The conflict is strongest, and the refusal theory most clearly supported by evidential experience, within the strongest of traditional masculine structures like the armed forces, the old-established public schools, or the Church. Regimental Sergeant-Major Kevin Croft threw away a lifetime's army career in March 1990 when he made sexual advances to a young recruit who had come to him to complain of sexual harassment from another regimental officer. At Croft's court-martial the youth testified that the older man had repeatedly said, 'I must be going mad, I just can't stand it any more.' Similarly homosexual priests report experiences which many liken to 'a kind of crucifixion', says Jesuit Father Robert Carter, one of 300 members of Dignity, a support group for gay and lesbian Roman Catholics in New York. To come out, as Carter has found, inevitably means the end of active parish priesthood: 'for a gay priest, private psychotherapy practice is one of the few ways to earn a living.' Yet to suppress all homosexual feeling and with it the right to any loving relationship brings 'forty years of hating yourself', according to Father James, a Roman Catholic priest in the English Midlands, 'with every year, sometimes every day, its own Calvary'.

It is of course simply another, disguised form of homophobia to suggest that all gay men are maladjusted, angst-ridden and bitterly unhappy. But no matter what their success as and among homosexual men, and despite centuries of misguided pseudo-scientific theorizing about 'inversion', 'the third sex', and so on, homosexual men are and remain men first, last and foremost and as such, like all men, never escape manhood's laws, rules and rites. Like all men, therefore, they pursue dominance and seek transcendence through the penis, with this added intensification of the principal feature of the masculine agenda, that in homosexual love not one but two penises may be enjoyed and exalted. 'I was sixteen, a girl's age,' writes Jean Genet. 'I loved Villeroy, who loved me':

I was more amused than anything else at his making love to me the first night, for I thought it a game despite the fact that his narrow, brutal face was drawn with passion. He was contented with this make-believe, but later, when one deep dark night I dug his tool into me, he almost passed out – and I too – with gratitude and love . . . We were children seeking our pleasure, he with his awkwardness and I with too much skill. Then I broke him in, I deflowered my pimp. The brute became quite timid when making love to me. One evening he even called his penis 'my brute', and mine 'your little basket'. We kept those names.[7]

Genet's odyssey from his foundling bastard beginnings through the sewers of the French penal system to his apotheosis as a widely-respected writer convinced him that as 'woman is the nigger of the world', so the homosexual who habitually takes on the 'female' or passive role in love-making will always be the most reviled and hated of men. Certainly within most prisons world-wide, where a great many homosexuals have spent time in the past, either because their 'vice' was against the law or because their deviance made them an easy target for the law-keepers, even 'normal' men (or perhaps especially such men) feel entitled to punish the 'cissy' for what he is. American academic Denis Altman writes of a friend arrested and thrown into the Tombs, Manhattan's House of Detention for Men, where for three weeks while awaiting trial (at which he was acquitted) he was repeatedly and brutally raped by prisoners and wardens alike: nevertheless 'all the rapists considered themselves straight, bragged of their adventures with women, and vehemently denounced faggots'.[8]

To be so violated, so dominated, so invaded, is to be cast back into the deepest psychic pit, the darkness of the primal struggle to be free of weakness and the terror of that weakness, and of the fear of the strength of the overwhelming 'other'. Small wonder then that homosexual males, like all men whose sense of oppression becomes too much to bear, will resort to any degree of violence to drive the demons back to the inferno and reassert the power of a man through the supreme, even life-and-death power of the penis:

I have decided that I think I should become a homosexual murderer, and shall get hold of young boys and bring them where I am staying and I shall rape and kill them . . . They will be killed by strangulation, after which I shall cut their throats and drink part of their blood and cut off their private parts and then cut it up. I will not stop before I have killed at least 30 boys. Most of them will be raped. It doesn't matter if I rape them before or after they are dead. When I have killed these 30 boys I will start a murder campaign against women.[9]

Ronald Frank Cooper, the author of this diary, was executed in South Africa in 1978 for the murder of a twelve-year-old boy he had tried unsuccessfully to rape. In England in 1989 four men were convicted of killing a backward fourteen-year-old youth during a homosexual orgy of such ferocity that the boy, the jury was told, 'could not possibly have survived'. Two of the defendants, it emerged at the trial, had had previous convictions for violently assaulting and buggering women.

Violence is not integral to homosexuality, nor homosexuality to violence. Yet even the most peaceable, well-adjusted and socially integrated homosexual male lives his life in and through the long shadow cast by the standard manhood agenda. As the lives of homosexuals show, from the great and the gifted to the nameless millions who never acknowledge all that they are, to be Mr Norm Average is only one of the ways of 'being a man'. But while 'being a man' remains predicated on homophobia and violence, homosexual males will fight in vain to be allowed to join the club. And while the classic manhood formula remains so tightly tied to marriage and fatherhood, even in an age of accelerating divorce, absentee fatherhood and an over-populated planet, homosexual men, even those as big, butch and masculine as Rock Hudson, are condemned never to be 'real men'.

'The bravest man amongst us is afraid of himself. The mutilation of the savage has its tragic survival in the self-denial that mars our lives. We are punished for our refusals . . . The only way to get rid of a temptation is to yield to it . . . You, Mr Gray, you yourself, with your rose-red youth and your rose-white boyhood, you have had passions that made you afraid, thoughts that have filled you with terror, day-dreams and sleeping dreams whose mere memory might stain your cheek with shame – '

'Stop!' faltered Dorian Gray, 'stop! you bewilder me. I don't know what to say. There is some answer to you, but I cannot find it. Don't speak. Let me think. Or rather, let me try not to think.'

Oscar Wilde,
The Picture of Dorian Gray (1891)

9   The Power and the Glory

Some people play the power game for money, some for security or fame, some for sex. Master players seek power itself, knowing that power can be used to *obtain* money, sex, security or fame. None of these alone constitutes power: but power can be used to produce them all.
Michael Korda

Success is sexy. Losing sucks.
New York subway grafitto

Blessed is the man who knows that egomania is not a duty.
Marianne Moore

When Elizabeth Garrett Anderson, who in 1870 became England's first woman doctor, was asked why she was applying for admission to medical schools instead of contenting herself with becoming a nurse, she replied: 'I should naturally prefer £1000 to £20 a year.' The same natural desire beats strongly in the breast of every real man, who knows for a fact that the degree of his reality in adult manhood will depend very highly, if not in some circles exclusively, on the amount of money, prestige and visible career success – in a word, power – that he can muster at the peak of his achievement.

The will to succeed, to 'be something' in the eyes of the world, runs both deep and wide. The nineteenth-century Liberal politician Lord Rosebery had three ambitions: to marry an heiress, to win the Derby, and to become Prime Minister. He achieved all three before he was 50, winning further renown for the brilliance of his literary and historical works. Such successful self-actualization, insisted Nietzsche in *The Will to Power*, whatever its field, would invariably produce the most remarkable and desirable psychological effects: 'Joy is only a symptom of the feeling of attained power. The essence of joy is a plus-feeling of power.' The opposite or loss of this happy state could be terrible indeed, as John Adams, one of America's Founding Fathers and second President of the USA, confided in a sombre letter to his wife:

The rewards of this life are the esteem and admiration of others –
the punishments are neglect and contempt. The desire of the
esteem of others is as real a want of nature as hunger – and the
neglect and contempt of the world as severe a pain as the gout or
the stone.[1]

Certainly when Lord Castlereagh, a forerunner of Rosebery as British
Foreign Secretary in the nineteenth century, lost the esteem he had
won through his vigorous and highly successful foreign policy against
Napoleon when he was universally blamed for the notorious 'Peterloo
massacre', the agony of mind he underwent was a major factor in his
subsequent suicide.

For life's winners, however, the rewards can be rich indeed. Aristotle
Onassis accrued some $1 billion during his lifetime, in addition to a
fleet of oil tankers, the yacht *Christina*, several Greek islands, and
other toys. World-class success also confers quasi-royal status, even a
touch of the divine: not only in his home country of Pakistan is
international cricketer Imran Khan treated according to a literal
interpretation of his surname, 'conqueror-king'. As this suggests,
eminence at the highest level confers almost unlimited power over the
lives and minds of others, something very actively but not always
attractively exercised by many successful men. As the most terrible of
the early Hollywood movie moguls, 'the biggest bug in the manure
pile' according to Elia Kazan, Harry Cohn boasted, 'I don't get ulcers, I
give 'em.' Asked why he had copied Mussolini's office strategy of
positioning his desk 30 feet away from the door where visitors entered,
Cohn replied, 'Simple: they're shitting their pants by the time they get
here.' When Cohn ordered a re-shoot on the 1939 film *Golden Boy*, the
director Rouben Mamoulian protested: 'Why? Give me one good
reason.' Cohn looked at him. 'The reason is – I am President of
Columbia Pictures.'[2]

The achievement of success not only implies but even demands
such dominance. As a result, the power conferred by undisputed
pre-eminence frequently finds its expression in extravagant, even
grossly excessive forms of behaviour. When the US Army overthrew
the Panamanian dictator General Noriega in 1989, inside his military
headquarters they discovered a Hitler-style bunker equipped with a
personal arsenal boasting almost a thousand automatic weapons of all
sizes. Equally prominent were portraits and statues of the Führer, a
library of Nazi lore, and a family of teddy bears in Nazi and Panamanian army fatigues. The successful man measures his achievement
by his ability to have whatever he wants. Onassis, said his personal

secretary at the time of the unexpected marriage to Jacqueline Kennedy, 'wanted to show the world that he could buy anything or anybody', that nothing was beyond his price, even when her financial advisers were demanding many millions of dollars for the hand of the world's most famous widow:

> Onassis felt he had made a pretty decent deal for Jackie. 'Do you think $3m is too much?' he asked me. 'Hell, no,' I said. 'You can buy a supertanker on that, but then you have to pay fuel, maintenance, insurance, and a lot of extras.' We used to call Jackie 'supertanker' around the office. Onassis didn't mind. It made him laugh. 'It's supertanker on the line,' I'd announce whenever she called. Jackie was an acquisition, nothing more or less.[3]

World players in the power game usually do not have to buy wives or girlfriends: when Jacqueline Bouvier married for the first time, the Kennedy clan got her for free. 'Power is an aphrodisiac,' observed a living example of the truth of his own aphorism, Henry J. Kissinger. Certainly this was so of Kennedy himself, whose compulsive rutting ('a pair of stewardesses in California', 'two mulatto prostitutes in New York' are typical extracts from FBI files) as revealed over the years since his death has demolished for ever the magical memories of the Camelot years and exposed the scumbag reality under the President's boyish, clean and shining façade. 'They use you and then they dispose of you like so much rubbish,' said Marilyn Monroe of both Jack and Bobby Kennedy shortly before her mysterious death in 1962.

Yet success remains sexy, even when sleaze is just around the corner. 'Being named the sexiest man alive was a bit embarrassing,' admits film star 'hunky' Harry Hamlin. 'But still, it was about time too!' Success is nothing without the public recognition of prowess: the successful man's demonstrable superiority in this field of sexual activity simply confirms his mastery in other areas. This prowess-display does not always take the simple, predictable form of compulsive conquest. For Mahatma Gandhi, sexual control, the public demonstration of the kind of man he wanted to be, lay in the refusal to indulge or parade his masculine sexual desire. In his early thirties Gandhi, long the prophet of non-violence, came to see sexual activity as another expression of man's ruthless, self-obsessed aggression, manipulation and domination. As a result he subsequently took the decision, in 1906 at the age of 37, to become celibate for life, after a prolonged trial to ensure that his resolution was strong enough for this lifelong test. Some 30 years later, nearing 70 and finding himself tormented by nocturnal emissions and the desire for intercourse,

Gandhi resolved on sterner measures to subdue the reluctant flesh. After years of prayer and meditation he embarked on a unique series of 'celibacy experiments'. These consisted of sleeping naked with women, one or two at a time: they included his grandnieces Abha and Manu, who was then only nineteen, his doctor, Shushila Nayar, and the wife of the prominent Hindu politician Jai Prakash Narayan. Gandhi's friends and fellow-politicians were extremely nervous about the impact of all this, and many advised against it. In the event, though, even Gandhi's bitterest enemies did not succeed in making political capital out of this 'celibacy', or in undermining the deeds and motives of the Mahatma.

For Gandhi, as for lesser men, perhaps the greatest attribute of undisputed power is the ability to realize not the limited repertoire of permutations on the sexual act, but the limitless realm of sexual fantasy. As a deeply repressed suburban youth struggling with acne, inadequacy, fundamentalist Christianity and a compulsion to masturbate, Hugh Hefner longed to believe that his desires were not disgusting but acceptable, that 'nice girls like sex too'. He dreamed of undressing a smiling, consenting, playful 24-year-old, with the wholesome reassurance of the girl next door, but also 'breasts the size of Ethiopia'. Beginning in 1953 with nothing but this dream to keep him warm and $600 to make it happen, Hefner created a world empire of fellow-dreamers: at his peak, three-quarters of a million men subscribed to the Playboy Channel on cable TV, seven million read *Playboy* in the US alone, while Playboy merchandising (anything bearing the famous bunny logo) brought in $240 million a year. The original playboy, Hefner himself partied for over 30 years, lurching from the Playboy Mansion's fabled 'love grotto' to its equally notorious big, round, rotating, vibrating bed. And even though Hefner himself has now followed the fashion of the nineties into post-AIDS respectability, even holy matrimony, it will be some time yet before his fans and co-fantasists accept that the party's over, for good and all.

All men are Fisher Kings [the wounded king of the Castle of the Holy Grail in the Parsifal myth]. Every boy has naïvely blundered into something that is too big for him, gotten half way through, realized he couldn't handle it, and collapsed. Then he is wounded, he is hurt terribly, and he goes off to lick his wounds. A certain bitterness rises in the boy because he tries so hard and actually touches his 'salmon' [the source of the Fisher King's wound and also of his strength] – his individuation – yet he cannot hold it. It only burns him. If you are to understand any man past puberty, you must understand this about him. Virtually every boy has to have the Fisher King wound . . . You only have to walk down the street and look at the faces to see the countenance of the Fisher King. We are all wounded, and it shows.

Robert A. Johnson,
He: Understanding Masculine Psychology (1986)

Hefner's story is a perfect illustration of the way a man may use the power of the present to heal the wounds of his past. The image of the wound, explains Jungian psychologist Robert A. Johnson, means that 'the man is wounded sexually': 'but it is not quite adequate simply to say that it is a sexual wound. *It is a wound to his maleness.*'[4] As the careers of Hefner and so many other successful men show, these early slights and injuries may be sexual, but are by no means invariably so; and whatever the wound, for such men, their success and the power it brings do not always have to find a sexual expression, but can become a source of pleasure and affirmation in themselves, comparable to or expressive of the sense of validation that satisfactory sexual experience conveys. As head of Columbia Pictures, Harry Cohn was once reviewing candidates for a low-grade job. 'Well, this one went to West Point,' his assistant began. 'Hire him,' interrupted Cohn. 'I always wanted to go to West Point. Now I can *hire* a West Pointer. It's *retribution.*'[5] In a similar vein Aristotle Onassis, whose appetite for new shoes was in the Imelda Marcos class, was said never to have forgotten the indignity of his barefoot childhood.

This theme, of the lifelong drive to comfort or repair some deep pain of childhood, surfaces again and again in the stories of eminent men. 'My earliest memories are rather sad,' says Lord Whitelaw, Deputy Prime Minister under Margaret Thatcher, with the masterly understatement of which the British are world champions. 'As a child of three I learned that my father had died as a result of wounds in the 1914–18 war.' The Whitelaw family had in fact been decimated in that war, with young William the only surviving descendant of what had been a family of four sons. The lonely and grief-shadowed childhood soon gave way to another acute distress, that of being sent away to school. 'I was desperately homesick, and formed a view which I have never had any reason to change, that small boys are extremely nasty to each other,' recalls Whitelaw. 'What is more, the lonelier the boy, the nastier the others will be to him.'[6]

From this basis of loneliness and despair, only the most strenuous effort can serve to restore the damaged ego. As the prominent industrialist Sir John Harvey-Jones explains his success in turning the giant ICI company round from profit to loss, the motivating force, he feels, sprang from far further back than his current position of commercial expertise. The spur was and had always been the misery of boarding-school bullying: 'I was unhappy beyond levels that I believed a human being could reach,' he told psychiatrist Dr Anthony Clare. 'It made me slow to grow up, and I was petrified of women – never met any. So I set myself standards of achievement. I simply *had* to succeed in my job.'[7]

'Boys don't "choose" to be strong, they "need" to be strong,' observe psychologists Connell Cowan and Melvyn Kinder: 'this relentless drive towards self-reliance helps boys overcome feelings of weakness or helplessness. It toughens them up, helps them better define maleness, and prepares them for the rigours ahead.' 'Maleness', here as elsewhere, both implies and demands worldly success:

> To be a loser is to suffer a terrible fate. In the course of therapy with men, we find that no matter how great their success, they are haunted by the specter of failure. Indeed it is our impression that men are driven much more by the fear of failure than by the desire to succeed![8]

Once again, to be a man it is not enough simply *to be*: a man must *do, display, prove,* in order to establish unchallenged manhood. Those who will never cut a swathe through the international worlds of business or finance must therefore find or create their own deeds of derring-do, through which they too can lay claim to manhood prowess, celebrity and success, if only for fifteen minutes. Jim Randi, of Boston, USA, holds the world record for sitting naked in an igloo (43 mins 8 secs), while Barry Kirk of Port Talbot, Wales, clocked up a record-breaking 100 hours at the considerably less demanding sport of sitting naked in a bath of baked beans. Other men have striven for supreme honours in the championship contests of welly-whanging, cowpat catching, and stuffing Havana cigars in the mouth (twenty-eight beats all comers). At least when French speleologist Michel Le Roux spent 203 days alone in an underground cave, he was doing it as part of an experiment for NASA. When another American, sociologist Maurizio

Montalbini, took on Le Roux's record and shattered it by a margin of seven days, he made no pretence of scientific experimentation. 'I just wanted to prove myself,' he said. 'I wanted to test my will-power.'[9]

Such bizarre and solipsistic acts of self-definition inevitably flourish in the absence of any genuine modern testing-ground for manhood, or challenge to heroism. And though at one level these activities may seem like play, to the men involved they are usually intensely serious, and their underlying model is always competitive and quasi-militaristic. In the shortage of modern wars, it seems, modern men make their own. Nowhere can the translation of life into war be seen more clearly than in the field of business success, as Cowan and Kinder stress:

> For some men, just making ends meet is a major achievement. For other, more affluent men, money becomes a measure not only of their ability to provide for a family, but also of their skill or cleverness at the game of power. Men tend to use the same terms to describe the pursuit of financial success as they would use to describe warfare or intense athletic competition. Managers fantasize themselves as field generals leading their troops into the fray. They 'nuke the competition', 'quarterback a squeeze play', 'make an end run' on 'the opposing team'. If a man has the skills necessary to survive in the corporate world, he is a 'winner'.[10]

Business, then, like so many other manhood activities, becomes a vehicle, a metaphor for the earliest struggles for survival, a struggle which at every stage some are destined to lose in order to enhance the prestige of those who win. To Sir John Harvey-Jones, industry is a permanent battlefield and as such inevitably claims countless casualties. 'It cannot be emphasized often enough that business is very much like war,' he says, 'despite the optimistic view that there is scope and space enough for everybody to be successful.' In the public world, as at school, competition, comparison and aggression are the primary barometers for measuring maleness. The men who from the outset of their careers are ready to risk themselves in this struggle will be rewarded by a progressive enhancement of their masculine image: both Richard Branson and Andrew Lloyd Webber, for instance, have over the course of their careers grown from long-haired young men about pop into paradigms of adult manhood success. Conversely the man who cannot or will not pick up this gauntlet, who shies away from the corporate rough and tumble, who can't play, won't play manhood's power games, will never be granted the same degree of approbation, envy, esteem, fame or fortune, will still risk being dismissed as a lightweight, even if his name is Yves St Laurent or David Hockney.

For many men of prowess, however, the call to battle is neither natural nor painless. 'Never was the effortless superiority of Edwardian unflappability so effortfully achieved,' commented a contemporary of the last great Conservative prime minister Harold Macmillan: the languid 'Mac' would frequently be violently sick before any major speech, and like Winston Churchill before him, was a prey to deep depression, often having to take to his bed for days on end with his 'Black Dog'. Nor can the successful man ever share his trials or the resulting distress: one of the definitions of a winner/leader/'real man' is that he is not vulnerable to feelings of softness, weakness or failure. In effect, the most 'successful' adult men are those who have most closely absorbed, and can most efficiently reproduce, the constant lesson of their boyhood: that emotions are dangerous because they are 'female', uncontrollable, and liable to provide others with a hold over you, and that in the final analysis they are unimportant, because they are invisible, internal and repressible, as against the 'real', external and public world that men must make their own.

And yet no amount of success in the world of public esteem can guarantee either to compensate for early suffering or relieve the sufferer from the compulsion to continue the fight. In the 'war of all against all', as Thomas Hobbes summed up the life of man, even reaching the summit of earthly power may never be enough. As President of the United States Lyndon Johnson had arrived at the position where he genuinely could at any moment 'nuke the opposition', and his power over the lives of his fellow-citizens was equal at every point to his powers of death. Yet the exertion of presidential dominance did not assuage but appeared to feed his truly cosmic sense of inferiority and insecurity, the product, it appears, of a grossly deprived and unloved childhood in which the nicest thing ever said about him was 'that Lyndon, he'll never amount to anything.'

As if in revenge on the whole of his universe, Johnson developed into a tyrannical bully of monstrous and legendary proportions. At glittering White House receptions, entertaining foreign royalty, nobility and heads of state, the elegant First Lady 'Lady Bird' Johnson could be downgraded to the status of a dimwitted domestic by the violent roar, 'Lady Bird, go get me another piece of pie!' For Johnson, that was the call of the sucking dove: political associates, even hardened men in their middle years, were regularly reduced to tears by his desire not merely to dominate, but to destroy those around him, to degrade them and drag them down. It is hardly coincidental that one of Johnson's favourite (and literally most revealing) tactics in this department was his habit of conducting political business while seated on the lavatory, a device also employed by some of the Hollywood movie moguls to similar effect.

The drive for autonomy and self-actualization and the mastery over weakness through the quest for personal power, has had a very good press over the years, ranging from epic poems hymning the odysseys of ancient heroes to admiring profiles of 'great men' in daily newspapers. Undoubtedly many men, growing in strength with maturity and reaching the peak of their powers, can make their personal journey a public triumph and vindication of all that they have sought to do. Who, however, questions the price of that triumph, or asks after the fate of those who do not succeed? Success itself depends on the resolution to engage in nothing but activities that generate feelings of strength, vitality and control, and an equal determination to avoid anything that could be a reminder of weakness or helplessness. Seeking action, shunning passivity, becoming effective, asserting independence, all these are the marks of manliness, which is the measure of success. Whether the success lies in fame and esteem or in wordly symbols like property, cars or other baubles, the message is the same: this is a man, a real man, one who knows how to 'fight, fuck, and make a lot of money', in Norman Mailer's phrase. Does anyone notice that as long as the standard masculine criteria, and all the effort that men expend to fulfil them, remain so explicitly work-and-action oriented, then every man will experience himself almost entirely in the public sphere and so be condemned to spending his life, and especially enjoying his triumph, quite, quite alone?

[Johnson had] a hunger for power in its most naked form, not to improve the lives of others but to manipulate and dominate them, to bend them to his will. For the more one learns – from his family, his childhood playmates, his college classmates, his first assistants, his congressional colleagues – about Lyndon Johnson, the more it becomes apparent not only that this hunger was a constant throughout his life, but that it was a hunger so fierce and consuming that no consideration of morality or ethics, no cost to himself – or to anyone else – could stand before it.

Robert A. Caro,
The Years of Lyndon Johnson: The Path to Power (1982)

So the very process of seeking success, fame or power to cure or compensate for the wounds of the past can in fact serve to replicate and even deepen those wounds. All these goals, once attained, isolate the achiever: attaining the 'top of the heap' means a solitary eminence whose fortifications cannot be breached except at the price of the loss of the respect which that eminence should bring. Success, therefore, can sentence its sons to a deep, lifelong, consuming loneliness. The process of seeking ego-reinforcement through the over-familiar worldly trappings (rich cars, fast women), the quest for self-affirmation and the insistent search for transcendence over the boyhood wounds of weakness, fear and failure, serve only to mimic the original dysfunction and condemn the sufferer both to perpetuating in himself and inflicting on others the pains he suffered in honour of the rites of man. 'I am myself, and if I have to hit my head against a brick wall to remain true to myself,' said Marlon Brando, 'I will do it.'

Inevitably, those who victimize themselves soon graduate to victimizing others. This victimization, however, of self or others, is never perceived as such. The rhetoric of sacrifice as the price of success is too deeply ingrained to be questioned: the division of the world into winners and losers too unthinkingly accepted by losers and winners alike. 'You got to have have-nots,' earnestly explains one of Studs Terkel's 'robber barons' in Terkel's magisterial study of the world of work, *The Great Divide: Second Thoughts on the American Dream* (1988). Additionally, as psychotherapist Philip Hodson observes, the successful man or leader cannot afford to acknowledge or even recognize the weakness underlying the impressive superstructure he has laboured to erect against any such thing: 'The "strong" male often lacks the strength of personality to confess to incompetence in the face of life's inevitable setbacks. Male culture enforces this as one of its most important characteristics. So official manhood incorporates moral weakness.'

Paradoxically this weakness, the fear of failure and natural revulsion at feeling under threat, will most characteristically express itself in successful/dominant men as an extreme assertion of strength. Andrew Neil, newly appointed by Rupert Murdoch to edit the *Sunday Times*, described the process by which he became known as 'the hard man of Wapping':

In the first speech I gave, I said I was sure there was a constituency for change, that the paper hadn't moved with the times and had to catch up. As I looked round the room I saw sullen resentment from people who had been entrenched in jobs for fifteen or twenty years. I knew I wouldn't win unless I went in with machine-guns blazing, so I got myself into a frame of mind I'd never been in before, and didn't quite recognize. I had to call on reserves of toughness and sometimes downright unpleasantness in order to survive. I hated it, and still do, looking back. I wasn't sure I had it in me, but I knew they'd have me for breakfast if I didn't. I made a lot of enemies, I had to deal with some unpleasant nasty people out to do me down and destroy me. They are the dispossessed now.[11]

Can power ever be asserted without some degree of violence and destruction, if only of the pretensions and hostility of those who dared to oppose it? 'I am proud to have played a major part in destroying Fleet Street,' Andrew Neil has said. 'It was a corrupt cartel of unions and proprietors which operated against the public interest. No one gave me more than six weeks when I took the job, so the fact that I'm in my sixth year gives me a certain comfort.' Dog eat dog, kill or be killed: the personal struggle takes on an inalienable echo of military combat at one end of the scale, and jungle warfare at the other.

These themes emerge even more clearly in the bitter power struggle which recently devastated the media world of Australia, when the heir apparent to the Fairfax chain of newspapers, television and radio stations and telecommunications interests fell out with his elders on the board. Forcing a confrontation with the senior and governing members of the family, young Warwick Fairfax borrowed millions of dollars in the attempt to take over by force what was destined to be his by inheritance anyway, and in the ensuing struggle to keep up the crippling interest payments, ended by selling off all the company's key assets, thus demolishing in months the cornerstone of Australia's multi-media industries and the country's oldest-established family business to boot. Although reviled nationwide as 'The Nerd' and cruelly lampooned for his weakness, timidity, devout Christianity and weedy physique, 'young Wocka', as Fairfax is known, nevertheless orchestrated a sufficiently terminal display of the violence of power to convince even his enemies that he had in him all the materials of a 'real man'.

I can take power too seriously to be totally comfortable with it. If all you have is personal desire, that's suspicious. You have to have a contribution to make.
      Mario Cuomo,
      Governor of New York

Only power, observed the American writer Alfred Kazin, can place people in a position where they may be noble. The world history of powerful men, however, from Ivan the Terrible to Pol Pot, suggests that nobility is frequently the last attribute to be activated by the access of power. And power is not an absolute, it is a relation: we do not speak of power in the absolute, but of power *over*, power *to do*. In the final analysis therefore, there is no power without the power to enforce. The greater the degree of attained and visible success, the greater that power of enforcement.

For millennia, it hardly needs stating, the classic victims of the coercion of male dominance have been the females of the species. Dominance requires submission: there is no passion without a victim. Historically this was expressed through the enslavement of captured females, the rape of the Sabine women, the 3000 'little lotus blossoms' held in concubinage for the emperors of China. And not only groups but individuals have felt the force of the masculine will to power. 'I've spent a lot of time on my knees,' said Marilyn Monroe in a confession not attributing her success with men to the power of prayer. The enduring resentment of the woman who has been so coerced, so exploited or emotionally raped, needs little amplification. What is not so clearly recognized, suggests US psychiatrist Dr Jim Francis, is the spur which drives a man who has so much, who in common parlance 'has everything', always to want more:

> For men, having the erect phallus accepted by a woman cannot be underestimated. It has to do with so much more than simply demonstrating the power of the phallus on an instinctual level. At certain times the acceptance of our sexual selves is like an acceptance of our *total* selves, and this holds out the promise of a complete healing and cleansing. A great deal of what we men struggle for in our sexual behaviour is really a quest to heal ourselves and find value in this world.[12]

'I'm still not sure, though,' continues Dr Francis, 'why we think this validation has to come through sexual contact with a woman.' Another American psychiatrist, Dr Peter Rutter, feels even more strongly that the men who seek to discover or exercise the 'plus-feeling of power' by enforcing the submission of women will always find themselves in 'the blindest of blind alleys':

> They can have the sexual contact if they insist: but it takes them farther and farther away from the healing they seek. Depression is an occupational hazard of men in power . . . all men in leadership

positions often hide chronic depressions for years behind a show of strength. These feelings of vulnerability and fear do not fit the approved masculine cultural image. Beginning in childhood when boys find themselves facing loss, they are encouraged to suppress the feelings inside, ignore them, or simply stop having them. They are often told that having feelings, especially painful ones, is a feminine trait. The men who successfully hide such feelings within are better equipped to become publicly acknowledged leaders and heroes. Yet there is a heavy price for this kind of masculine success.[13]

And not only for the men of power themselves. Those who pay more, and pay again and again, are their masculine victims. For victimizing women is less than half the story. As with violent crime, those who most feel the impact of this expression of manhood tend to be other men. Nowhere can this more clearly be seen than in any of the armed forces, any time, anywhere in the world. As a raw recruit to the US Army, Roger Hoffman recalled unwittingly attracting the attention of his sergeant-major during evening roll-call. 'He squeezed off a look at me and spat. My heart thudded,' he writes. '"Hoffman," he purred as he leaned down and got into my face, "What *have* we here?"' Hoffman's girlfriend had been unwise enough to send him a perfumed stocking, in a playful re-run of a 1940s war movie she had seen. The sergeant decided that this 'Half-Man' recipient of effeminate female favours needed a lesson in manhood:

> On command I removed helmet and glasses. Two giant hands hauled the stocking down over my head. It bent the tops of my ears and flattened my nose. My lips felt stapled together. Everything looked underwater. I wondered how people wearing stocking masks robbed banks. Lucas loaded the glasses back onto my noseball and ear stumps and thwocked my helmet to eyebrow level. 'You smell *gooood*, Half-Man, real good. Now drop on down and low-crawl over to the Pit and do some laps for that Big Ranger in the Sky.'[14]

After this and more in boot camp, Vietnam, Hoffman found, was a breeze.

The story of violence and brutality in the armed forces is nothing new – Hoffman's treatment is mild indeed in comparison with the days of keel-hauling and the cat-o'-nine-tails – and could even be defended as part of the process necessary for turning a raw rookie into a good fighting man. In war, too, it is argued, humanity, even the most basic of human considerations, constitutes a luxury that the harshness of the time cannot afford: 'When you're up to your arse in alligators,' says British army officer Captain Fred Holroyd, 'you don't think about draining the swamp.' The whole of a boy's life, in Holroyd's view, was only a rehearsal for this, the real thing: 'We practised gang tactics from the age of seven. You had your rites of passage. They put you inside a tractor tyre which was manhandled on to the roof of an air-raid shelter and then bowled off at speed!'

Arguably the armed forces are the last remaining bastion of official, sanctioned, widespread, adult male violence. Films like *Rambo* or *Red Dawn* contrive to invest armed conflict with sexiness, success and the potential for death in a lethal mix guaranteed to impair the judgement of even the most hardened consumer of today's cultural cocktails. More pernicious, because less widely recognized, is the extent to which all adult manhood, all success, all power in today's world is predicated upon and entwined with a routine and systematic violence that few even seem to recognize, let alone to challenge or wish to change.

For today, every man has come of age. No longer are men kept in the psychological bondage of childhood by the power of Church or state: no longer must they defer to the concept of the father-god, jealously guarding his power and privilege against lesser mortals. Through science, through technology, through his mastery of the world of nature, man has made himself the central source of power and ultimate authority on this earth. He is the centre of his sinful world: nothing else counts. Man-come-of-age does not need to practise humility and resignation before the face of any external source of power: he can and must affirm his domination, and the easiest, most common and most successful way of doing that will all too often be, in some form or another, the expression of violence.

Of course there are thousands, hundreds of thousands, many millions of successful, powerful men who have never expressed physical violence, and who would rarely admit even to experiencing the slightest sensation of it. Yet for evil to triumph, as the eighteenth-century politician Edmund Burke is said to have observed, all that is required is for good men to do nothing. And while manhood, maleness, success, power and prestige remain so inextricably entangled with 'winning', 'scoring', 'nuking the competition', in short establishing superiority at the expense of everyone else, then violence, in all its hydra-headed variety, will continue to flourish, for these reasons:

● Although the majority of men achieve success without violence, they always feel in however tiny a corner of their minds the desire to retain the right to it, in case it should ever be necessary.

● When men hear about a colleague or competitor, or even a total stranger who has resorted to violence, their reaction is rarely one of wholesale revulsion and disgust, but is more likely to be at least a *frisson* of interest.

● If the violent action has been successful, especially in a business or competitive context, the reaction will more often than not be one of approval rather than disapproval.

● Men who are never violent live vicariously through the exploits of those men who are. 'In a tribal sense,' says Dr Peter Rutter, 'it is as if men who violate the forbidden zone are the designated surrogates who live out these fantasies for the rest of the men in the tribe.'

● Because the stimulus of violence is so closely allied with that of sex, men gain both pleasure and a quasi-sexual satisfaction from thinking or talking about violence, whether sexual or not, and do not wish to be deprived of this.

● Because so many men engage in violence (physical, emotional, financial, corporate and legal), each episode and each tacit vote of approval of that episode generates like a virus an infectious atmosphere of acceptance which lowers the resistance of men trying not to act on or even acknowledge the violence of their inner lives.

● And because the deepest possible drive towards worldly significance and success, the endless quest for transcendence and the triumphant epiphany of maleness, together with the desire to see penis-power confirmed as the final answer to fears of weakness and the wounds of boyhood, all lie behind the attraction of and for violence, *men will not give up either the attraction of violence or their imputed right to violence, until they learn other ways to find what they seek.*

Let us remember: what hurts the victim most is not the cruelty of the oppressor, but the silence of the bystander.
Elie Wiesenthal

IV THE RAPE OF REASON

Immer neue Schmerzen
(always new pain).
Günter Grass

10 Fatal Attractions

What has the Man not been able to talk about?
What is the Man hiding?
Nietzsche

There's a darkness inside all of us . . . you, me, the man
down the street. Some have it under control. The rest of
us try to walk a tightrope between the two.
Clint Eastwood

Unde fames homini vetitorum tanta ciborum est?
[Where does it come from, man's great hunger for
forbidden fruit?]
Ovid

Life, says the young American novelist Brett Easton Ellis, is the game
that moves as you play. Perhaps this is why so many men, once
possessed of the goal for which they have striven from childhood, find
that it is not what they want after all. It is one of the most painful
paradoxes of the construct we call 'man' that adult manhood success as
defined by tradition and convention (that is, by other men) so often
proves to be both too much, and still not enough. Indeed the very rules
of manhood which govern the efforts to 'make it' or 'get there'
(competition, exclusion, progression through the hierarchy of achievement to the rewards of success) encourage men to keep striving, to
keep wanting more, and to feel entitled to more. The knowledge that
convention and tradition (in short, other men) have set a boundary to
how much a man may legitimately have, only serves to increase the
desire and to whet the cutting edge of the determination to enjoy it.

This desire is not the urge of a Galileo or a Tom Paine to challenge
tyranny and publish by example the rights of man. Rather it is the
concealed, even furtive compulsion to commit wrongs, to break the
rules, especially those controlling sexual conduct. It is the impulse
which makes a respected politician regularly turn to prostitutes, or a
vicar revered for his odour of sanctity fall to feeling up his choirboys. It
is the prompting which makes every married man at some time or
other 'commit adultery in his heart', in the words of former US
President Jimmy Carter's unfortunate personal admission, if not in a

more receptive part of the human anatomy. The attraction of all this lies in its forbidden nature – and such attractions can be fatal to a man's marriage and his family, to his career or status, to his peace of mind, even to life itself.

All men, all sentient human beings it may be argued, have illicit fantasies, and not always do these lead to doom or despair. 'I am a slave and my wife is an empress', wrote a 38-year-old vicar to Deirdre Sanders, agony aunt of the *Sun*:

> I am lined up with a number of other male slaves and she inspects us all intimately. She chooses me and leads me to her private quarters. She wants to do exciting things to me, but green or not, I can be in control and masterful, and do what I want to her![1]

A couple such as this, happily engrossed in what must be a welcome change from the trivial round of Mothers' Union meetings and confirmation classes, may in the eyes of some conform rather too bleakly to the Swiftian definition of marriage ('the capacity for being mutually well deceived') but they are unlikely ever to be a menace to the health of the nation, or a danger to one another.

And any man who confines his sexual attentions purely to his wife is one up (or more accurately, several down) on most of the rest of the adult male population. For monogamy is one of the hardest of all man-made rules for the average man to keep. 'From the time I was fourteen or fifteen, I've always just *had* to turn my head whenever I heard high heels tapping along the ground,' said Martin Grove, a research scientist. 'You can't switch all that off just with a half-hour ceremony. You don't really want to, anyway. Well, you want your wife to be married to you, but you can't stand the idea of being tied down to her! It's a real killer to feel like Darby and Joan when you're not even thirty.'

'They are not long, the days of wine and roses,' wrote the Victorian poet Ernest Dowson. Reluctance to accept that the carefree bachelor days are a thing of the past is only one of many complex reasons why a man feels compelled to break out of the charmed intimacy of marriage and introduce a fresh pair of legs into the game, according to psychiatrist Dr Alan Gessler. 'Some men feel – or claim they feel – that one woman simply is not enough to "satisfy" them. On examination, they prove to be biologically no different from any other normal male. But if you think you're hungry, I guess you're hungry.' To feed this hunger, some men will go to extraordinary lengths. Until his recent detection, Glaswegian James Hood kept two wives, sixty miles apart, meticulously sharing himself between them, for twenty years. Only when illness and redundancy brought exposure and a prosecution for bigamy in March 1989 did Hood agree to settle down with the woman of his first choice.

As an extension of this argument that the desire for variety is just a normal masculine need, or polygamy a natural male instinct, many men will deny that their infidelity does any harm, says Dr Gessler. 'In therapy, male patients will repeatedly say, "It's a natural thing, how can it be wrong when it feels so right?" They swear that they are not hurting their marriages, and often claim that they are in fact strengthening them: and above all, they insist that they love their wives and families, and believe that the wives should have no problem in believing this too.' One of the most prominent exponents of the 'I love you, what's the problem?' line of argument in recent years was the Australian prime minister Bob Hawke. Challenged during a television interview in March 1989 about his reputation for being 'a womanizer', Hawke frankly admitted that he had committed adultery. But he then immediately directed the conversation away from himself and towards his wife, 'an incredible woman', he declared, who 'understood that it was just a part of a pretty volatile, exuberant character' and who 'knew my love for her would never change'.

I cried for madder music and for stronger wine,
But when the feast is finished and the lamps expire,
Then falls thy shadow, Cynara! the night is thine;
And I am desolate and sick of an old passion,
    Yea, hungry for the lips of my desire:
I have been faithful to thee, Cynara! in my fashion.
> Ernest Dowson,
> 'Non sum qualis ero'

If 'normal' and 'natural' masculine behaviour bears any relation to what the majority of men actually do, then infidelity is one of the most normal and natural of male activities. For many men, it is also vital in enhancing their self-esteem, even if only in their own eyes. 'He cheated on me with men and women,' said the Indian film actress Anna Kashfi of her marriage to Marlon Brando, 'and was quite proud of his huge appetite for sex of all kinds.' Dr Annette Lawson, a British sociologist now at the Institute for Human Development at the University of California, Berkeley, and the author of *Adultery* (1988), found that 78 per cent of the husbands surveyed for that study had committed adultery, as against 47 per cent of a comparable group in 1965. 'These figures compare well with other studies,' she says. 'People today are speedier off the mark.' For Dr Barbara Adie, Fellow of the Institute for Psychosexual Research in London, this is probably an underestimate: 'I'd say 80 to 90 per cent of men have had at least one episode of infidelity during the course of a marriage or partnership lasting longer than three years,' she says. 'Most men, however, do not class this as adultery. They will tend to use that term only for a longer, more fully developed relationship or affair.' Perhaps fidelity itself is a problem, an unreasonable demand to make of a normal, healthy male? Not so, Lawson contends: the problem stems from the conflict between 'the Myth of Romantic Marriage', enforcing coupledom and proscribing solo adventuring, and 'the Myth of ME' ('Monogamous love' + 'Egotism', the conviction that getting whatever ego gratification you want is both an inalienable right and an essential part of personal development).

And whatever a man may want, some woman, somewhere, it seems, is waiting to minister it to him. 'I never go out looking for it, I never have to,' says James Curwin, an architect from South Wales. 'There are so many more adventurous women around these days, it just seems like an explosion of opportunity. I feel as if I've been waiting for this all my life, and I don't see why I should miss out.' Today's greater sexual freedoms, while they may not provide a convincing reason to explain the rising tide of infidelity and adultery, will at least supply the perpetrators with a plausible-sounding excuse, suggests psychologist Dr Andrew Stanway:

> Most men when asked say that they are not on the look-out for extra-marital sex, but that if it presented itself they wouldn't fight off the woman too hard. This means that men are open to offers outside marriage because there are many women who are sexually available and see all men, married or not, as fair game. Clinical experience shows that most men would like to be monogamous, but find it difficult, if not impossible, not to go in for a 'touch' of adultery from time to time.

Yet the clearest possible sign that, in adultery, the unfaithful man is not getting what he wants is to be seen in the number of repeat offenders. 'I'm looking for a return of that thrill, the spurt of excitement you get when you see a woman the first time,' explains David Price, a computer sales manager. 'Nothing can touch for me the indescribable moment when I first get my hand on a woman's breast –

it's almost better than all the rest. But it never lasts. It can't really, can it?' 'Like a junkie', then, in the words of his own savage self-assessment, David has to keep finding the new 'fix'.

And what exactly are men searching for or acting out in adulterous liaisons? 'For men, sex is a gender-underliner,' suggests Carol Clewlow, author of *A Woman's Guide to Adultery* (1989). 'They need it for their egos.' When this is the need, whole battalions of willing women will hardly serve to assuage it. 'Lyndon Johnson loved all his people,' said Lady Bird of her husband's time in presidential office, 'and over half of his people were women': a closer-to-home version of Lord Rochester's quip about the libidinous Charles II, that 'the King was truly a father to his people or at least to a good many of them'. For the man who is not and never will be King of England or President of the USA, the need to assert masculinity and reinforce ego-reality is arguably even more acute. When individual masculine identity is all but submerged under the roles of husband, father and breadwinner, a man really needs to hold on to the one thing he can call his own.

Leave off with the blushing, bury the shame, you are no longer your mother's naughty little boy! Where appetite is concerned, a man in his thirties is responsible to no one but himself! That's what's so nice about growing up! You want to take? You take! Debauch a little bit, for Christ's sake! STOP DENYING YOURSELF! STOP DENYING THE TRUTH!
    Philip Roth,
    Portnoy's Complaint (1971)

'I love women, I just can't get enough of them,' said Picasso. 'If God invented anything better, he kept it for himself.' Yet love, as many of today's psychosexual professionals will contend, really has very little to do with it. The psychology of men who betray (and with over 98 per cent of the adult male population of Britain essaying marriage at least once in their adult lives, almost all male promiscuity takes place within the framework of marriage) is usually explained in terms which flatter the male, implicitly defend his right to conquest, or invite us all to share the nudge-and-wink assertion that boys will be boys: 'I've got a very strong sex drive', 'I'm still a bachelor/playboy at heart', 'It's only natural', 'It's quite separate from my marriage and what my wife doesn't know won't hurt her', 'It's all part of today's climate, and besides, I love women'.

The men say, the women say. 'By Grand Central Station,' lamented Elizabeth Smart in her memoir of betrayal, 'I sat down and wept.' Not only professionals in the field but hundreds of thousands of wives and girlfriends tell a different story. 'Oh, I shall commit violence,' wrote Emma Goldman to her faithless lover, Dr Ben Reitman. Goldman had discovered that while she was engaged in the radical political activities that made 'Red Emma' 'the most dangerous woman in the world' to the US authorities in the 1890s, Reitman had been compulsively unfaithful to her with practically every woman he met. 'I am raving, feverish, ill with anxiety,' she wrote. 'Your love is all sex with nothing left when that is gratified. And while I suffer, you are with someone else.'[2]

In the nature of things, even the most discreetly conducted extramarital relationship cannot be guaranteed to remain secret. When it breaks, many men, it seems, have gambled on their wife's acceptance: 'I just couldn't believe she would throw everything away, the house, the children, everything, for something so casual and meaningless,' said Philip Hayes, the 38-year-old art director of an advertising agency. When one of his 'admittedly many' flings ('hardly flings, more fling-ettes') came to light through 'a moment of idiotic carelessness' with an American Express slip, Philip was aghast to discover that what was meaningless to him was supercharged with meaning for his wife. After a deep depression lasting nearly a year, she asked for a divorce. 'She said I made her nothing,' Philip said, 'and all our life together had been nothing as well.'

Few women in this situation are capable of the Jerry Hall counter-strike, the retaliatory affair with millionaire Robert Sanger with which the gorgeous Texan model took her revenge for the infidelity of her partner Mick Jagger. Most women put up and shut up, deciding to soldier on and forgive, even if they can never quite forget. Others do not, and the marriage becomes a casualty of the inability on one side or the other simply to carry on. The psychic pain and waste of all this is incalculable: 'If I could cure the husbands of playing around, I wouldn't need to treat the wives for depression,' commented one GP. 'The nation's drugs bill, for everything from tranquillizers to stomach pills, would be cut by half.' And to reverse again the common perception of women as the victim sex, the wives, mothers and girlfriends of compulsive Casanovas are not the only victims of these entanglements. Despite the admiring notion of the man who 'plays away' or 'gets plenty' as super-macho, a winner, somehow ahead of the game, there is a mass of evidence to show that in illicit amours, whether they go right or wrong, men bleed too.

'The problem with adultery is that it is inherently a self-punishing, self-defeating exercise,' says Dr Gessler:

At one level, however fervent his protests to the contrary, the adulterer is doing his best to spite his wife, specifically in her symbolic role as Mother: she isn't giving him what he wants, she doesn't seem sensitive to his needs, she's too engrossed in her job, the house, or most revealing of all, her 'other' children. Yet adultery is essentially a fantasy flight to find the 'real' mother, the woman who will offer him unconditional, all-embracing love, who will provide the nourishment he desires, who will serve his bodily needs as instantly, adoringly, as he dreams she must have done in his primal heyday. Whether his biological mother did so or not, is immaterial. The craving is there. Yet he can only answer it by an action which, once the flush of romantic devotion is over and his lover starts treating him like a normal human being again, simply replicates the original loss, the first betrayal. Consequently every act of infidelity (and most adulterers are repeat offenders), however apparently successful, is a reminder of this, at however deep a level. And every time he tries to 'lose himself' in a woman, he is condemning himself to enduring again the moment when he has to re-emerge, and so re-open the psychic wound.

So in the height and heart of adulterous pleasure lurks an inescapable pain, suggests Philip Hodson:

Promiscuity is not inherently corrupt, for there are men and women with very high sexual drives, impeccable manners, a horror of commercial entanglements, a penchant for sensuality, a disinclination for matrimony, a scrupulous regard for questions of consent, a diligence in matters of hygiene and a gift for intimate friendship. Yet it has to be said that such paragons are few and far between. More common are Casanovas with chips on their shoulders.[3]

The model is not of adult love, then, but of infantile longing, recast as 'imperial greed – the lust for conquest'. As a result, men in adultery abuse their female partners as a means of achieving dominance over women and over themselves. In so doing, they abuse themselves as well, for every act chains them afresh to the treadmill of relentless pussy-hunting, and exposes them to the perils of polygamy. 'And however hard you try,' says Hodson, 'you cannot fuck everyone, so your vaunted domination is doomed to remain incomplete.' With every encounter, men are fated 'to lose more than they gain, turn sex into work, and flirt with the "new impotence" of satiety'.

Entering an adulterous relationship with an unacknowledged axe to grind blunts the edge of judgement, discretion, even basic self-respect. In a striking example of this, Lyndon Johnson was legendary among his staff for his combination of macho posing and puerile exhibitionism, when he used to wander naked out of the shower with his penis in his hand grunting, 'Well, I gotta give ol' Jumbo here some exercise, I wonder who I'll fuck tonight.' Another self-proclaimed super-stud was the Belgian author Georges Simenon, creator of Inspector Maigret. Looking back on his life from the vantage-point of his sixties, Simenon announced that he had made love to 10,000 women, an average of over three a week, 52 weeks a year, during the whole of his adult life. As Hodson drily observes:

> Even a slow-witted detective could see that a man who was *also* producing three and a half books a year in the same period was either skimping on his work, which on the evidence would seem unlikely, or somehow failing to investigate the in-depth personal reality of his paramours. The author's alibi for his gluttony would convince neither judge nor jury. He suggested that he had 'loved women' all his life and claimed to be perennially interested in 'human communication'. The prosecution is quick to reply that 'love' like that merely gives abbreviation a bad name, and if he wanted to communicate so much, why leave so little time to talk?[4]

Simenon's vaunted 'love' of women did not withstand the subsequent revelation that, as with so many sexually compulsive men, desire for him keyed into dominance in a particularly seedy way. The great sage, honoured for his work throughout the world, sought out shopgirls and secretaries for sex, and paid in cash for the majority of his insultingly brief encounters. The root of his compulsion, records his biographer Fenton Bresler in *The Mystery of Georges Simenon* (1979), was a sense of inferiority to women, a consequent fear of them, and a rage at that fear: he was convinced that all women were laughing at him, and he could only take his revenge and kill the fear by dissolving the imagined sneer on every female face into a real-life expression of sexual ecstasy.

Anger and fear: these themes recur in almost all the approaches to the subject of male promiscuity, whether in the professional and academic literature or in the memoirs of survivors. One of these is American writer Peter Trachtenberg, whose self-confessed 'romantic and sexual compulsion', his 'addiction to women', is charted in his book *The Casanova Complex* (1989). Trachtenberg recounts reeling out of a hotel in New Mexico, 'unable to sleep though half-drunk on mescal', and scouring the city for a woman to screw. After a brief connection 'with a newly-divorced schoolteacher from California', he writes, 'abruptly I excuse myself and scramble up to my room, not sure whether I have been saved, or dragged back into my prison cell after an abortive escape. I am on my honeymoon.'

Such furious, ruinous behaviour can only stem, Trachtenberg argues, from a rage to destroy: an anger against women so deep that both the Casanovas and their chosen partners become its victims. Men compelled to repeat their romantic and sexual conquests may look like glamorous creatures enlivening a drab and conventional world – some of them, like Frank Sinatra, Warren Beattie, Eddie Murphy and Mikhail Baryshnikov, are among the leading heart-throbs of the twentieth century. But their love, their sexual attention, says Trachtenberg, are in reality nothing but a kind of cannibalism: 'they want to *ingest* their victims, for them women are a sustenance, like food.' Promiscuous men are therefore condemned to mimic female eating disorders like anorexia and bulimia in their relations with women, an alternating cycle of bingeing and vomiting, indulgence and recoil. Such behaviour is, and increasingly becomes, more and more addictive: 'the importance a woman has is not as a person, it's the importance a bottle of Scotch has to an alcoholic, characterized by a lot of fear and anger.'

For Trachtenberg the root of this 'fear and anger' is an overwhelming anxiety, amounting at times to an existential dread: 'men use women as drugs to sustain some coherent sense of self, to anaesthetize personal disquiet, to shore up the sense of what it is to be a man, to be lovable – in extreme cases, what it is to be a human being. Some of the more disturbed men I spoke to suffered from existential doubts of whether or not they existed. For me it was compulsive, a message I sent to myself that I was a man, that I was desirable, that I was virile.' Yet by one of the perverse tricks that the human psyche loves to play, the greater the search for validation through the female, the greater the fear of getting too close to the thing that is woman, of falling into her power, of becoming feminized:

> To ward off this fear, Casanovas must deny their mother's power while casting off all that is feminine within themselves. While they often display superficial insight into women (a result of their early identification with their mothers and one of the chief reasons for their romantic prowess) their attitude to them is informed less by empathy than by triumphant contempt . . . If

these men see women as weak, passive, emotional and dependent, they categorically reject such traits within themselves. Instead they cling to an ego-ideal that is strong, cool, active and self-sufficient – macho or hypermasculine . . . In their relations with women these men observe a strict economy, allowing themselves to do and feel only what is 'manly', while assigning all that is soft, irrational – in a word, 'feminine' – to their partners.[5]

Yet when men make women the repository of all they fear and hate about themselves, once again the real problem, it seems, lies not in women but in the male disgust with all that it is to be a man, the rejection of human masculinity and masculine humanity in favour of the crude and self-punishing stereotypes inherited from boyhood and even earlier. Living in mortal fear of defencelessness and aban-donment, promiscuous and unfaithful men are nevertheless com-pelled to re-enact the ritual motions of rapprochement, intimacy and severance. Constant copulation, as a defence against defencelessness, condemns the philanderer to a continuous replay of his feelings of vulnerability and loss, inferiority and powerlessness, 'a position that deprives us of attachments we secretly covet,' comments Philip Hodson: 'the masculine man's lack of emotion is often paradoxical evidence of powerful hidden desires. They have the greatest possible hunger for love, and go to the greatest lengths to conceal their appetite. They suffer from the maximum sense of insecurity in the process.' And every little high brings ever nearer the final, all-time low.

Men have affairs because they are afraid of dying.
Moonstruck
(MGM release, 1988)

If the pull of the forbidden liaison is so strong, the drive to seek connection so overriding, how much stronger must these be when the woman herself is a forbidden one, a 'sister of sin, and daughter of the game'? History and literature alike are studded with stories of men possessed by what the French call the *nostalgie de la boue*, the urge to plunge and wallow in the mire of conscious sin, to seal the deed of darkness with a woman of the night. On the simplest level, a call-girl, prostitute or professional expert is generally credited with being more skilful, more forthcoming and more experienced than the average amateur. 'I went to a prostitute because I thought she would suck me off,' said Dennis, an accountant. 'In fact she did absolutely nothing, just took her skirt off, opened her legs and lay there staring at the ceiling. I couldn't even get an erection.'

As the general run of prostitutes offer nothing but short-order sex, leaving the discipline, golden rain, french fries and garnishings to their specialist sisters, many men could be sharing Dennis's disappointment. A 1988 survey by the Central Birmingham Health Authority showed that around 30,000 men were visiting the city's prostitutes every year, a total of almost 15 per cent of the adult male population between the ages of 16 and 75. 'The women claim to see around 18 clients a week,' said the District Medical Officer.[6] Birmingham, 'Britain's Second City' or 'the arsehole of the mean and filthy Midlands', according to the British Tourist Authority and D. H. Lawrence respectively, may not appear to have much in common with the elegant and cosmopolitan Swiss capital of Geneva. But in an attempt to grapple with the shock revelation that Switzerland now leads Europe in the rising incidence of 'SIDA' (AIDS), Swiss research from the Federal Office of Public Health reveals that between 200,000 and 300,000 Swiss men regularly use the services of a prostitute. This translates into between 10 and 15 per cent of the adult male population between the ages of 20 and 70, a surprising similarity with the Birmingham figures.[7]

For men bowed down or simply bored with the burdensome roles of husband, father and breadwinner, the appeal of the woman who makes no demands, who can be picked up and dropped like a blow-up doll, can be very tempting. When the woman concerned is more sophisticated, enthusiastic or accommodating, possibly not even a professional but a good-time girl of the type in which every social and political hot spot abounds, then she has an edge which can make her almost irresistible. And when a man is heavily occupied with a post of prestige and power, when his days are long and his moments of rest and relaxation short, then the lure of the forbidden woman can be an attraction fatal to his career prospects, public prosperity, even peace of mind, for the rest of his life.

Alone among political leaders William Gladstone repeatedly and publicly associated with prostitutes without damage to his political career. Protected by his professed desire to rescue 'fallen women', his deep Christian piety and secure family life, Gladstone survived even an arrest for soliciting as well as the sniggers, sneers and whispers of those less high-minded than himself. For other men in public life, however, the association with any kind of illicit amour is so generally disastrous as to call into question the sanity, or at least the judgement, of any man who attempts it – and yet they do, they have, and they always will.

In the nineteenth century, a woman did not even have to be a prostitute for an unfortunate attachment to cost a man almost all he held dear. Two key figures of the Gladstone era, the Liberal Sir Charles Dilke and 'the uncrowned king of Ireland', the Home Rule party leader Charles Parnell, both fell from high office to become political pariahs after being cited as co-respondents in divorce cases. In the twentieth century, the epitome of the living sacrifice offered raw and bleeding to the great British public in one of its periodic fits of morality must be the Minister for War of the Macmillan years, John Profumo.

By the standards of any age (Chinese emperors could order up any number or combination from among upwards of 3000 concubines, while their Roman counterparts thought nothing of having 50 or 100 slaves in attendance for every episode of lust, boys as well as girls) Profumo's affair with the 'good-time girl', nineteen-year-old Christine Keeler, was not much for anyone to get excited about, hardly even the participants. 'An affair!' Keeler herself has written:

> What was this affair that became tainted by the filthy minds of the creeps in their two-up, two-down, semi-detached suburbia? What was this 'impropriety' which became the talking point of the world? Does proof of impropriety lie between striped sheets? This was a brief affair, with little real communication. It had no more real meaning than a handshake or a look across a crowded room.[8]

How brief, Christine later confided to *Daily Mail* journalist Baz Bamigboye: 'It happened twice with John Profumo. It wasn't great.' But in 1963 (the year, according to Philip Larkin, when sex began), Keeler also had sex ('Once – and I can't remember what that was like either') with Eugene Ivanov, a Russian naval attaché and possible spy. No one has ever seriously alleged either that Christine Keeler knew anything of value (not even the simple secret of looking after number one), or that Profumo imparted to her one shred of information which could have been transmitted to Ivanov. But national security was never really the name of this game. Profumo had broken the rules, then lied about it. Worse, he had shattered the British establishment's most cherished myths about itself. 'Ostensibly about security risks and betrayal of trust,' wrote Tony Parsons in the spring 1989 issue of *Arena* magazine, 'the scandal was really about sex and class. It destroyed for ever the old feudal notion of some people being one's *betters*.'

As the Macmillan government sputtered towards the end of a second term in office still relying on the rapidly failing slogan responsible for powering them into office in what was increasingly beginning to seem like another world, 'You've never had it so good', Profumo was called to account and ruined. Public reaction to the affair handed Labour a 20-point lead in the opinion polls and destroyed Macmillan's standing, as well as that of his administration. The 'Profumo Affair', argues Parsons, changed the course of British political history. 'It killed off for ever the old patrician Conservatism of Macmillan, Rab Butler and Douglas-Home. The scandal paved the way for slick, cynical Socialists and selfish, brutal Tories. What Christine Keeler had between her legs was Harold Wilson and Mrs Thatcher.'

With Profumo, in fact, went a whole way of life, and a school of political thought and conduct that had endured a century and more. But where the rules are concerned, nothing is too high a price to pay. At 45, a pillar of society, the father of two young sons and husband of one of the nation's sweethearts, the film actress Valerie Hobson, a woman who singlehandedly put the 'fragrance' into wifehood before Mary Archer was invented, John Profumo saw, touched and fell to the temptation of forbidden fruit: at which Nemesis, the oldest tart of them all, hoisted up her skirts and ground into action in the service of her most faithful clients, the men who had not been caught out and were determined, come what may, to hound into oblivion all those who ever are.

Is sex dirty? Only if you're doing it properly.
Woody Allen

For most men, whatever psychiatrists, feminists or disgruntled wives may say, having sex outside marriage remains a perfectly normal thing to do. Indeed with the weight of statistical evidence on its side (more men have affairs than play golf, support a football team, go fishing or drink beer) the balance shifts from normality towards inevitability as an aspect of male behaviour. The promiscuous adulterer, like any other high achiever, is rewarded with esteem: Frank Sinatra dubbed John F. Kennedy America's 'cocksman emeritus', a tribute the President was happy to return. Even an entanglement with a 'good-time girl' or the questionable descent to tarnishing a palm or two with silver falls within the concept of normality of the normal average man. What has he to say, though, to his fellows whose fantasies are not of more-or-less reciprocal acts with grown women, but dreams from an altogether darker region, of dominance, dirt and destruction, of S&M, bestiality, little girls, little boys?

'What's taboo?' asks Barry, a London night-club owner whose other interests include escort agencies offering both male and female companionship: 'Especially today. Once you've broken the first rule, everything else just follows.' Hugh Hefner began with the wholesome desire to make love to Miss America, at least in her sweet and clean incarnation as the girl next door. At the peak of his priapic pride, an average evening's entertainment at the Playboy Mansion, Hefner's so-called 'Magic Kingdom', went like this:

> Hefner was frolicking in the water with his economy-sized bottle of Johnson's Baby Oil, gently massaging all the girls . . . Lila took Linda's hand and together they put on a little lesbian show; the others gathered round to watch and offer suggestions. Then Linda was held out of the water and Chuck [Linda's boyfriend] demonstrated how he could insert his whole fist into her body, finger by finger. This performance produced muted cheers, and Lila tried the same trick. The fun ended with Hef having anal intercourse with Linda. Chuck was delighted.

This, however, was only the *hors d'œuvres*:

> Chuck was saying how they had this dog back home in Florida called Rufus, and Linda just couldn't get enough of him. Hef said he'd seen Linda's dog movie, he had a copy of it in his collection. Not long afterwards Linda was appalled to learn that Rufus had arrived at Playboy Mansion West.[9]

Linda, as she later told author Russell Miller, had been kept in line by incessant beatings and 'every conceivable kind of sexual humiliation'. Part of her training, however, was at least to pretend, and to pretend well, that she was enjoying it. The same requirement, arguably more perverse than the perversion itself, is frequently made by men engaged in degrading women, girls, boys, even babies, for the satisfaction of their unsanctioned desires. 'You like this, don't you?' is a common question of the obscene telephone caller as he pours his masturbatory drivel into a paralysed female ear. In a similar vein MGM mogul Arthur Freed, producer of *An American in Paris* and *Gigi* ('Thank heaven for little girls') was all smiles when he welcomed the eleven-year-old Shirley Temple to his office to audition for a new part, and ceremoniously exposed himself to her. 'I laughed,' she recalls. Freed flew into a terrifying rage. 'What's the matter with you?' he screamed. *'Get out!'* Temple exited, only to find that across the hall, Louis B. Mayer was trying to seduce her mother.

Why do they do it? 'It makes a man feel potent,' says David Briggs, a Sheffield psychotherapist who has set up a clinic to help sex offenders. 'It makes him feel that he and his sexual prowess can make an impact.' Dr Christopher Cordess, a forensic psychiatrist at St Bernard's psychiatric unit in London, agrees: his patients, who range from sex pests to full-blown rapists, experience through their actions 'a wonderful feeling of omnipotence'. The feeling of potency is even greater when the sexual target is a child: 'Child sex abuse arises out of enormously powerful emotional forces in adults,' comments Dr Geoffrey Wyatt, the Middlesbrough paediatrician involved in the Cleveland cases of 1987, 'and it produces enormously powerful emotional reactions in children.' What can be the depth of darkness, of fear, of impotence, out of which this uncontrollable hunger for potency, indeed for omnipotence, must so disastrously spring?

Whatever it is, for many men it is too great to be allayed by public triumph and professional success. It cannot be slaked by the comforts of home or the pride of paternity: most child abusers in fact are either the children's father or in some other close quasi-paternal role. It cannot, in the teeth of centuries of pious sentimental fiction, be cured by the love of a good woman: the role of father, the taking of a wife, will only serve in the case of these men to re-open the files, to restart the primal drama and shape it ineluctably into its finished form of tragedy.

And for men trapped on the darkening downward spiral of fatal attractions, forbidden fruit, what hope of recovery? Precious little, it seems, when there is so little recognition of men in danger, men at fault. Only when the damage has been done (a marriage destroyed, a wife hospitalized, children in care) or an offence has been committed (a four-year-old boy with a torn anus, a seven-year-old girl with gonorrhea) will the powers-that-be react. But how can patriarchal authority restrain the power of the father, the husband, the man, to do what he wants, how he wants, when he wants, for as long as he wants? When gamekeepers are poachers too, what hope for the native wildlife? 'History, if we read it right,' says Max Lerner, Professor of US Civilization and World Politics at Brandeis University, 'is the record of the attempts to tame Father. The greatest triumph of what we call civilization is the domestication of the human male.' On this record, civilization has a good way yet to go. For as our twentieth century ages towards extinction, on the pattern of man's life overall, like any dying animal it threatens us with an ever-increasing ferocity in its furious refusal to go gentle into the last good night.

Light breaks where no sun shines;
Where no sea runs, the waters of the heart
Push in their tides;
And, broken ghosts with glow-worms in their heads,
The things of light
File through the flesh where no flesh decks the bones.

A candle in the thighs
Warms youth and seed and burns the seeds of age;
Where no seed stirs
The fruit of man unwrinkles in the stars,
Bright as a fig;
Where no wax is, the candle shows its hairs.
        Dylan Thomas

11 The Unplumed Serpent

All stories, if continued far, end in death, and he is no
true storyteller who would keep that from you.
Ernest Hemingway

I am not one of these complacent ancients. I detest
being old, resent almost every aspect of it.
J. B. Priestley

Can't go on, must go on –
Samuel Beckett

Pop star Pete Townshend, 'talkin' 'bout his generation', hoped he'd die
before he grew old. Many stars in the rock music firmament have lived
out the seductive fantasy of being beautiful and damned, 'too fast to
live, too young to die', and some, like Keith Moon, Jimi Hendrix and
punk prodigy Sid Vicious, have died for it too. Pop idols like Townshend or the freakishly youthful Cliff Richard may be luckier than most
men in working with the young in a youth industry that provides them
with a means, motive and opportunity to keep the years at bay. 'But
come he slow, or come he fast', as Sir Walter Scott observed, 'it is but
death that comes at last': and death not alone, but attended, as he has
always been, by his faithful lieutenants disease, degeneration and
decay. When masculinity has always been predicated on potency, and
measured by visible strength and success, what will it mean for a man
when the dark days come upon him: when, in the words of Ecclesias-
tes, 'the grasshopper shall be a burden, and desire shall fail: because
man goeth to his long home, and the mourners go about the streets'?
    For many men, possibly even a majority, the tragedy of growing old
can descend before they have even completed the process of growing
up. Pop stars like Mick Jagger, Bill Wyman, Eric Clapton and Elton
John, castigated by their friend and chronicler Jackie Collins as 'ageing
idols prancing around in clothes which look ridiculous on men twenty
years younger, trying to live up to some pathetic image they think they
have to maintain', are not the only Peter Pans of modern society.
Professional sportsmen, too, have perfected a way of life which allows
them to refuse to grow up, but remain instead in the golden world
where every boy can enjoy the never-ending thrill of the game, even

if it is only Subbuteo. And even the highest of achievers in the public world will always have known one domain where they can continue to be 'boy eternal', that of their home: with the involvement of most men in the domestic labour of their establishments either minimal or non-existent, their home remains what it has always been, a place where food, warmth, clothing, rest and sustenance are simply, unproblematically provided, just as they always were from infancy.

But no mother, whether real or symbolic, can in reality hold back the years, any more than can even the best wife, partner, companion or full-time home-maker. And caught between the Scylla of a waistline inexorably inflating, and the Charybdis of a face advancing steadily upwards over the head, the man who is still King of the Lost Boys in his heart must play his part for all it's worth now, before his time runs out. The Peter in him is still the same hungry boy, seeking ever more urgently as his clock ticks away a Wendy of his own and the all-embracing, all-transcending love of his primal infant kingdom. But the Pan is driven by darker desires, and an even older article of faith – for while the Greek god may have been man and musician from the waist up, the nether parts were all goat. A raw ruttishness then, a pungent, aggressive, even offensive sexuality can disfigure the latter years of the lives of a great many more men than society has ever found it comfortable to acknowledge. And even as the hostile forces of degeneration are massing on the horizon and beginning to close in on the camp, not a captain within but is not resolving to go down fighting, to make one, just the one, last stand.

> When I get older, losing my hair,
> Many years from now,
> Will you still be sending me a Valentine,
> Birthday greetings, bottle of wine?
> John Lennon and Paul McCartney,
> 'When I'm Sixty-Four'

'Given the choice,' asks retired headmaster George Gracewell, 'would any man go bald? To me it's the worst part of getting old. I loathe it, I just can't accept it gracefully. It makes you less of a man, even less than human somehow.' Losing his hair may not be a man's first intimation of mortality – a certain slowing down, a thickening of the midriff, a reluctance for late nights, may all have been observed and accommodated – but it is more loaded, more irreversible, than any of these. In the days when men invariably wore wigs, perruques, hats or head-coverings of all kinds from the breakfast bonnet to the final flannel nightcap, hair loss began earlier, due to the unhealthy, usually ver-minous state of the scalp. But whatever the private cost, publicly it mattered much less, since it could so easily be camouflaged and thus denied. Even today in certain parts of the world, local custom permits a man to conceal what otherwise would radically change his image, and hardly for the better: who for instance realizes that beneath his threatening headgear the charismatic Yasser Arafat, leader of the PLO, is virtually bald?

In the western world, where there is little cover to be found for a thinning pate and the cult of youthful virility is running stronger than ever, a rampant industry has sprung up from the fertile bed of men's insecurity, longing and loss. The professional hair-restorers, or 'trick-ologists', in the phrase of one aggrieved client, are rich in suggestions if not in solutions, and blithely ready to pursue them to any lengths of a man's tolerance or his wallet. Bats' droppings, chicken shit, rats' piss and sundry less savoury slimes and sludges are enthusiastically peddled and as vigorously applied: the fact that these potions have a shining record of inefficacy stretching back to the days of Tutankha-mun and Aeschylus, whose undefended skull reportedly split open under the impact of a tortoise dropped by a passing eagle, has no adverse effect upon sales.

How could it? As long as a flourishing head of hair (*pace* Yul Brynner and Steven Berkoff) is the beacon of masculinity, and masculinity means fighting, striving, and 'staying on top', men must struggle to revive, replace or renew the flagging energy and volume of their most visible sexual member. For despite the compensatory myth of masculi-nity that baldness is caused by an excess of the male hormone testosterone ('bald is sexy'), in fact baldness only occurs when nature decrees that a man has passed his sell-by date, and the genes obey their programmed instructions to shut down follicle production.

The drive to turn back a tide as irresistible as the waters of the moon produces some truly lunatic devices and desires. For the increasingly desperate sufferer, the outside of the head can come to dominate what lies inside it. Chemistry characteristically gives way to surgery in the search for the wonder cure, and the miracles of modern technology now offer balding men the hope of hair renewal by transplantation from the back of the scalp, the armpit, or the groin. There are only two drawbacks to this procedure, according to Jonathan, a 42-year-old advertising manager who underwent a hair transplant in 1989, if you discount the first two, the cost and the pain: 'One is that at least half the bits they plug in to the bald patches don't actually take, and the other is, when they do, they don't look remotely like hair anyway.'

Jonathan, like a number of other men who have sought this treatment, has been left severely scarred both physically and mentally as a result. His head is disfigured by a hideous grid pattern of visibly distinct circlets of feebly-sprouting tufts drill-punched across an otherwise inescapably bald dome. He is now having psychiatric help to cope with the trauma of what he sees as his self-induced mutilation: 'I was one hundred per cent a volunteer for all this,' he says bitterly. As an indication that access to the best of these treatments that money can buy will be no guarantee of success, witness the unsuccessful operations undergone by comedian Russ Abbott and perhaps the most celebrated of failed hair transplant victims, Elton John, who never now appears in public without a hat. 'The other day a woman asked why I'd had a hair transplant. I asked her why she wore lipstick,' said John Cleese. 'I have had more attention from women in the last few months than in the whole of my life, and about time too.'

> Middle-aged life is merry, and I love to lead it,
> But there comes a day when your eyes are all right
>   but your arm isn't long enough to hold the
>   telephone book where you can read it.
> Ogden Nash

For a man of any masculine pretensions or even human pride, the loss of hair is only one of a series of losing battles against his dwindling physical faculties. Eyesight, hearing, prostate, performance, all may fail without reducing in the least the old man's desire to carry on as in the days of his youth – indeed it often seems to intensify it. At 89, worried about his failing eyesight, David Garnett, Bloomsbury survivor and author of *Aspects of Love*, did not contemplate giving up driving: he merely hired a young woman to be on hand for the moment when he could no longer see. Garnett at least demonstrated some sense of responsibility in connection with his declining powers. In a related case which came before London's Old Bailey in 1989, a London pensioner who ran over a deaf mute and killed him was proved to have been driving with such bad eyesight that he was only able to read a number-plate, with his glasses, at 8.1 metres, instead of the legally-required 20.5. After sentence, William Slater, aged 66, accepted that 'he should never have been behind the wheel'.

For all that, however, the moment of truth must come for all men, and often earlier than they imagine it will. 'So we'll go no more a-roving,' wrote Byron:

> Though the heart be still as loving,
>   And the moon be still as bright.
>
> For the sword outwears its sheath,
>   And the soul wears out the breast,
> And the heart must pause to breathe,
>   And Love itself have rest.
>
> Though the night was made for loving,
>   And the day returns too soon,
> Yet we'll go no more a-roving
>   By the light of the moon.

In a less poetic vein, Giles, 'an affluent insurance broker in his mid-forties, with thinning hair', had this dismal experience at a disco, as he confessed to Anna Ford, when he was only thirty: 'There was this absolutely divine eighteen-year-old in velvet hot pants. I thought, this is tremendous, I *must* go and dance with her. So I walked across the floor looking frightfully cool – I thought – and she turned round and said, "Piss off, Grandad!"'[1]

Arguably the wise man protects himself from such cruel rebuffs as he ages by sticking to his own wife, or at least to women who are aware of ageing too. But however well he handles it, as the years dwindle down every man is forcibly returned to the uncompromising biological reality of his individual and sexual origins: that the male is the less successful of the two human sexes, and that he is therefore doomed to fight as hard and harder in his final years as he had to at the start of his life. Just as the embryonic boy only survives as a result of his furious early struggle against the disadvantages of being born male, so now must the ageing man buckle on all the armour he can muster to combat all the ills his flesh has made him heir to, simply by virtue of being male.

For where ageing is concerned, nature hands out two packages, his and hers. 'Hers' means that she will live longer, by up to ten years, an autumnal bonus of extraordinary sweetness at a time when the years may be golden, but there are far too many behind, rather than still to come. In an eerie echo of Mother Nature's decree that more males than females must die in the earliest years of life, so too in the latest does she sacrifice the men and spare the women. As the bio-systems run down, the greater vulnerability to disease which men show throughout their lives increases by leaps and bounds: older men are far more susceptible than women to life-threatening viruses like influenza, while pneumonia, the killer of the 57-year-old Jim Henson, creator of the Muppets, is known to doctors as 'the old man's friend'. When a new or mutant viral strain appears, like Legionnaire's disease, three times as many men as women fall victim to it, and of the fifteen principal causes of death (heart disease, cancer, cerebrovascular disease, homicide, suicide, accident, etc) only diabetes claims the lives of more women than men.[2]

As time goes by, even if he escapes the grim reaper's extended repertoire of fun tricks, the average man has a harder time than his wife even in trying to maintain an average standard of fitness, since a woman's metabolism ensures that her body converts food more efficiently than the equivalent man and so produces more energy and in particular, more long-term stamina. Partly at least as a result of his inferior energy reserves, a man of 60 can exercise only up to 60 per cent of the capacity he enjoyed at 20, while a woman of the same age retains up to 90 per cent of her youthful ability to take exercise. The man who nevertheless bowls up to his century will find himself outnumbered by women in the ratio of four to one, a fact observed with shuddering dread by Irma Kurtz's father in his retirement home. 'You see how it is,' he told *Cosmopolitan*'s agony aunt, *'only the old men die.'* At the greying of the world then, men must unexpectedly, unaccountably and terrifyingly learn to lose: so superior in every trial of strength, competence and mastery, they prove at the last so poor at the ultimate test of staying alive.

I kept sucking away, but as soon as he got hard, he'd get soft again ... what could be more poignant than a liberated woman eye to eye with a limp prick? All history's greatest issues paled by comparison with these two quintessential objects: the eternal woman and the eternal limp prick ... the prick which lies down on the job ... the prick at half-mast ... the

atomic war-head prick which self-destructs ... no
wonder men hated women.

> Erica Jong,
> *Fear of Flying* (1973)

Among the countless, hopeless miseries of growing old, undoubtedly
the greatest for every man is the soft, resistless tread of the advance of
sexual impotence. Strictly speaking, the term itself only refers to the
fact that the penis cannot become erect. But the word, and the concept
which lies behind it, implicitly take in a man's whole life and being, in
the way that failures of other organs simply do not. Sociologists may
publish admiring papers on the sexual capacities of octogenarians, care
workers may caringly incorporate double suites in sunset homes, but
for all too many of the intended recipients, this humane bounty can be
little more than a black joke. 'When it goes, it goes,' said Ted, a retired
Warwickshire farmer in his eighties, 'and it don't come back. And the
worst is the thought that everyone's laughing at you.' The fear of this
particular form of ridicule drove Hemingway, when he was only 38, to
a physical attack on fellow-writer Max Eastman, who, he falsely
believed, was 'saying he was impotent, and playing into the hands of
the gang who were saying it'. Later (much later) Hemingway was able
to acknowledge honestly, if obliquely, the reality of his problem.

Although regularly whispered from woman to woman between the
discreet sheets of the world's agony columns ('My husband has
developed a problem that worries us both very much'), for men
impotence has always been the thing that dares not speak its name. No
man can pass into or through adult life without at least one episode of
erectile failure, more commonly several, some sustained. The causes
are very common, and well-known (alcohol, tiredness, overwork or
overweight, emotional shock, too many cigarettes, even a long day in
the saddle or distance bike-riding). Yet every man feels isolated,
devastated, uniquely blitzed when his male machine won't work. 'It
happens,' observes the smooth New Yorker in *Midnight Cowboy*,
coolly studying her cigarette. 'It ain't never happened to *me*!' is the
Midnight Cowboy's painful retort as he contemplates for the first time
the prospect of a future stripped of his studhood and with it the
meaning of his life.

Yet impotence and its afflictions are no modern phenomenon. After
the disastrous wedding night in 1795 on which he collapsed, paralytic,
into the fireplace, the Prince of Wales had the greatest difficulty in
whipping up any 'warmth of sentiment' for his bride, Princess Caroline
of Brunswick. Dynastic anxiety in the king and court mounted to fever

pitch, and the princess was delicately sounded out. She confessed that after the first week or two of marriage, she and the prince had lived 'not at all as man and wife', and that 'Prinny' now treated her with 'the highest aversion'. 'If I can spell her hums and haws', the elder statesman entrusted with this unappealing task wrote to his wife, 'I take it that the ground of his antipathy was his own *incapacity*, and the distaste which a man feels for a woman who knows his *defects* and *humiliations*'.[3]

The unfortunate Prince Regent had at least the excuse of a wife so unwholesome, so stupendously unfragrant, that on first embracing her he almost passed out and had to be revived with a timely glass of brandy. The impotence associated with old age is no respecter of female beauty, and its origins as a human problem are lost in the sands of time. In ages past, the loss of potency of a priest, king or shaman was a cause of severe anxiety to all his tribe. 'Now king David was old and stricken in years,' records the First Book of Kings, so 'he gat no heat':

> Wherefore his servants said unto him, Let there be sought for my lord the king a young virgin: and let her stand before the king, and let her cherish him, and let her lie in thy bosom that my lord the king may get heat.
>
> So they sought for a fair damsel throughout all the coasts of Israel, and found Abishag a Shunammite, and brought her to the king.
>
> And the damsel was very fair and cherished the king and ministered to him: but the king knew her not.

Similarly Picasso, rendered impotent in his eighties through a prostate condition which he refused to have treated, became incapable of sex with even the most beautiful of his models, abandoned painting, and so degenerated into the pornography of the final years.

Today's men, facing what one called 'the ultimate failure' and denied recourse to the Abishag or any other attractive solution, generally approach it unprepared and quite alone, afraid to seek help or even to acknowledge what is happening to them. They feel like pariahs, outcasts from the race of man, and like dying animals isolate themselves from the rest of their species. Yet the truth is that this condition is endemic to the species, as common as masculinity itself. It goes with the territory. More men consult their doctors about impotence than about anything else. Over two million of these, according to the medical literature, are suffering from 'permanent or intractable erectile dysfunction'. Even this is not the whole story. 'These figures have to be on the low side,' comments Robin Penberthy of the London Diagnostic Centre, an independent clinic specializing in this field, 'as so many men do not seek help. US research, especially random surveys, in casualty departments, during health or dietary checks and so on, shows that the true number of intermittently or functionally impotent men is far higher than this.'

These numbers must inevitably increase as more and more men survive to a greater and greater age. Yet almost no consideration has been given to the future of *homo* no longer *erectus*. 'When age unsexes a man,' writes Irma Kurtz, 'it does a thorough job. It castrates him.' The failure to produce an erection, to 'perform', challenges the very essence of selfhood and sexual identity in a way that women, even after the menopause, never have to face.

To combat this, in a poignant parallel with the hair loss industry, a vast range of responses has sprung up to offer the sufferer everything short of a penis transplant. From reputable medics to shameless mountebanks, the dick-deliverers will supply creams, sprays, potions and lotions, ointments, tablets, and 'natural herbs'. Sex aids freely advertised ('an important breakthrough ... unprecedented success') include pillow books, 'stimulating underwear', 'penis enlargers', 'Dr Blakehoe's Energizer Ring', 'the Big Brother Vibrator', the 'Constant Power Ejaculator' and the 'Triple-Ripple Three-Edged Dildo' ('just plug this into your woman and give her the feeling of being opened up to you as never before!').[4] 'The problem is so enormous, some men will literally try *anything*,' says Robin Penberthy, whose company Genesis Medical Ltd also supplies the Correctaid Erection Assistance Product through the London Diagnostic Centre: 'pipes, pieces of metal, anything to allow them to penetrate. They're dangerous and unpleasant, for the female, and some of them for men too, like rubber bands – that's one of the oldest solutions, the geishas used to use rubber bands – but these and other things can lead to gangrene and amputation.'

The depths of quackery into which the desperation of the unmanned man may lead him have to be plumbed to be believed, as have the gruesome, almost unimaginable acts of self-mutilation recorded. In a case reported in the *Journal of the American Medical Association* in 1989, a man who injected cocaine into his penis to enhance sexual performance subsequently had to have nine fingers, both legs, and his penis amputated. In a similar vein, the British man who injected paraffin into his scrotum and all around the shaft of his penis (*General Practitioner*, 31.7.81) seems to have been serving it with an ultimatum: 'This is positively your last chance! Stand and deliver, or it'll be the end of you!' Even the reputable modern treatments, although developed by qualified doctors and tested under medical supervision, reveal the immeasurable extent of men's desire to be normal and potent again, or even bigger than before. The Correctaid, a soft rubber condom which creates an erection by producing a vacuum, has no working parts to go wrong. When the device has to be returned by a dissatisfied customer, the most common complaint is that it is 'too big'. Since fit is of the essence, the aid comes in 23 sizes, from 3¾ inches in length to 7½ inches, and all purchasers measure themselves. Even at this stage, therefore, some men are still seeing their penis not the way it is, but the way they want it to be, and are unable to resist ordering up a new improved version before they have succeeded in restoring the old one to working order.

Where does it come from, this terrible tyranny of the penis, this dominance of a small organ that, even when it won't stand up, won't lie down? The decline in this, as in any other physical function, is natural, inevitable, and only to be expected. Yet no man ever seems to expect it. It should never come as a complete surprise: on the contrary, the angle of erection begins to decline visibly from 10 per cent above the horizontal at the age of 20, to 25 per cent below it at 70. From 40 onwards, the manufacture of testosterone dwindles, until by 70 again the average sperm count is only half of what it was at 35. But no man seems to know this, or to prepare for its impact. Even the clumsiest clown has heard by now of the clitoris and has some idea of its whereabouts. Yet even educated and intelligent men can be staggeringly ignorant of the workings of this most vital part of their own bodies.

But then, whoever tells them, asks Irma Kurtz, what they need to know?

Women talk to each other and write relentlessly in newspapers and magazines about the menopause. Would any man's magazine dare to tell its readers that long before the age of seventy most of them will have no more sex life at all? Or that over the age of fifty-five or so a third of them will no longer be capable of strong or regular erections?[5]

And more, much more. Whoever tries to free the sufferer on this wheel of torment from the 'genital terrorism' which dominates his every thought and act? The enforced pursuit of phallic infallibility locks the man who would be King Dong, effortlessly, terrifyingly erect, back into the relentless cycle of measuring equipment, techniques, output and performance as in the bike-shed and locker-room days way back when. In boyhood and adolescence he had learned to obtain his warmest feelings of strength, power, achievement and manliness in the eyes of other males through his genital activity. Now, with all this slipping, and threatening to bring a psychic landslide down with it, what does a man do but make ever more strenuous demands on his three-, five- or seven-inch self than those it could cope with in the first place?

Yet what else has he ever done? How can an old dog learn new tricks, or unlearn the rites of man? At every crisis of life men suffer, and alone, because other men have always preferred to see individuals blub or bleed in corners rather than question the insane diktat that all men must be all-tough and all-strong, all-powerful and unyielding. Once again, in what must be a familiar enough situation by now, the lonely male finds himself sacrificed for other males' greater good, or rather for the common myth of male solidarity. When solidarity itself is the problem, maleness must still prevail. Mae West was not alone in her fervent faith that a hard man is good to find. A genuinely good man, in this context, one who can spare others and himself from this painful communal fraud, is even harder to discover.

Paradoxically, the impotent man's frantic secret search for a remedy ties him into the very same game of which he is a victim. The insistence that impotence must be cured by medical or surgical treatment absolves the sufferer from having to contemplate the problem of what identity he may have outside his genital reality. As long as he remains fixated on his cock, his better-red-than-dead proof of manhood, he never has to examine what in him is simply human, or how much he might share with the females of the world. To avoid this, he will go to any lengths, any pains: tumescent injections directly into the penis, obtainable only on prescription at £50 a shot, with the risk of uncontrollable, agonizing priapism necessitating surgical intervention after four to eight hours, or penile implants of stainless steel rods ('the very *essence* of male identity management' according to Dr Michael Kimmel) which can fester or fail to work. All this is worth enduring because it insists on the curability of the impotence and hence the inevitability of the return to full manhood status. By its obsessional concentration it also reasserts the centrality of the penis and its demands, and so re-states all the cardinal articles of masculine belief, the faith in penis-power above all, and the conviction that with enough will, drive, effort and 'fight' he can transcend whatever weakness is undermining him and holding him back. In brief, it preserves his masculinity in the teeth of its spectacular collapse, helping him to hang on to what makes him a man, even when it has lain down and died.

He never had to worry about diet or exercise. Instead he worried about my imaginary lover. You'd think that with his looks and all the success and adulation he had known he wouldn't have been so desperately insecure. Cary was complicated and tortured – nothing like the suave debonair characters he played on screen. In the end he became impossible to live with.

Maureen Donaldson, Cary Grant's last love,
An Affair To Remember (1989)

Even those the gods love grow old and tired and sad. Those who do make another painful discovery, that impotence may not be merely physical. In his old age, Churchill's 'raging Black Dogs' gave way to paralysing depressions when he was powerless to move for days on end. And as with physical impotence, the descent into depression finds most men pitifully unprepared. 'What I want to be is a wise old man who won't bore,' Hemingway told the *New Yorker*'s Lillian Ross in 1950, in a sunny sketch mapping out all his hopes of the golden age to come. He would see all the new prize-fighters, bull-fighters, ballets, sons of bitches, big international whores and bottles of wine, and never have to write another line about it. He would write 'lots of letters' to his friends, and get lots back, and 'make good love' until he was 85. Then, in an effortless transition, he would make 'the prettiest corpse since Pretty Boy Floyd' – a tragic underestimate of the decay, the impotence both physical and mental, the failure of both art and nerve that drove him to make himself one of the ugliest corpses to be found outside a slaughterhouse.[6]

As this suggests, depression cannot come unheralded, and many men approaching the sadness of age find that when sorrows come, they come not as single spies, but in battalions. Among the Navajo, the man who reaches the age of 45 ascends to a new hierarchy of respect and authority over the young: in our more 'advanced' society he is more likely to be reduced to the reactionary fury of an Allan Bloom fatuously inveighing against the 'nonstop, commercially prepackaged masturbational fantasy' of modern culture (*The Closing of the American Mind*, 1987). Age can become a time not for gently letting go, in the spirit of T. S. Eliot's 'Song for Simeon' ('My life is light, waiting for the death wind / Like a feather on the back of my hand'), but a violent rearguard action against loss, defeat and death. In Britain, a 72-year-old former regimental sergeant major, Percy Jones, was convicted in 1989 of trying to kill a policeman by ramming a police car when finally cornered after a 105 mph car chase. In the same year Jack Kelm was arrested in Greeley, Colorado, for nearly a dozen armed attacks on banks, all committed since his 80th birthday. Kelm, now 82, was said to have 'gained the confidence' to embark on armed robbery only recently, after lying low since escaping from a chain gang over 40 years ago.

For many men, the hardest of all the mental and psychological afflictions of growing old is the loss of work. 'Othello's occupation's gone', one of the profoundest laments of western literature, is echoed in a minor key a thousand times a day up and down the world wherever a man has to leave a job which has been, as it is for so many men, his life. Churchill's truly annihilating depressions did not set in until after the end of World War II, when the advent of peace stripped him not only of his job, but of his role, function and divine purpose, as he believed. A later prime minister, Harold Macmillan, likewise confessed to ending his career feeling 'old, incompetent and worn out', and of the Profumo affair which ended his premiership he later confessed to his deputy, 'Rab' Butler, that 'it was a wounding thing, a sad thing' and 'his heart was *broken*'.

As long as manhood continues to be defined by what a man *does* rather than what he *is*, there can be no escape even for men of far less power and significance from this peculiarly painful form of bereavement. When the loss of office is compounded by a spectacular fall from grace, then the stage is set for an exceptional degree of mental distress. When the American TV evangelist Jim Bakker, facing a possible 120-year sentence on charges of million-dollar frauds from his PTL religious empire, appeared in court in North Carolina in 1989, sobbing, distraught, and apparently mentally unhinged, lawyers and commentators alike were quick to smell a sympathy stunt. But even the experienced New York reporter John Cassidy had to admit, 'If Bakker was acting, it was an Oscar-winning performance.' Given his situation, Bakker would have had to be mad *not* to feel the pain of it, rather than the other way round.

For the mature man, losing a cherished post may in fact provide one of the few opportunities in his life of expressing his emotions openly and without pretence. Summarily sacked as Director-General of the BBC, Alasdair Milne observed that he passed through disbelief, distress and shock until cold realization brought 'anguish, followed by despair'. Receiving a similar 'professional death sentence' over a breakfast pair of particularly well-poached eggs at Claridge's, Peregrine Worsthorne noted with equal honesty feeling 'sick with indignation and shame' when the 'acute shock' of this 'paralysingly painful blow' sank in. Deeds as well as words can vividly convey a loser's rage, humiliation and loss of face. At 73, suffering from the effects of a stroke as well as the megalomaniac delusion of any dictator that he can and must rule for ever, Prime Minister P. W. Botha was forced out of power in South Africa by his cabinet and colleagues in the most publicly humiliating way possible. Loathed by his former colleagues, ridiculed throughout his country, Botha orchestrated his departure as one all-engulfing death-wish, splitting his party, throwing its electoral chances into the lap of the opposition, endangering the constitution and undermining the stability of the state. He at least was never going to wander off into the sunset and cultivate his garden.

Die at the right time! He that consummates his life dies his death victoriously.
Nietzsche

In keeping with the heroic fantasies which govern so much of male thought and action, there is a general assumption that a 'real man' will die 'like a man', at the height of his powers, striding out to meet his fate, not shuffling round death's anteroom for years in carpet slippers. For this reason too many men refuse to contemplate the prospect of their own age and enfeeblement, to accept diminution or to face encroaching fragility. In his mind every man wants to go with a bang not a whimper, as soon as his useful work is done. Mapping out his political future after the Conservatives failed to win the election of November 1885, Lord Randolph Churchill, the father of Winston, told a friend, 'I shall lead the Opposition for five years. Then I shall be Prime Minister for five years. Then I shall die.'[7] The inner conviction of redundancy, of inbuilt obsolescence, the bitter certainty that the world has finished with you when you retire, breeds a lethal fatalism: the majority of men retiring at 60-plus in Britain and America are dead within three years.

It is a poignant reflection on any man's three score years on this earth that all he can think of to do after giving up work is to die. For some men, it can indeed become a grim race, a kind of terrible competition. 'I bet I make it to the barn before you do,' the dying Gary Cooper told the dying Hemingway in May 1961. Cooper won his bet, despite Hemingway's final resort to a short cut.

Like many men before and since, Hemingway could not wait for death to come and call of its own accord. 'What does a man care about?' he asked shortly before he shot himself, 'Staying healthy. Working good. Eating and drinking with his friends. Enjoying himself in bed. I haven't any of them.'[8] As men are more susceptible in age to the whole spectrum of afflictions, mental and physical, so now are they more likely to commit suicide. At the twin peaks of suicide attempts, during the teen years and again in the over-sixties, men easily predominate over women in both successful and unsuccessful suicides. In youth and age, then, at key times of insecurity and transition, men find it harder to hold on to their sense of self and purpose, easier to reach for the false certainty of the terminal conclusion which provides them with a solution no matter what the cost to anyone else. For men growing older, the manhood code of fighting and winning, strength and success, is bound to fail, and may indeed serve as an increasingly unbearable mockery. 'There is no remedy for anything in life,' Hemingway argued with the blind self-absorption of the mutilated ego: 'Death is a sovereign remedy for all misfortunes.'[9]

Antique platitudes like this may be as close as we are likely to get to what is one of the last of the male mysteries, what makes a man kill himself. In a poignant case from the end of 1987, as a highly successful solicitor, a former mayor of Beaconsfield and owner of a £50,000 Maserati, among other good things of life, Hugh Simmonds apparently had everything to live for. Although married, he was planning a holiday with the woman with whom he had been having a long-standing affair, whose parents later said that the couple had been 'very much in love'. Shortly before they were due to leave, Simmonds was found dead in his car from carbon monoxide poisoning. It subsequently emerged that at least £3.8 million belonging to Simmonds's clients could not be accounted for. 'I believe he killed himself because he was going to be found out,' said the solicitor leading the formal investigation. 'He could not face life after that.'

Suffering the pain of a personal blow or the humiliation of a business defeat may be the overt reason for this irreversible step. Yet what greater misery can there have been than for the Jews in the concentration camps, where suicide was virtually unknown? Jews and non-Jews alike had a harder time surviving the peace than the war: British statistics for 1946 show a steep rise in successful male suicides. And when the moment comes, it comes like all the other key moments of men's lives, in silence and in pain. 'He never betrayed his emotions, his sadness,' said the concierge of the apartment block where the Italian writer Primo Levi threw himself to his death at the age of 68. Many years earlier, Levi had survived Auschwitz, an experience which convinced him that 'the aims of life are the best defence against death'.

At the end, though, his world view was as bleak as a Polish winter. 'We live and die for nothing,' he wrote. 'The skies perpetually revolve in rain.'[10]

Chatting amiably to the concierge only moments before his fatal plunge, Levi gave no indication of his intention and so took with him into eternity the secret of his death. Whatever the immediate impulse, suicide has at least the clear rationale of preserving a man still in the prime of his pride if not of his body, from the fear and pain of dying nature's way. 'My flesh began unto my soul in pain,' wrote the seventeenth-century metaphysical poet George Herbert, 'Sicknesses cleave my bones . . . ' In his intensely personal memoir of his own fatal illness, *A Voice At Twilight: Diary of a Dying Man*, writer and publisher Jeremy Warburg also turned to poetry to express his light, ironic, unafraid reflection on this theme:

> *Cancer – the Crab*
>
> I've always liked crab –
> the meat, that is
> makes me feel good
> the iodine
> makes me sleep soundly
> no waking in the small hours
> perhaps that's why I didn't run
> feeling it settle on the seashore of my body
> clamping its claws about my bones
> catching me
> alive
> eating me
> to death

Yet physical pain, as Warburg found, may not be the worst of the afflictions of a dying man. A growing helplessness and unavoidable dependency, a reduction to a nursery diet of soothing liquids and ice-cream provoked, just before his death, the sardonic observation: 'Just like being an infant. Others ministering to one. Everything via other people. Birth and death. Very near each other. Same thing really.'[11]

Nor will these physical associations be the only unwelcome evocations of infancy. As he approached his own death, Henry Miller became increasingly tormented by terrible memories of his mother's. A harsh, domineering woman, she had provoked her last fight with him on her deathbed, when in the struggle to restrain her, Miller found his hands around her throat before he was able to break away, 'sobbing like a child':

> When we were burying her, they couldn't get the coffin angled right to lower it into the grave . . . she was still resisting us. Even in the funeral parlour before that, where she was on view for six days, every time I bent over her one of her eyes would open and stare at me.[12]

For Warburg, too, the nearness of death brought back all the most painful of primal themes as he struggled to explain and understand the reasons behind his illness: 'See it as being gripped in a vice between the claws of irreconcilable conflict and intolerable despair.' The roots of this he traced to his induction into the world:

> For me it may well have been that I was *afraid* to display my creative talent to the full. Terrified of showing, let alone using it. In relation to my mother, first and foremost. 'Put him down a peg or two!' she always tinkled. Ringing in my ears. An expert tinkler. Most certainly succeeded at that. If you can call that sort of thing success. Put him down. Stop him. Kill him!
> And my father. Not that much better. Left me at the age of two to tender mercy of my mother. *Force majeur!* Of course.
> My siblings too. My brothers . . . [13]

Father, mother, siblings, infant – only one key element is missing from the dying man-child's recreated world, and it is hard to imagine that the star of the show called Everyman would disappear before the final curtain without taking even one last bow. Anecdotal evidence in fact abounds to establish the importance of the phallus in the final hours or minutes of a man's life. The onset of death, it is said, produces an engorgement of blood that results in a truly stupendous erection, especially if the man has died by violence. This, local experts darkly hint, is what witches and grave-robbers sought from the corpses of dead men, rather than the fingers or toes more chastely supposed removed on these occasions.

Hard evidence of any of this, needless to say, is difficult to come by. But one incontrovertible example exists, from an impeccable source. As he recorded in the *Phaedo*, Plato attended with other close friends the execution of Socrates in 399 BC. Condemned to drink hemlock, Socrates refused the escape planned by his friends, and 30 days later drained the fatal cup with perfect cheerfulness. As the poison took effect, the jailer began to feel Socrates' feet and up his legs, demanding to know if he had any sensation there. When the probing hand reached Socrates' groin, the philosopher threw aside his robe to reveal an erection. 'We owe a cock to Asclepius, pay it, don't forget!' he said, and died. In telling his friends to sacrifice a cock to the god of health and healing, Socrates was making a characteristically coarse sexual joke: an erection on my deathbed! Thank you, God! The fact that the cock was also the standard gift from man to man at the start of a homosexual love-affair also draws the jailer into the joke and demonstrates that, even at the last, Socrates' mind was as playful as his penis.[14] How far the less well-endowed of his fellow-men can hope for as much of nature's bounty in their closing moments must remain, for the present, in doubt.

You're as old as the woman you feel.
  Groucho Marx

Socrates was not alone in welcoming the touch of a friendly hand in his hour of need. His demand has been echoed by many men, with just two further provisos, that the hand should be female, and not over the age of 24. As the phallus has played such a key role at every stage of a man's life, so now does it often enter, in the final act, its finest hour. And for men determined to keep death at bay through vigorous rearguard action and the regular exercise of their principal weapon, not simply a female, but a very special female may be required.

Ibsen, Hardy, George Bernard Shaw, Sartre, Charlie Chaplin, Groucho Marx, Cary Grant, Dr Spock, Lord Reith, André Previn and Andreas Papandreou, Gary Hart and Bill Wyman, John Derek and Hugh Hefner – what could these men have in common but the compulsion that was always known in more indulgent times as 'a weakness for younger women'? How many lesser men share with these celebrities the thing that makes all men brothers, a hopeless susceptibility to the demands of the penis and especially the wayward dictates of the waning dick? All these men, and millions more besides, have suffered, and inflicted, the peculiar delights and disasters that beset any ageing man in thrall to younger women. Lord Reith, who as the first head of the BBC would sack any staff who got divorced, could nevertheless embarrass his hosts and friends by arriving at important functions accompanied by a succession of young women while his wife remained at home. He told his daughter, who resented her mother's public humiliation, that he had discovered too late that life was for living. 'Is there no age limit?' groaned Shaw, although he knew the answer even as he asked the question. 'Intellectually, I knew that some marriages fail,' admitted Margaret Papandreou, wife of the 70-year-old Greek prime minister who left her for a woman less than half his age. 'But emotionally, it was unbelievable to discover my husband's erotic desire was so important.'

There are as many perspectives on the May/December scenario as there are would-be performers. 'Infirm lechery is a male dementia,' says Irma Kurtz. 'When the sex act has been only an allegory of power for a man, he is bound to grow old in cantankerous denial of impotence.' On the physical side, medics stress, an uncritical, athletic, enthusiastic 24-year-old is much more likely to supply the stimulation the ageing man now needs than the mumsy wife of his own age and weight. 'I go for shapely blondes,' says John Cleese, recently disencumbered of wife number two: 'Doesn't everyone?' Yet even as he drowns himself in bimbos, no man's mother is ever far away. 'Men may think they are rejecting their aged wives because they remind them too much of their mothers,' explains Barbara Gordon, author of *Jennifer Fever: Older Men, Younger Women* (1988). 'But what they have is an inexhaustible desire for the uncritical love which young women give so freely.' The real problem with the old wife, then, is that she has usually become someone else's mother, possibly too even her own woman by now, no longer centred adoringly and exclusively on him as the new young love will be. And the new 'mother' will have the added bonus for her man that she will once again be the age she was, when as an infant he first fell hopelessly in love with her. 'You are a figure from the dreams of my boyhood,' Shaw wrote to his adored Mrs Patrick Campbell. 'I want to have a woman's love on the same terms as a child's':

> to take it for granted that I am a child and want to be happy, and suddenly find myself in the arms of a mother – a young mother, and with a child in my own arms who is yet a woman. All this plunges me into the coldest terror.[15]

Shaw's terror, though rarely so clearly seen or honestly expressed, is the driving force behind all geriatric amours: having a younger lover makes them feel that they are farther away from death. The Shaws, the Cary Grants and Paul Hogans can at least afford to buy the favours they crave – Bill Wyman reportedly spent £1 million on a London house 'to give Mandy a home of her own', Hogan $2 million on 'Linda's love-nest' in Australia's exquisite Byron Bay. But the men who cannot follow their example do not necessarily abandon the phallic quest. In a case prosecuted at Exeter Crown Court in May 1989, a 71-year-old pensioner was accused of raping a 16-year-old girl taken on holiday as companion to his elderly wife, asleep nearby. His defence was that she seduced him. In the following month, a 59-year-old retired man was convicted at Cardiff Crown Court of indecent assault, attempted rape, and rape, on a series of girls between the ages of seven and twelve, over a period of ten years. He had set up a riding stables as a 'honeypot' to attract the girls he needed for his sting. Men in their sixties, seventies, and late eighties are regularly convicted of sexual offences against women, girls, boys, even toddlers and babies. *Why?*

Why do they need to fight off the fear of death by phallic bravura and genital display, amounting, with any coerced or purchased partner, to a form of phallic terrorism? Why can they not come to terms with winding down, with yielding to softness and weakness? Why must they remain to the end locked into the rhetoric of fighting, winning, refusing reality in favour of the fantasy of omnipotence and immortality? 'I've licked the Big C,' boasted John Wayne. If anyone could have, the world would have wanted it to be the Duke. But no man beats death in the final round. What is this drive, this essence of maleness, this thing hidden in the heart of masculinity that makes even respectable grandfathers, headmasters, priests behave so? What is it but the thing that has been there all along, the unanswered, unanswerable lust capable of making any regular ordinary guy into a killer male?

Oh would I could subdue the flesh
  Which sorely troubles me!
And then perhaps could view the flesh,
As though I never knew the flesh
  And merry misery . . .

Get down from me! I thunder there,
  You spaniels! Shut your jaws!
Your teeth are stuffed with underwear,
Suspenders torn asunder there
  And buttocks in your paws!

Oh whip the dogs away, my Lord,
  They make me ill with lust.

Bend bare knees down to pray, my Lord,
Teach sulky lips to say, my Lord,
That flaxen hair is dust.
John Betjeman,
'Senex'

12 Killer Male

We are an old-fashioned conscript army ever eager to
obey our leaders' orders . . . we automatically hit those
who hurt us . . . We don't hesitate to kill.
Philip Hodson

Oh! what action so voluptuous as destruction . . . there
is no ecstasy like the one we taste in giving ourselves up
to that divine infamy.
de Sade

The seeds of every crime are in every man.
Tolstoy

Before his death in 1924, Lenin predicted a century of violence to come.
With less than a quarter of its course to run, nothing can now prevent
his prophecy from coming true. In an age where science and technology, medicine and industry, have conjoined to offer the first real
hope of freedom from want, disease and distress that our world has ever
known, we have contrived to continue the threat to human life and
happiness by escalating aggression and violent action to levels which
are past comprehension and, for those who have died, past cure.
Despite the apparent ending of the Cold War as the nervous 1990s
made their bow, the loss of fifty million men in two world wars, the
continuance of global conflict, the mushroom cloud overhanging all
Einstein's children since the atomic devastation of Hiroshima and
Nagasaki in 1945, all numb the mind and induce a false sense of
inevitability, of hopeless resignation, of existential despair.

But each act of violence, from the brick in the face to the initiation of
global war, traces back ultimately to one individual. That man can deal
in violence and death only through a suspension or breakdown of his
common humanity, a failure of imagination on a truly terrible scale.
But equally, every successful or unpunished act of violence argues an
even more terrible cause, the moral and political failure of the wider
society. Most men are not killers. But most men are, in some way,
contributors to or consumers of violence, and until this fact is both
accepted and understood, we will make no headway against what is
rapidly emerging as the principal life-threatening disease of our time.

What makes a man violent? That which makes him a man. What do the child abuser, sadist, sexual murderer, serial killer have in common? Masculinity.[1]

'For some reason,' observes Cambridge criminologist Dr Donald West, 'all the well-known sexual deviations are much commoner in men than in women.' For this common-sense observation, there is an equally common-sense explanation: biology. Man is the aggressive animal: 'it's their hormones'. Yet if masculine aggression were caused by the 'male hormone' testosterone, as produced by the testes, why is aggressive behaviour widely reported in boys long before the age at which they have any hormones, or indeed testes, to speak of? 'Violence goes back a long way,' comments psychologist Oliver James. 'Violent boys think about forms of violence, and fantasize about inflicting violence, even when they are much too young, weak and powerless to do it.' 'We must look at what does not vary,' write Deborah Cameron and Elizabeth Frazer in their study of sexual murder, *The Lust to Kill* (1987):

> The common denominator is not misogyny, it is a shared construction of masculine sexuality, or even more broadly, masculinity in general. It is under the banner of masculinity that all the main themes of sexual killing come together: misogyny, transcendence, sadistic sexuality, the basic ingredients of the lust to kill.[2]

If the testosterone flood is so unmanageable in adult life, why do soldiers and sportsmen have to psych themselves up to an emotional frenzy with drills and chants invoking an obviously very absent sexual potency ('This is my weapon, this my gun / One's for business, one's for fun') before going into action? If the superior muscle groupings of the male's arms and shoulders explain why they fight, batter and strangle, why do women, with their vastly stronger legs and thighs, not go round kicking people to death?

In practice, as Cameron and Frazer show, 'hormones' are used to explain aggression, which is then traced back to 'hormones'. It can hardly be stated frequently or firmly enough that the simple possession of the male hormone testosterone has no direct or causal link with aggression, or all men would be violent. Nor is testosterone an exclusively male property: women possess it too, and women's level of testosterone in the blood is found to rise with participation in any dominant role. Aggression is an attitude, not a biological imperative, and as such it is heavily taught, initiated and encouraged in boys from birth, and certainly from well before puberty, the first time they have any testosterone to speak of.

It is also insufficiently acknowledged that men can and do choose what they do with their aggression. Dr James Dabbs of Georgia State University told the American Association for the Advancement of Science Annual Congress in 1989 that a survey of men in different professions showed that vicars displayed the lowest levels of testosterone, while 'actors and American football players' had the highest. A linked study of 1700 American men funded by the US National Institute of Health in 1990 showed that 'socially successful and dominant men' in business, industry and the arts had higher testosterone readings than the unsuccessful. In two studies of tennis players, male and female, testosterone levels increased in the winners and decreased in the losers. When the same chemical substance can create or sustain a man or woman as a head honcho or Wimbledon champion, its days as a catch-all explanation for aggressive, criminal or violent behaviour in men only are surely numbered.

Biology, then, offers no real answer to the escalating problem of today's violent aggression. Such crude, outdated biological reductionism has become in fact a shorthand evasion of genuine analysis or the political will to make change. Violent aggression, though its manifestations will generally be obviously and brutally physical, is not a physical act like eating or walking, and it cannot be explained away by a physical cause, or dealt with by physical action. Too many attempts to grapple with violent crime in the past have been bedevilled by the deep-rooted conviction that they are caused by the men's 'uncontrollable urges'. Treatment has therefore focused on chemical, hormonal or surgical (i.e. physical) treatment. 'Of course castration works,' observe Cameron and Frazer drily, 'just as the cutting off of hands terminates the career of a pickpocket. But no one argues that theft only arises from the possession of a pair of hands.'

The belief that 'the hormones' can account for and even excuse male violence and aggression dies hard, however. When the 1950s film actress Susan Cabot was murdered by her son in 1986, the defence offered was that the 25-year-old man had been receiving hormone treatment. For beating his 59-year-old mother to death with a weightlifting barbell, Timothy Scott Roman was convicted of 'involuntary manslaughter', and given a suspended prison sentence. Even when the 'hormone argument' loses ground, another genetic excuse for violent men is waiting in the wings. In recent years the chromosomal make-up of males has been linked to violent crime, most explicitly when a number of US prisoners were found to have chromosome abnormalities, in particular an extra or damaged 'Y', the 'male' chromosome. Disappointingly enough for the champions of biological determinism, however, further research showed that the possessors of the 'supermale' extra 'Y' chromosome in fact commit fewer offences of violence against the person than 'normal' men.[3] And if the standard issue of the 'Y' gene, plus gonads, testes and testosterone were the *sine qua non* and key to the mystery of male aggression, why are not all men wife-beaters, child molesters or sadistic rapists?

The myth of males' 'overpowering urges' is wholly proof, it seems, against such questions. From pop biology to lay psychology is an easy glide. Violent men on this line of reasoning are not normal, they are psychopaths, they are insane. Again Cameron and Frazer point to the curious circularity of the argument – psychopaths are men who commit terrible crimes, and the reason that they commit such crimes is because they are psychopaths. Equally, it is taken for granted that the vast majority of psychopaths will be men: there are five male psychopaths to every female in Britain's special hospitals. Yet no one ever questions *why* this should be so – or why their illness should take the form of killing women.

And it is worth remembering that the original 'Ripper' who terrorized the streets of London in the 1880s was never caught. So-called psychopaths are usually found to be functioning fully in society, as the 'Yorkshire Ripper' Peter Sutcliffe did, holding down 'respectable', even demanding jobs, and successfully covering their tracks. Sutcliffe himself, like the 'Moors murderers' Ian Brady and Myra Hindley as well as many other violent robbers, rapists and murderers, evaded detection for years, during which they aroused no suspicion in their everyday lives. For madmen, in fact, psychopaths are remarkably sane. Neurological and brain tests on convicted sexual murderers show no abnormality or disturbance, even in those who have committed the vilest of crimes. Peter Sutcliffe was not considered mad by any of the psychiatrists who examined him after his arrest: one, Dr Terence Kay, even argued that Sutcliffe, who assaulted his victims sexually with anything from a screwdriver to a Stanley knife, who rammed a plank up one woman's vagina and raped another as she died, was *not* a sexual sadist.

The truth of male violence is that maleness itself provides the key. 'The aggressive boy has been brought up to see harsh physical power as an effective means of getting what he wants,' says Oliver James. 'Violence is the masculine expression of anger created by dreadful experiences, and for some men it becomes a way of life.' All preoccupations, all 'urges', all beliefs, even of the deranged, are drawn from the social and value systems to which they have been exposed. All behaviour, even that of the maddest of madmen, has a function and purpose. As the linking thread between violent offenders is that they are male, then it is to masculinity itself that we must look for the answer to its origins and for any hope of its remedy. If we are serious about addressing the question of violence in contemporary society, we must confront what we are doing in the making of our men, from their earliest years.

Men never leave the playground.
Philip Ridley,
screenwriter of *The Krays*

'A 20-year-old thug,' comments Vivian Ellis, an experienced Crown Court prosecutor on England's Northern Circuit, 'has been a thug for at least ten years. That's his *job*. It's a bit late to try to get him out of it.' When Lee Costello, aged sixteen, was convicted at Birmingham Crown Court in 1990 of the murder of an eleven-year-old girl, the prosecuting solicitor said, 'It seems perfectly clear that the attack was premeditated: from documents that came into the possession of the police, the accused had planned to commit a rape and murder.' Not until the age of ten is a boy deemed old enough to judge between right and wrong, and so become morally and legally responsible for his actions. Yet the child who comes to the attention of the police at ten has already had ten years of training in aggression and antisocial behaviour. And what he will have learned will be no different from all the other boys of his age.

He will have learned, to begin with, that woman (as mother, carer, nurse, grandmother or teacher) is the primary source of all his most powerful feelings, good and bad. And a mother's place is in the wrong: for the rest of his life he will resent her power, either the power of her warmth (too engulfing, too reminiscent of his powerlessness), or the arctic winter of her coldness (too abandoning, too life-threatening). He will have been driven out of the house of women, and so denied access to the regular expression of unforced feeling. He will have learned instead the hardening of pain, humiliation and aggression, the art of fighting as self-expression, and the price of losing. His manhood training, while purporting to toughen him up, will have done nothing to address his anxieties about 'making it', 'measuring up', the fear of fear which is at the core of male identity. It will indeed all too often have confirmed his doubts about his self-worth, institutionalized the psychic fissures that arise from a profound self-hate, and driven him, even at this young age, into a position from which he has to take charge of the violence which has been done to him. Only by owning, mastering and returning it, by casting off the role of the victim of it, will he feed the gnawing angst, the hunger within.

This hunger – for proof of manhood, for meaning and significance, for transcendence of fear and pain – is at its greatest in those who have least to begin with, and aggression is its classic response. The young males of every underclass have to reach higher, strive harder to be 'real men', and hence are unable to avoid embarking on what they know from the outset will prove to be a collision course with violence, brutality, and masculine authority. The arrogance of a too-early, uneasy machismo, the social and educational disadvantage that has already triggered a string of petty delinquencies, all these make inevitable the hostile attention of an embattled state. For men of colour in both Britain and America, that will be the least of it. 'A black male teenager is twice as likely to be unemployed as his white male equivalent, and six times more likely to be murdered,' reports US journalist Mark Cooper. In Los Angeles alone 'there have been nearly 3000 gang-related killings and 15,000 woundings since 1980.' The young black looks forward, then, to an adult future prematurely deformed, and promising strikingly higher rates of illness, early death, imprisonment and criminal victimization than the lowliest of his white compatriots will face. He will also have markedly lower employment, earnings, prospects and opportunities of every kind.[4]

In these circumstances, argues Ice Cube, chief rapper with the LA band NWA (Niggers With Attitude), criminality is the only sane and logical response. 'The people I went to school with are some of the worst people I know. They dropped out of school in the eighth or ninth grade, can't read too good, can't get a job, their girl had a baby; these kind of problems stack up but you've got to survive, so the best they can do is steal, sell dope and dodge the police.' Gun-fighting is a way of life: 'if you sat on this porch at night and listened real hard you'd hear nothing but gunfire.' The harder it gets, the more essential to survival, both physical and mental, is an almost hysterical reiteration of a hardline machismo, the rhetoric if not the reality of unassailable manhood. Ice Cube uses his raps like the chart-topping 'Gangsta Gangsta' to reach for the invulnerability he and others like him so desperately crave to cloak the terror of their vulnerability:

> I'm the mother-fucker that you read about,
>   Taking a life or two,

That's what the hell I do,
    If you don't like the way I'm living,
Fuck you!

Ice Cube's ruthless survival ethic leaves no room in his life for
women, who appear only as gold-digging 'bitches' in all the NWA raps:
'You're only vulnerable if you let yourself be, and I wouldn't let myself
be vulnerable to anything . . . I wouldn't lose no sleep over no person
other than my own family.' Yet females, whether 'bitches' or
'respectable girls', continue to be both a private thorn in the young male
flesh, and a public excuse for ritual aggression and combat. 'When two
men fight over a woman, it's the fight they want, not the woman,' said
Dylan Thomas. In Britain, rival gangs of Muslims and Sikhs regularly
clash on these grounds. 'It centred on the belief that young Sikh girls
were being taken against their will and being sexually abused by
Muslim boys,' said Christopher Hotten, prosecuting one such race riot
between the Shere Punjab gang of Birmingham and their rivals, the
Aston Panthers, in June 1989: 'Both groups came to the stage where
they were prepared to take the law into their own hands.' On this
occasion, only the intervention of the (unarmed) local police between
the two gangs, both heavily weaponed and out for blood, forestalled
their mutual lust to kill.

Manliness . . . it is a hideous and crippling lie; it not
only insists on difference and connives at superiority,
it is also by its very nature destructive – emotionally
damaging and socially harmful.
    The youth who is subverted, as most are, into
believing in the masculine ideal is effectively separated
from women – it is the most savage tribal logic – and he
spends the rest of his life finding women a riddle and a
nuisance.
        Paul Theroux,
        'The Male Myth'

From the riddle, the nuisance, the threat and the danger of woman,
where should the young male recoil but back into the bosom of the
gang? So the move towards individuation in reality serves only to

reinforce group loyalty and the tyranny of male bonding. Yet for those who cannot go with the growth opportunity that the first approach of womanhood provides, the male group is destined to become ever more dysfunctional. For traditional masculinity, as enshrined and idealized among immature or under-developed men, is a complex of positives and negatives, harsh blacks and whites, whose contradictions impose impossible tensions on blacks and whites alike. Success, strength and power are starkly opposed to failure, weakness and submission: he who does not achieve the one is automatically consigned to the other. The fear of that failure keeps the young inadequate running with the pack for the warmth of its solidarity, condemning him to an ever-escalating level of violent action and ritual manhood display.

For the gang at this stage has, like each of the young men in it, put away childish things and become either semi- or wholly criminal. Boys who formerly hung out together for want of anything better to do now meet for the express purpose of 'wilding', the word a horrified America had forcibly added to its vocabulary in the summer of 1989, when a gang of youths carried out the notorious rape, sodomization and vicious battering of a 28-year-old investment banker jogging in New York's Central Park. The term 'wilding' – New York street slang for 'raising hell' – may have been new, but the offence itself has a well-established modern pedigree. In 1983, a gang of 'wild things' descended on a Diana Ross concert, beating and robbing more than 180 people (imagine that at Woodstock, or indeed any of the 1960s pop concerts). In 1985 a 'wolf pack' attacked a charity march in Central Park, snatching chains and purses, injuring children as they went. In 1989 a young German tourist was foolish enough to stop a group of youths in Times Square to ask for directions. The gang chased him down the subway and threw him on the line.

New York, it will be argued, is a special case. Londoners, however, have watched in disbelief as their once-admired underground train network has been overtaken by 'steamers', whose violence is all too often only a hair's breadth away from murder. In a 'steaming' attack by the Mean Machine gang of north London in March 1989, one passenger who resisted narrowly escaped death when a knife, aimed at his heart, glanced off his breastbone. As the gang, thwarted, swept off the train, an Algerian student, newly arrived in the city, was casually knifed to death *en passant*, a random proxy for the first equally random victim.

Murder, however, is not the end in itself. The drive, conscious or unconscious, is towards the transfiguration it provides, the elevation into a new, highly-select élite, as the Polish scholar Jan Kott, a veteran of the Polish underground of World War II, explains:

The terrorist Chen in Malraux's *La Condition Humaine* utters one of the most terrifying sentences written in the mid-twentieth century: 'A man who has never killed is a virgin.' This sentence means that killing is cognition, just as, according to the Old Testament, the sexual act is cognition; it also means that the experience of killing cannot be communicated . . . But this means also that the act of killing changes the person who has performed it; from then on he is a different person living in a different world.[5]

In the absence of other rewards of the successfully established man, the thrill of blood, the power of life and death, become the reward so keenly sought and, once obtained, an addiction as strong as heroin or alcohol. 'Many young men lust after violence,' says David Robins of the Oxford Centre for Criminological Research. 'Some people hanker after sex or success at work, but others hanker after blood. It gives them a real thrill. In fact they glory in it.'

When the lust for blood and death is compounded by a clinical addiction, the results are beyond calculation, even beyond belief. In a series of raids throughout England's wealthy Home Counties over a ten-month period during 1989, crack addict Brian Tomlinson extorted £150,000 to fund his addiction. Tomlinson, who answered only to the names of 'Zorro' or 'Rambo', armed with a Bowie knife and cut-throat razor and supported always by chosen members of his gang, attacked women alone with their children after their husbands had gone to work, systematically applying violence and torture until enough money was raised to induce him to leave. In one attack he split open the head of a one-year-old boy with an iron bar, then caused the child's eight-months-pregnant mother to go into labour by sitting on her stomach. 'To call your behaviour animal-like,' said the judge who sentenced Tomlinson to seventeen years' imprisonment, 'is an insult to animals.'

Such horrors are not new – Julius Caesar, Goya, the women of the Holocaust or Vietnam, could all bear witness to the truth of the ancient Eastern proverb, 'Women are the grass that gets trampled when the elephants fight.' What is new is the random eruption of barbarous male sadism into peacetime, prosperous suburbs, in the clockwork orange pursuit of recreational savagery for its own sick, sweet sake. Only in such acts, it seems, can a significant proportion of today's young men locate themselves in the late twentieth-century hierarchy of male expectation and demand; only thus can they bridge the abyss between their aspirations and their reality; only through the blood, pain and suffering of those weaker than themselves can they achieve those idealized masculine norms of strength and dominance which they are lacking in every other respect. Aggression, criminality, by creating a pitiful weakness and vulnerability in its victims, allows the young aggressor to transcend his own. The assumption of power, however brief, over others, offers him a kind of heroism, a starring role, a naïve dream of self-realization through the truth of pure behaviour untrammelled by conscience, reason, or even hesitation. How naïve then it is of us to believe that imperatives like these can ever be restrained or abolished by vigilante patrols, new laws, more police.

New York's 'wilding' gang, London's Mean Machine, and Brian 'Rambo' Tomlinson were all black. Race however, though a key theme, is not the explanation of young male violence. Glen Ridge, New Jersey, is a whiter-than-white community of upper-middle-class families whose sons are blessed from the cradle with money, opportunity, education and prestige. When a retarded girl was sexually assaulted by a group of local youths in March 1989, the initial reaction was one of stark disbelief: the accused were all star members of the local high school football team, and included a pair of 18-year-old identical twins who served as the team's co-captains. Early opinion in Glen Ridge blamed the girl, who must have 'led the boys on'. Police investigations revealed the existence of a 'team within the team', an élite gang styling themselves 'the Muscleheads', whose members were both local sports heroes and school bullies. 'In between playing football and beating up their fellow-students, the Muscleheads allegedly watched pornographic videos,' reported *Sunday Times* writer Mark Hosenball. The group assault, when the girl was enticed into a cellar and abused by five of the youths while others looked on, only came to light when the Muscleheads were heard bragging about it in the school locker-room. Explicitly linking the Glen Ridge case with the notorious New York Central Park assault, Hosenball comments: 'Both incidents demonstrate that gratuitous sexual violence among teenage American males transcends racial boundaries . . . the number of sexual crimes committed by American boys has soared in recent years.'

What is the drive that fuels such acts of violence? What is the appetite that they feed, but also fan? Reading backwards from the forms of expression they take, it is clear that these acts, however apparently 'unnatural', 'mindless' or abhorrent, merely repeat in an exaggerated form all the key themes and inescapable imperatives of 'normal' masculinity: the fantasy of heroic endeavour, the competitive urge to dominate and excel, to 'get ahead', the need to blunt all tender feelings, the search for significance through the transcendence of fear and weakness, the centralizing of the penis and its demands, the resort to penis-power and phallic control as the first and final weapon at moments of stress or need. How can we continue to make a hard and fast distinction between 'normal' and 'criminal' when both are located along the same spectrum that we call 'man'?

Bloodshed is a cleansing and a sanctifying thing, and the nation that regards it as the final horror has lost its manhood.

Patrick Pearse,
Irish patriot

The battle hymn of the republic of men may be more clearly audible in the war chants of the druggies and the dispossessed than in the rest of the young male population. But as any acquaintance with the literature makes plain, neither race nor deprivation holds the key. The drive to create cruelty springs from the primal recesses of male consciousness, and can only be increased by the passage of time. For violence rapidly becomes functional – the ten-year-old boy obliterates his own fear and weakness in the act of pulling the wings off flies – and with experience violent men learn to depend on the constant renewal of that pay-off, the validation of manhood prowess that they seek. Worse, they come to enjoy the process, and to take pleasure in inflicting pain, to need the erotic reward of watching another's dreadful, even terminal suffering. It is no coincidence that the majority of sexual deaths occur by strangulation, the perfect method by which the killer can derive the maximum satisfaction both from a 'hands-on' killing and from watching the tortured face below him in every moment of its final agony.

Violence, then, repeats itself, and always must; if successful, because it supplies the psychic need, or if unsuccessful, until it does so. For this reason violent crime is condemned to follow an ascending pattern of severity, with sexual offences in particular subject to this dismal law of diminishing returns. Battered wives invariably report that their beatings started with a push or a slap; rapists, even if never previously caught, characteristically have a history of offences often leading straight back to 'simple' indecent exposure, although the convictions are not invariably of a sexual nature: robbery, for instance, especially breaking and entering, is frequently implicated as a run-up to rape. A London prison survey of 40 convicted murderers demonstrated that they had all beaten their wives over a considerable period of time, progressively stepping up both the range and the viciousness of the assaults, a result widely borne out by other studies in Britain and the USA.[6] If we could find the way to cut into and arrest the violent man's career while he is still an apprentice to pain, we could immediately save at least two lives, both his and his first victim's, for the normal, ordinary life of the average twentieth-century citizen.

'The main point to grasp about male violence,' comments Dr David Drewett, a consultant psychiatrist discussing his work at a private London clinic for violent men, 'is that *what they do falls within the range of normal male behaviour.* Psychiatry has no solution to this. Either the violence must be limited, or the norm redefined.' Twenty-one-year-old Steven Beaumont of London told the woman who left him in 1988 after a five-month relationship that if he ever caught her with anyone else he would kill her. When she found a new boyfriend he climbed into her flat at night and mutilated her with four different knives in a sustained attack during which she almost bled to death, and which has left her scarred for life on the throat, breasts, sides, back and stomach. At his trial at Southwark Crown Court, Beaumont denied attempted murder, but agreed that his aim had been to inflict grievous bodily harm. What are the norms which in today's world permit such behaviour? *Primus inter pares* must be the law of male domination – no man so mean but expects to be master of his own woman, in his own house: indeed the lowlier his station, the more serious the threat to his claim to that status, the greater will be his need for support and validation in that intimate arena, and the more violent his revenge if denied it. Ten thousand years of human history have invested the rule of patriarchy with the force of a law of nature. Yet the feminist challenge of the last twenty years has shown that this right of man is based neither on natural law nor on superiority in nature. The impact of this on the lives of men like Beaumont has been incalculable.

Or rather, still uncalculated, for great numbers are still engaged in the painful process of surveying the battlefield and enumerating their losses. The older man has one lament: 'I've been stripped of my importance, the man should be number one, the breadwinner, with everyone looking up to him', the younger man another: 'I don't think I'll ever have the respect my father had, it's like America, we used to be the biggest thing on the earth, now suddenly we're nothing special, the enemy even.' But the loss is the same. Men have lost their territory as women have invaded their world of work, demanding money, excitement, and a piece of the pie. They have lost their home comforts as each Angel at the Hearth has spread her wings and taken off in search of independence and a little fun before she's playing a harp for good and all. And none of this feels like it's supposed to for a real man.

Undoubtedly the worst of the wounds of feminism, though, lies in its successful challenge to the male right of sexual exclusivity and exclusive, lifelong sexual possession. No longer may a man choose a girl and have the reassurance that he will be her first and only lover: no longer can he relax in the comforting knowledge that in the country of the one-prick princess, his one-eyed man will always be king. After marriage, too, the old security has gone: adultery among wives in Britain and the USA is now running somewhere between 25 and 40 per cent, while divorce petitions brought by women in Britain account for a staggering 82 per cent of the total.[7] Not surprisingly, men in general can suffer intensely from a marriage break-up, and measurably more than women on almost every criterion available. An EEC survey of 1989 found that over 50 per cent of divorced men regretted losing their partner, as against less than 25 per cent of the women. Divorced men, especially those who remain unmarried, display soaring rates of cerebral and coronary thrombosis, cancer, career breakdown, mental distress, insanity and suicide.[8] 'Love *hurts*,' says writer Andrew Davies, discussing his novel *Getting Hurt* (1989). 'In fact the fields are littered with wounded soldiers in the sex wars.' When a woman leaves a man:

> You are back feeling as sick and strange and incomplete as you did at the start, but now you *know* what you want, and nothing will do but to bury yourself in her, merge with her, dissolve into her, you just have to be touching her all the time. Just when she feels so stifled by you she can hardly breathe, you make new demands on her, you want somehow to pin her down, fix her, make her yours . . . If it is bad enough you will have to kill her to hold her still.

Inevitably violence of some sort will be the response to such violent feelings. When women are assuming autonomy, usurping male authority, men must strive harder for dominance if they are to re-establish the boundaries under threat. And the means to do so, the weapons of sexual terrorism, are never far away. The patriarch at bay usually has to look no further than the ends of his arms: in a grim ascent from the solitary sexplorations of boyhood through the companionable pub years raising a glass with a gang of mates, beating the wife, 'teaching her a lesson' or 'just giving her a reminder' becomes 'what your right hand is for'.

Force is only used when power is in jeopardy.
Hannah Arendt

Violence within marriage arises from men's power and women's resistance to it, real or imagined. In one case investigated by the American sociologists R. Emerson and Russell Dobash working at the Institute for the Study of Violence at the University of Stirling, a woman who had made a birthday cake for her son gave her father the first slice. For this her husband broke her wrist. Alternatively, the wife or female partner may be attacked for exerting her own power, real or imagined, for usurping initiatives, economic and/or sexual, and undermining the husband's manhood by encroaching on his male prerogative and privilege. One woman who after a prior discussion with her husband went on her own to buy a dishwasher, was stripped naked and had a kettle of boiling water poured over her head. Whether supposedly resisting or exerting power, women are overwhelmingly the targets of men's violence: the Dobash study shows that nearly 80 per cent of all intra-family violence is perpetrated against wives. Not only are wives or live-in partners more likely to be attacked and killed than any other member of the family; these attacks are also more likely to be systematic, sustained, varied and sadistic. If violence expresses the male right to dominate, this meaning is accepted by the vast majority of the recipients, since most battered wives do not report the crime or even consider it to be one; nor do they leave the relationship, fight back, or turn to anyone else for help.

By staying silent, or simply by staying, these women sentence themselves to continuing, usually escalating, attacks. In one case known to a London Women's Refuge, a husband cut off his wife's little finger with a pair of secateurs: in his next attack, he tried to saw off her arm. Another man who had previously attacked his wife with scalding coffee and tea, covered her in white spirit and set fire to her with a blowtorch. These cases are not exceptional. In the London area alone, more than 100,000 women a year need hospital treatment after violence in the home. Most of them will be familiar, if occasionally unrecognizable, faces in their local casualty departments: the average number of beatings per woman sustained by those admitted to refuges in England and Wales, is 35.[9] Apart from bruises, bloody noses, broken teeth, split lips and cauliflower ears, that also means innumerable fractures of everything from skulls to feet, cigarette burns, wire whippings; and worse, far worse.

What are these women doing to provoke or merit such extreme punishment? Nothing, contend Rebecca and Russell Dobash. Excuses of provocation offered by violent men in reality merely rationalize a deeper need. Marriage alone confers the rights of ownership and domination which this type of husband must exert if he is to be a real man in the eyes of others: 'it cannot be stressed too much that it is marriage, the taking on of the status of wife, that makes woman the "appropriate victim" of violence aimed at "putting her in her place", and that differential responsibility and authority give the husband both the perceived right and the *obligation* to control his wife's behaviour.'[10] This assumption of ownership and control lies behind the sexual jealousy and possessiveness which dog so many relationships, often with disastrous results: Ian McCallum, a Bedfordshire publican, was jailed for life at St Albans Crown Court early in 1990, for killing his wife after she left him to set up home with one of his 'regulars'. McCallum told the court that he began his murderous attack when his wife informed him that he was not the father of their eleven-month-old daughter whom he had brought up as his own.

In extreme cases this lust for possession, this inability to recognize the separateness of 'his' female, leads the husband to the conviction that the wife has no need of life without him, and no right to life apart from him. One man stabbed the woman who had left him, at the christening celebrations of their baby daughter. In a dissimilar but related case, a pensioner, wrongly convinced that he had cancer, killed his 71-year-old wife with a hammer, seeing her as an extension of himself and so at his disposal. Professionals in the field are accustomed to this close, indeed extreme form of identification. Social worker Jean Renvoize reports a batterer who proudly displayed his wife's bruises, pointing out the worst: 'they were *his* bruises, *he* made them, and he is obviously possessive about them . . . in this way he has made her flesh *his* flesh, and for a little while he rests secure.'[11]

Man and wife is one flesh, runs the Elizabethan proverb recalled by Hamlet in his disgust at his mother's remarriage (IV.iii.55). But the 'one-flesh' that the damaged and damaging man seeks here is not that of wife, partner, friend or equal. Only in the cradle did he know that kind of closeness, that right of command, and only in the marital relationship will he relive those primal conflicts. The all-consuming infantile rage can find its target against the mother-wife at any time, any age: a 74-year-old retired vicar beat his wife to death when, in an attempt to re-tune the radio, she lost the reception of his favourite programme, *Desert Island Discs*. 'It seems that they experience their marital partners as attempting to annihilate their very being,' says Jean Renvoize.

Reproduction, marriage and child-rearing is the only one of our activities which absolutely demands sustained generosity and selflessness; it is therefore not surprising that if either or both partners are unable to give, their handicap will be revealed, and violence is one way in which the anguish of such failure will be expressed.

Dr P. D. Scott,
psychologist

'My father used to make us bring his food to the table, wait on him, like, then if he felt like it he'd break the plate over our heads. He liked it best when it was custard, because it was hot,' one north of England daughter of a violent father reported. Fifties film star Jerry Lewis, one of America's best-loved comedians, beat his sons 'till the blood ran', according to his eldest boy Joe. It is not hard to imagine how an adult woman, privy to a man's most intimate fears and failures, could catch him on the raw (traditional advice on how to keep a husband happy always insisted, never say you're no good at your job, you're no good in bed, or you're getting to be just like your father, advice many women knowingly and maliciously disregard). But a child? How can a child trespass on any of this?

Simply, it seems, by being born. The adult manhood themes of ownership and control in fact come through even more clearly in the case studies of violence against children, especially sons. 'Once, my father found me on the street,' says actor Rupert Everett. 'I hadn't seen him for months. I said, "Hi, dad," and he just hit me really hard on the head and walked on. I understand him now.' Another son, in a case described by Philip Hodson, was given $25 by his father for a graduation present, driven to the station, put on a train to New York and told, 'I hope I never hear from you again.' And parallel with the contemporary epidemic of divorce, the recurrent stories of fathers kidnapping their 'tug of love kids' suggest that even the men who reconcile themselves to losing 'their' woman will not readily abandon their rights or claims in their offspring.

Yet fatherhood can prove for many men anything from a deep disappointment to an intolerable burden, and one above all for which they have never been equipped. The average school-leaver of eighteen will have had thirteen or fifteen years of intellectual training, which may include subjects as abstruse as Higher Maths, Sanskrit or Ancient Greek. Over the next few years he will be trained for some occupation, and he will learn how to handle money, to get a house, to get on. But he will be taught nothing about fathering, the most important job of his life. On the contrary, he must, in the words of one father, 'make it up as he goes along'. All he has behind him will be his own experience of being fathered, a training which may prove not only inadequate but deeply destructive. For however dim, distant or unassertive the father, the role itself carries expectations of primacy, centrality and authority which even the youngest of fathers subconsciously assumes will be his by right in his turn. Any challenge to that authority will be bitterly resented and immediately put down, however wide of the mark it may be: 'He really hates me', 'She doesn't want me, she kicks me off with her feet, I can tell', and 'He looks at me as if to say, "Go on, just you try and make me"', battering fathers claimed of children as young as three to six months old.[12]

A man's right of violence over his women reaches back into history, and is only recently being challenged in the societies of the West. Further east, an older law still applies, and may even be renewed: Iraq's Revolutionary Council issued a new decree in March 1990 'to strengthen ethical values', abolishing any legal process or punishment against men who kill female relatives of women caught in adultery, and permitting men now to kill with impunity their mothers, sisters, daughters, female cousins, mothers- and sisters-in-law, nieces and aunts. The right of violence against children has had an even longer life and is still being vigorously defended today, as a logical extension of the father's right to do with his child what he will.

Yet the expectation of unquestioned, unbending, omnipotent male authority, the public and symbolic equivalent of the Teflon erection, is only part of the story. At another level, the penis-that-is-man craves above all the primacy that was once his by right, and could be, *would be* his again were it not for this other baby, this interloper, this cuckoo in the nest, this thing which has arrived and come to stay, this ET. The child in him is foredoomed to fight the child who is usurping his childhood, commandeering his right to be 'boy eternal', his need to be fed. Danny Palmer was only sixteen in 1988 when social workers let him set up home as father to his girlfriend's baby in a damp, squalid London bedsitter. For the unprepared youth, 'the novelty of being a father turned sour when taunted that the child was not his – suspicions subsequently confirmed by tests', it was stated at his trial in 1989, when he was convicted of killing the child after breaking the seven-month-old baby's wrists, gouging his eyes, and beating him with a banister rail or rounders bat. In the same month in London Robert Johnson, aged 29, was convicted of attacking his three-year-old son Liam on Christmas Day 1987, with such ferocity that the child's spine was completely broken and 'open like a hinge', the pathologist told the court. The injuries were caused some three weeks before the little boy died, said Professor James Cameron, 'and must have made his last days a live agony'.

As these and numerous related cases show, the desire to remain child can readily co-exist with the will to be father. Joel Steinberg, the New York lawyer and assailant of the pitifully brutalized Hedda Nussbaum, was so determined to become a father that he exploited all the resources of his legal training and $3-million-dollar fortune in the illegal adoption of two children, both of whom he beat and tortured and one of whom, six-year-old Lisa, he killed. Yet part of his abuse of Nussbaum, his long-standing partner, consisted of forcing her to write out lines, 'I must care about Joel's hair', or 'I must take care of Joel's teeth'. Mothers normally enjoy taking care of their children. Steinberg's lawyers said, 'We are not denying there were beatings. We say she enjoyed it.'

How far the victim must be in reality from enjoying such violence emerges from one father's account. His attacks on his daughter began when he found himself teaching in an 'oppressive' inner-city school, where the violence of the boys resulted in regular outbursts like the pitching of desks through plate-glass windows. His own failure to control this left him feeling 'completely inadequate', and at the mercy of a fear which grew greater every morning. After one cataclysmic day, without premeditation, he attacked his daughter:

She was the most charming, lively and completely inoffensive little girl, then aged about five or six, and nothing she would ever do could have warranted my onslaught of brutally heavy slaps around the face and head.

Her complete vulnerability and incomprehension of why she was being attacked seemed to provoke me to further slapping and violent shaking. My wife's protests, far from stopping me, seemed to act as a perverse sort of encouragement.

The next evening, after another humiliating and hopeless day at school, I came home and the scene was repeated. This time there were two or three attacks, again without the slightest provocation.

I realized that I was speculating in quite a detached way about how I could hurt my daughter, not in a spontaneous fit of anger, but in a more thoughtful and calculated manner.[13]

Suffer little children, said Jesus: and they do. According to the annual figures of the National Society for the Prevention of Cruelty to

Children, allegations of child sex abuse in the UK rose by 24 per cent in 1989; and 95 per cent of the allegations were later found to be true, said Dr Alan Gilmour, the director of the society. Proven cases of child sex abuse have doubled in the last five years: the financial resources of the society, and its number of trained and qualified inspectors, have not. NSPCC figures for sexual abuse are supported by government figures for all forms of child abuse: a 1989 survey by the Department of Health showed that one in four children had been abused, physically, or sexually, or both. Figures from previous years also showed that the number of children either at risk, or currently under abuse, is rising every year.

As worrying in a different way is the changing pattern of child sexual abuse. In a move which displays a chilling parallel with similar developments in adult sexual crime, attacks on children increasingly display elements of the sadistic, the voyeuristic and the bizarre. In a case at Stafford Crown Court in December 1989, a 25-year-old man was convicted of buggering a four-year-old boy, and of almost biting off the child's penis, an injury so severe that it had to be surgically repaired under a general anaesthetic. In another prosecution, at the Old Bailey in London in March 1990, a father convicted of incest with his two daughters pleaded guilty to making the 12-year-old sleep with him every time she menstruated in order to avoid 'defiling the temple of her bedroom', and to forcing her younger sister, as soon as she reached the age of 12, to eat 'spells and potions' before intercourse so that he could 'watch the devil come out of her'. Children thus robbed of their childhood become adults before their time: Dr Jane Wynne, whose work in exposing child abuse in Leeds led to the conviction of a sex ring involving 35 men, reports a sixteen-year-old girl with cancer of the cervix after multiple sexual abuse from the age of nine, and girls and boys as young as three with venereal diseases. The victims of today make the new victims of tomorrow, says Dr Wynne: 'Between 40 and 60 per cent of male abusers were abused themselves as children.'

Women, children, boys, girls, lovers, strangers – the dance goes on. Of all the acts of sexual terrorism, abuse within the family, by father, brother, grandfather or 'Uncle Charlie' is arguably the worst, involving as it does so much silent, repeated, and intimate pain, in the tenderest and most unprotected years. Yet undoubtedly ahead in the public mind, in the fear felt by women and in the status accorded to the man, stands the figure of the sexual assailant as hero, the rapist-murderer. In the act of killing, argued the French writer and homosexual Jean Genet, 'the murderer destroys the laws of God and man by becoming God'. And in the act of rape he makes all the world bow down before his God, the jealous god who can brook no other idol of worship, his penis.

All acts of violence, all questions of manhood, return ultimately to this. The penis rampant stalks through history, making war, breaking peace. Rape has fuelled pogroms, invaded ghettos, strengthened empire-builders against natives and freedom fighters against imperialists, and its fear now lives with almost every woman, as familiar to her as her closest intimate, dictating too many of her everyday actions, too many days of her life. Rape and its threat of death can call upon world-famous stars like Connie Francis and Kelly McGillis just as much as the vicar's daughter from Ealing: unlike the popular press, the 'Yorkshire Ripper' made no distinction between prostitutes and 'respectable women'.

For the erect penis, as the saying goes, has no conscience. Nor will he ever have, as long as he lives in a world where his primacy, his supremacy, his stupendous, larger-than-life magnificence are exalted, while the real needs of his host-machine, the thing called man, are systematically denied and perverted in the name of making him a man. Men, as human beings, will not flourish, and violence will, as long as they are subjected to the brutal manhood training of an outmoded masculine agenda: as long as they are forced into competitions pre-equipped with a built-in structure of failure: as long as they need the reassurance of constant potency, are empowered as men to demand it, and can only obtain it through fighting, winning, and beating others down in the endless battle of the sexes and the wars, outlasting all others, of a never-satisfied virility.

What makes a killer out of an ordinary regular guy? What makes a man a man? His rites of passage, and his faith in his rights. Time to rewrite the rites of man.

Epilogue

Surely there must be some meaning beneath all this terrible irony.
George Bernard Shaw

The study of history and culture teaches that all the world was mad in the past; men always thought they were right, and that led to wars, persecution, slavery, xenophobia, racism, and chauvinism. The point is not to correct the mistakes and really be right; rather it is not to think you are right at all.
Allan Bloom

Man is a failed species. I look forward to a future where the unabating bellipotence of the male will cease, and women will create a new universe.
Jeremy Reed

Let our son go free,
  Let him go onward
Until he emerges
  And goes forth over the bay.
Let him go forth
  Into the dawn
And onward into the world of light.
Maori chant

'Today,' writes the Christian philosopher Jacques Ellul, 'Man has come of age.' No longer subject, in the West at least, to the tyranny of religious bigotry, the might of an unjust state, or the daily threat of death through sickness and starvation, he has the chance, for the first time in history, to live his own life, not the standard hand-me-down version of the past, nasty, brutish, and short. And he must live it now by new rules. Many of the former conditions legitimizing violence in both men and nations no longer apply. Many of the calculations of former times (the end justifies the means, the price is not too high, *dulce et decorum est*, it'll all be over by Christmas) have been exposed for what they are, tales told by idiots. Twentieth-century man, caught now on the cusp of a new millennium, is on his own.

And never more alone. 'I am a spirit roaming the night,' wrote the American serial killer David Berkowitz, the self-styled 'son of Sam', in one of the obscure missives with which he tormented the police for many months before his capture in 1983. Invaded at work, diminished at home, abandoned in marriage and threatened by the monstrous moms, the regiment of women now suddenly committing adultery and petitioning for divorce, the average man finds himself fighting space-age wars armed only with the emotional equivalent of the pike and blunderbuss. Great strains evoke powerful responses, and violence has always been a first, rather than the last, resort of traditional masculinity. The posturing pen-pusher Jean-Paul Sartre spoke for many with his inflammatory bleat: 'It is only through mad fury that the wretched of the earth can become men.'[1]

How could men, and women too, even in the sixties, have fallen for this rad-chic 'power-grows-from-the-barrel-of-a-gun' rubbish? Because they needed to. That need, coupled with the wish-fulfilment belief (Sartre again) that 'violence, like Achilles' lance, can heal the wounds it has inflicted', has brought us to the edge of this abyss. Thirty years on, the wretched of the earth are no less wretched, individually and collectively, than they were. Man can put a girdle round the earth in four minutes, but he cannot feed all his children, or prevent them from killing one another: woman can watch heroes walk on the moon, but cannot find the man who can offer her any better than a one in three chance of staying married to him. Meanwhile the victims of our sins of omission and commission go forth and multiply as the hungry young look up and are not fed. Violence feeds such children. 'I've pent up all my aggression, kept swallowing it and swallowing it,' said Mark David Chapman after shooting down John Lennon in December 1980.

For every John Lennon there are a thousand, a million unknown soldiers who go unsung to their graves in the ceaseless round of manhood's wars. Current statistics show:

- figures for offences of violence and sexual offences increased by 20 per cent in Britain in 1989, even though figures for other offences showed a decrease. Preliminary figures for 1990–1 show that 'we are facing the worst year since the war for percentage increase in recorded crime', said Paul Condon of the British Association of Chief Police Officers.

- the greatest increases came in rural areas hitherto deemed relatively safe, like Norfolk (26 per cent increase in crimes of violence) and Dorset (74 per cent increase in sexual crimes).

- America's murder rate is surging towards a new record level: by the end of 1990, almost a quarter of a million people will have died by violence in the decade since 1980, which had itself marked a previously unprecedented 'all-time high'.

- over 90 per cent of murderers are male.

- males also constitute the majority of murder victims (53 per cent in Britain, 74 per cent in the USA).

- 8 out of every 10 women are subject to some form of sexual abuse or offence in their lives.

- of nearly 3000 rapes reported in Britain in 1988, only just over 1000 went to court, and there were only 420 convictions, although over 60 per cent of rape victims knew their attackers.

- rape is the most rapidly rising crime of violence in the USA, showing a 50 per cent increase over the last decade.

- over a third of all married women suffer violence and/or the threat of violence from their husbands.

- one-third of all murdered women are killed by their husbands or lovers.

- police in the UK make arrests in only 17 per cent of 'domestic disputes' involving physical injury, rising to 20 per cent in 'life-threatening cases'.

- the number of young offenders (14–20) is rising, while the age at which boys first offend is dropping.[2]

Do these figures show a real increase in the volume of crime, or are they simply the product of wider reporting due to increased public awareness? The frequent posing of this question has itself become a tactic for distracting public attention from the figures, as if 'increased reporting' makes the known amount of crime somehow less real, or means that we have less to worry about. Of the two realities, the volume of crime and the public perception of it, the volume of under-reported crime in the past (obscurely perceived as 'the real figures') is hardly likely ever to be established by an age which cannot even discover the volume of unreported crime in its own time. The concept of 'under-reporting' in itself has also provided a convenient distraction, and a way of fudging the figures, for while women had and have very good reasons for failing to report a sexual assault, there is no reason to assume that the figures for offences of violence have leaped up because men and women are suddenly no longer shy about being mugged, robbed, or attacked in streets and pubs. The figures that we have demonstrate the size of the problem – in the case of sexual assaults at certainly less than their true level – and we should be seeking ways to deal with this, not shadow-boxing with the notion of the way things used to be.

The soaring statistics have another significance, however, which has received little attention from our political masters apart from the passing tribute of the odd windy sigh. Both crime and the fear of crime have permeated the very fabric of western life, and the rising volume of complaint is the clearest possible signal that the people of the countries affected are no longer prepared to tolerate this. Historically many practices (judicial torture, slavery, genocide) were considered completely acceptable, and were so widely practised as to be considered normal, even civilized. Until an aroused public opinion began to see them as wrongs, until governments and rulers began to move against them with all the legal and social sanctions at their command, they remained normal and natural, seamlessly integrated into the fabric of national, social and personal life.

The same is now true of male violence. 'We cannot doubt that we are a highly aggressive species,' wrote Konrad Lorenz with the sick smirk of self-congratulation that characterizes so many of men's pronouncements on violence. Who 'we'? Over 50 per cent of the population can't play, won't play a game whose rules insist that the players must trade in violence and cruelty, and are forbidden to doubt or question any of its underlying assumptions. The tenacity with which even good, kind, sane, normal and responsible men cling to the idea of aggression as their biological birthright is one of the major obstacles to its removal. Yet with the safety of each new-born boy or girl, the fulfilment of individuals, the happiness of families, with even the life of the planet at stake, can anyone seriously doubt that for bulging biceps and hairy chests, for the master of the house and Marlboro man, for *homo erectus* and his hand-held gods Phalles and Priapus, above all for every downhome Doctor Death, the day of reckoning has finally come?

Most men are fucked up, whether they know it or not. And their aim in life is to try to fuck women up, whether they know it or not.
Andrew Davies

> It is tragic how few people ever possess their souls
> before they die.
>   Oscar Wilde

What remedy for men, maleness, masculinity, manhood? First we must accept that whatever is currently being done to control this behaviour of men, it is not working. Pundits relieve themselves in public with loud calls for more penalties, more police. This limited, short-term, essentially reactive thinking has been characteristic of all official approaches to the issue, and is at least in part responsible for its escalation. No one argues with the view that criminals should be caught and punished. But the *post hoc* knee-jerk reaction, however swift and terrible, serves only our need for a violent response and for retribution, and does nothing to eradicate violence, or to protect future victims.

The need is to acknowledge the roots of violence, and to cut into the process higher up the causal chain. We should be asking what purpose these crimes serve in the lives of the perpetrators, in direct opposition to the mindless media rhetoric of 'mindless, meaningless crime'. For there always is a meaning, and with less than 2 per cent of sexual murderers found to be in any way abnormal, a perfectly normal one. A perfectly normal, indeed super-normal male meaning, that is. Violent men are always seen and explained as deviant from the masculine norm. 'Tony Maclean is surely by definition mentally ill,' wrote reporter Minette Marrin of the 1989 'Notting Hill rapist', a fifteen-stone body-builder versed in military tactics from his training as a paratrooper who was found guilty in April 1990 of multiple charges of rape, attempted rape, indecent assault, robbery and burglary. 'Sane people do not terrorize single women in their own homes or rape them or tie up teddy-bears in the bedrooms of pretty strangers. As an amateur, I feel sorry to think that he will be sent to an ordinary prison.'[3] In reality, Maclean, who attacked women undetected for eight years, was simply doing what every other man in England was doing at the time, trying to make himself feel more of a man. Only his techniques diverged. His aims were the same, or greater. For violent men, however small or weedy in body, are invariably found by psychologists to be over-conforming in mind to masculine norms, over-determined by the 'fight-'em-fuck-'em-forget-'em' ideal of manly conduct, and so much in thrall to the concept of male domination that they do not and will not regard rape as any kind of crime.

But as long as the majority of men are not criminals, not likely to prey on women in dark streets or on boys behind bike-sheds, why should the entire sex stand impugned? How can there be anything wrong with a system that is eight or nine times as likely to produce a captain of industry, a selfless leader, or at the least an 'ordinary regular guy' as it is to spew out a man who will rape a boy with a broom handle or keep a woman in an abandoned pit-working until she quite literally dies of fright? What is wrong with the way we make men now? Only what is wrong with much else that has endured unexamined for a great many years: an outmoded system, inappropriate to the needs of the present or to the hope of the future, and too deeply implicated in creating the problem for which it purports to be the solution.

For manhood training, by its very nature, creates the climate in which violence can flourish, and a society in which, despite its pious protestations, a level of violence is always tolerated, indeed expected ('boys will be boys'). Draconian laws against rape are meaningless when so few rapists are caught or if caught, prosecuted, or if prosecuted, convicted: prosecuting ten, twenty, fifty football hooligans does nothing to stop the hundreds, thousands, who every Saturday tear apart the fiction of our ordered society, and increasingly those of other countries as well. The acceptance of violence at every level, from the highest reaches of the judiciary and executive to the unemployed youth or boy of ten, the fatalistic conviction that aggression is unanswerable, a law of nature, may be seen in all the official responses to the problem – including the utter failure to identify it as a problem.

Governments in Britain and America mount multi-million-dollar, multi-media campaigns against drugs, which, serious as they are, affect a much smaller proportion of the population. Yet no policy, no government funding, no political will, no real thought or commitment goes into a sustained drive against domestic violence (in itself a belittling euphemism) or child abuse. 'If we can persuade more women to come forward and report domestic assaults, it's possible we may be able to stop the incidents escalating into serious woundings or even killings,' said John Patten, Minister of State at the Home Office and chairman of the inter-ministerial group on women's issues. If we could persuade ministers to think, or even to read their own Home Office statistics on the low rate of police intervention in 'domestics', could they possibly do better than this?

We need to acknowledge that the seeds of violence are in every man, therefore their education should be devoted to training that out, not beating it in; that aggression is contagious, and that watching it, taking part in it, reading about it, and expressing it will never reduce it, and consequently that all arguments for 'letting off steam', 'just enjoying a bit of a rough-house', 'sublimating violence' or 'providing an outlet for aggression' are spurious and corrupt; that the passion of violence will always, must always demand a victim, and that the victim will always, must always, be someone weaker, smaller, and lower in the hierarchy of violence, if not of suffering. As long as aggression is admired (in business, in love relationships, in Clint Eastwood and Sylvester Stallone), so long will men be the victims of their own dreams and delusions and of the danger around them.

These victims, of what we must learn to recognize and acknowledge as the victim sex, will include men and boys like these pitiful human fragments whose heads tossed for a little while above the tidal wave before it drew them down:

- Hollywood agent Jennings Lang, shot in the groin by film producer Walter Wangel in a car with his client, the film star Joan Bennett, Wangel's wife, when Wangel suspected an affair.

- Daryl Hawkins, a student of Leamington Spa, attacked from behind with a rounders bat as he stepped out of a pub after a quiet evening with friends, leaving him 90 per cent brain-damaged, doubly incontinent, and mute.

- John Gordon, a Yorkshire headmaster, who was arrested for soliciting in a man's lavatory by a member of the local police vice squad and hanged himself to avoid the disgrace.

- Ed Phillips, who shot himself on the set of *Dallas* in despair over business deals involving the actor Ken Kercheval ('Cliff Barnes').

- Vinson Harris, a US federal prisoner, told 'This is Alabama, nigger, and we're going to teach you to keep your mouth shut': dead of suffocation after his mouth was sealed with duct tape.

- Eddie Banks, explosives expert of Bolton, Greater Manchester, who blew himself up in front of his wife after leaving his girlfriend, following a row about her kitten when he told her 'You think more of that cat than you do of me.'

- Sakander Ali, a Birmingham ten-year-old found hanging from a swing in the playground where he normally played.

- David Hosanky, 18-year-old heir to a French fortune, who repudiated his lover when she told him that she loved him, because he could never feel safe with a woman who admitted that, then threw himself from the balcony of his luxurious Riviera apartment.

- Ronald Goodwin, 33, an electrical fitter, killed at Totton, near Southampton, by a gang of youths when he tried to stop them vandalizing a German-made car after England's defeat by West Germany in the 1990 World Cup.

Shall we go on?
Or is it time to stop?

Let the old man lie in the earth
(he has troubled men's thoughts long enough)
let the old man die,
let the old man be of the earth,
he is earth,
Father,
O beloved
you are the earth,
he is the earth, Saturn, wisdom,
rock (O his bones are hard,
he is strong, that old man).
H.D.

A twenty-first-century blueprint for boys' survival must begin at the beginning. We must:

● bring the father of every baby boy into the close circle of his care from the moment of birth, loosening the Oedipal knot and giving the child a same-sex parent worth modelling himself on.

● help the boy to be genuinely strong and independent, teach him how to love and care for himself, so reducing his dependence on the female, on the gang as a substitute for the female, and his demand for constant service and centrality as a precondition of living.

● reconsider and reorganize schools, syllabuses and sporting activities in order to eliminate all violence and bullying as well as their systematic structures of failure; recognize boys' enormous diversity, and find more fruitful outlets for their energy.

● allow, encourage, and teach boys to honour their emotions as much as they do their anatomical attributes, and return them to the manhood traditions of earlier times: Achilles wept, Luther wept, Dickens wept, Jesus wept!

● help boys fully and frankly through the terrors of adolescence, with honest and loving sex education in the family in place of the current twenty minutes with the biology teacher or games master.

- restore the ideal of one true, loving, lifelong partnership, in which the woman is seen as a valued and cherished equal, not as a caretaker, mother-substitute, or sparring partner.

- pick up the vulnerable boys early on in their school lives, where they are always known to teachers, from the age of seven onwards. If enrichment programmes can be offered for the gifted, why not even more for the boy who is failing, and so falling dangerously towards manhood violence?

- widen the basis both of men's acceptability and of our definition of success, so that fighting and winning cease to dominate every man's agenda.

- love men more as they are, and less as we would all like them to be.

For the violent few, we, and they, need:

- far more extensive and sophisticated research into masculinity, aggression and violence, abandoning for ever the study of middle-class white boys in university labs who are hardly likely to demonstrate in front of a white-coated lady researcher what pornography really makes them do.

- far better record-keeping of offences of sex and violence, with an 'at risk' register of offenders, as well as of their victims.

- swift, stern and non-negotiable enforcement of existing laws against violence, in every case.

- new laws where the old have proved to be inadequate, like the protection afforded to rapists who attack women and men with a weapon, however horrific (bottle, chisel, hockey stick), since only the penetration of the penis can legally make the violation a rape.

- a sustained, fully-funded attempt to change the men who are caught and convicted, confronting them with their victims and introducing them to the concept of reparation.

- programmes and penalties of escalating severity for repeat offenders.

Too costly? Families on welfare, children in care, men's alcoholism, accident rates, premature disease and death cost the 'advanced' countries millions. Too long-drawn-out? We have eternity ahead. Too difficult? For many men, could it be more difficult than it is now?
Shall we begin?

'I have no name:
I am but two days old.'
  What shall I call thee?
'I happy am,
Joy is my name.'
  Sweet joy befall thee!
        William Blake,
        'Infant Joy'

Notes and References

Full details of works cited will be found in the Select Bibliography on pp. 247–51.

PROLOGUE

1. Hemingway, *A Moveable Feast*, pp. 188–9.
2. William Walton's comment, and that of an even closer source, Hemingway's younger brother Leicester, are taken from Brian, *The Faces of Hemingway*, pp. 181 and 23 respectively. Zelda's attack appears in Meyers, *Hemingway*, p. 164.
3. *The New Book of American Rankings*, FY1 Information Services (Facts on File Publications, New York, 1984), p. 165.
4. US statistics come from the US Department of Justice Report to the Nation, *Crime in the United States*, UCR 1987 (1988), US Department of Justice, Washington DC, pp. 7, 19, 24. British figures are taken from the British Government Home Office Statistical Bulletin of the Statistical Department for 1989, 7/89, March 89, pp. 4 and 5.
5. Sirhan Sirhan, *Time*, 13 April 1981; John W. Hinckley, *New York Times*, 9 July 1982.
6. A. L. Rowse, *Homosexuals in History*, p. xii.
7. Brent Staples, 'A Brother's Murder' in Klein and Erickson, *About Men*, p. 60.
8. Figures taken from US Department of Justice Report (1988), p. 28, which also reports (p. 32) that of all US violent crimes against strangers, 70 per cent were against males.
9. Harry Brod, 'A Case for Men's Studies', in Kimmel, *Changing Men*, p. 271.
10. *The Sunday Correspondent*, 17 September 1989. For French statistics, see *The Daily Telegraph*, 11 September 1989: for American, *Time*, 23 March 1987.
11. Nelson Bryant, 'The Sorcery of War' in Klein and Erickson, p. 221.
12. Hodson, *Men*, p. 135.
13. Report to the Nation, p. iii.

1 THE PRIMAL EDEN

1. Metcalf and Humphries, *The Sexuality of Men*, p. 19.
2. Nicholson, *Men and Women*, p. 46; King, *Women and Work*, p. 4.
3. Hodson, pp. 26–7; Oakley, *Subject Women*, pp. 42–5.
4. Oakley, p. 43.
5. Oakley, above; Swiney, *Women and Natural Law*; Montagu, *The Natural Superiority of Women*; Gould Davis, *The First Sex*; Ounsted and Taylor (eds), *Gender Differences*.
6. Nicholson, p. 17; and see Oakley, ch. 5.
7. O'Faolain and Martines, *Not In God's Image*, p. 19.
8. Belotti, *Little Girls*, p. 52; Nicholson, p. 17; Oakley, pp. 94–6; Olivier, *Jocasta's Children*, p. 54.
9. Freud, VII, p. 223.
10. Gathorne-Hardy, *The Rise and Fall of the British Nanny*, pp. 163–6.
11. Olivier, p. 82.
12. Raven and Weir, *Women in History*, p. 14.
13. Phillips, *Maori Life and Custom*, pp. 170–1.

14. Olivier, p. 40.
15. Olivier, p. 26.
16. Hodson, p. 26.
17. Olivier, pp. 40–1, 61–2.
18. Pichois, *Baudelaire*, pp. 349 and 361.
19. Humphry and Tindall, *False Messiah*, pp. 10–12.
20. Lawrence, *Lady Chatterley's Lover*, p. 210.
21. Dinnerstein, *The Rocking of The Cradle and the Ruling of the World*, p. 41.
22. Cameron and Frazer, *The Lust To Kill*, p. 18.

2 THE DAWN CHORUS

1. Roth, *Portnoy's Complaint*, pp. 1–2.
2. Ayling, *George the Third*, p. 27.
3. de Mendelssohn, *The Age of Churchill*, p. 385.
4. *The Independent*, 31 October 1989.
5. Hayman, *Kafka*. Quotations, in order of appearance in the text, are taken from pages 13, 39, 18, and 1.
6. Hibbert, *George IV*, p. 2.
7. Millgate, *Thomas Hardy*, p. 16.
8. Proust, *A la recherche du temps perdu, Swann's Way*, p. xii.
9. Ginny Dougary, 'Relative Values', *Sunday Times* magazine, 23 April 1989.
10. Firestone, *A Book of Men*, p. 85.
11. Forman (ed.), *The Letters of John Keats*, I, 156.
12. Leilah Farrah, 'Relative Values', *Sunday Times* magazine, 25 May 1989.
13. Lawrence E. Gary, 'Predicting Interpersonal Conflict Between Men and Women: The Case of Black Men', in Kimmel, p. 233.
14. Henry Miller, 'My Life And Times', in Firestone, p. 12.
15. Schreiber, *The Shoemaker*, pp. 27–8.

3 PARADISE LOST

1. Henry Vaughan's lines are taken from 'The Retreat'; William Wordsworth's from the Ode 'Intimations of Immortality from Recollections of Early Childhood', and the 'Lines composed a few miles above Tintern Abbey'; and Thomas Gray's from the 'Ode on a Distant Prospect of Eton College'.
2. Reiss, *Joseph Goebbels*, pp. 1–3, 12.
3. Humphries, Mack and Perks, *A Century of Childhood*, p. 23.
4. Oliver and Neneta Marin, *Hello*, 3, 10, 17 June 1989.
5. Crick, *George Orwell*, p. 64.
6. Olivier, p. 89.
7. King, p. 11.
8. de Mendelssohn, p. 54.
9. *Ibid.*, p. 77.
10. Franks, *Goodbye, Tarzan*, p. 123.
11. All statistics and research figures are taken from King, pp. 4–5, and Maccoby and Jacklin, *The Psychology of Sex Differences*, *passim*.
12. Oakley, pp. 111–12; and see King and Maccoby and Jacklin, *passim*.
13. Klein and Erickson, p. 27.
14. Meyers, pp. 12, 13.

4 BEATING THE BOUNDS

1. Gathorne-Hardy, *The Public School Phenomenon*, p. 41.
2. Crick, pp. 68–71. Note that Crick suspects some exaggeration in this account, but does not doubt its essential veracity.
3. de Mendelssohn, p. 45.
4. Sutherland (ed.), *The Oxford Book of Literary Anecdotes*, p. 271.
5. Humphries, Mack and Perks, *A Century of Childhood*, p. 122.
6. Humphries, p. 122.
7. Klein and Erickson, pp. 247–9.
8. *The Times*, 16 June 1989.
9. Badinter, *Man/Woman*, pp. 75–6.
10. Farb, *Man's Rise to Civilisation*, p. 72.

11. Suttie, *The Origins of Love and Hate*, p. 87.
12. Lee, *The Blind Side of Eden*, p. 5.
13. Hodson, p. 25.
14. Ronald Hayman, 'It is time to listen to Freud', *The Independent*, 12 October 1988.

5 MAN'S BEST FRIEND

1. Humphries, p. 159.
2. Crick, p. 51.
3. Reich, *Passion of Youth*, p. 212.
4. Survey led by Dr David Forman at the Radcliffe Infirmary, Oxford, for the Imperial Cancer Research Fund's Epidemiological Clinical Trials Unit, reported in the *British Medical Journal* (April 1989) and in *The Independent* and *The Daily Telegraph*, 28 April 1989.
5. Franks, p. 36.
6. Marsh, *Eye to Eye*, p. 201.
7. Hayman, pp. 39–40.
8. Johnson, *He*, p. 25.
9. Deidre Sanders, *The Woman Report on Men*, pp. 12, 165.

6 MAJORITY RULE

1. Nicholson, pp. 67–8.
2. *Woman's Own*, 7 March 1989, pp. 20–2.
3. All these statistics, and the research studies that produced them, are detailed in Nicholson, p. 44.
4. Freud, XIX, p. 252.
5. 'Nude Awakening', *Elle*, August 1989.
6. Vilar, *The Manipulated Man*, pp. 74–5.
7. Metcalf and Humphries, p. 31.
8. 'The Game', *Esquire*, April 1989.
9. Ian Penman, 'Who's Afraid of Norman Mailer', *Arena*, Summer 1989, pp. 130–4.

7 ECCE HOMO

1. de Mendelssohn, p. 71.
2. Terkel, *Working*, p. 24.
3. 'Tootsie Taught Dustin Hoffman about the Sexes', *New York Times*, 12 December 1982.
4. Russell Miller, 'Maestro in Hell's Kitchen', *Sunday Times*, 30 July 1989.
5. Jim Stodder, 'Confessions of a Candy-Ass Roughneck', in Shapiro and Shapiro, *The Women Say, the Men Say*, pp. 40–4.
6. *Daily Telegraph*, 15 April 1989.
7. *Sunday Times*, 26 November 1989.
8. Dobash and Dobash, *Violence Against Wives*, p. 3.
9. For the account of Lord Byron's courtship and marriage, see Hartcup, *Love and Marriage in the Great Country Houses*, pp. 128–30; for the Prince of Wales's wedding in 1795 to Princess Caroline of Brunswick, see Hibbert, pp. 146–8.
10. Alvarez, *Life After Marriage*, pp. 29–30.
11. *Daily Mail*, 7 March 1989.
12. Metcalf, p. 33.
13. Ford, *Men*, p. 101.
14. Kimmel, p. 89.

8 PLATO'S CLUB

1. Franks, p. 127.
2. Williams, *Memoirs*, p. 20.
3. Wilson, *Lawrence of Arabia*, p. 189.
4. Boswell, *Christianity, Social Tolerance and Homosexuality*, p. 197.
5. Boswell, p. 62.
6. Ellmann, *Oscar Wilde*, pp. 448–9.
7. Genet, *Miracle of the Rose*, p. 113.
8. Altman, *Homosexual Oppression and Liberation*, p. 15.
9. *True Detective*, January 1979, cited by Cameron and Frazer, pp. xiii–xiv.

9 THE POWER AND THE GLORY

1. Adams, *The Works of John Adams*, VI, p. 234.
2. Gabler, *An Empire of Their Own*, pp. 151–2.
3. Heymann, *A Woman Named Jackie*, p. 508.
4. Johnson, p. 12.
5. Gabler, p. 151.
6. *The Sunday Times Review*, 30 April 1989.
7. *Reader's Digest*, August 1989, p. 87.
8. Cowan and Kinder, *Women Men Love, Women Men Leave*, p. 169.
9. *Time*, 27 July 1987, p. 23.
10. Cowan and Kinder, p. 169.
11. *Options*, June 1989, pp. 40–1.
12. Rutter, *Sex in the Forbidden Zone*, pp. 60–1.
13. Rutter, p. 95.
14. Klein and Erickson, pp. 226–7.

10 FATAL ATTRACTIONS

1. Sanders, p. 11.
2. Chris Reed, 'The Red Queen and the Hobo King', *Guardian Women*, 8 January 1985.
3. Hodson, p. 80.
4. Hodson, p. 81.
5. Trachtenberg, *The Casanova Complex*, p. 196.
6. *The Independent*, 19 May 1988.
7. *Sunday Telegraph*, 30 April 1989.
8. Keeler, *Scandal!*, pp. 104–5.
9. Miller, *Bunny*, pp. 174–5.

11 THE UNPLUMED SERPENT

1. Ford, p. 240.
2. Hodson, p. 11.
3. Hibbert, p. 161.
4. Metcalf and Humphries, p. 63.
5. Kurtz, *Malespeak*, p. 70.
6. Aronowitz and Hamill, *The Life and Death of a Man*, p. 21.
7. de Mendelssohn, p. 65.
8. Meyers, p. 559.
9. Meyers, p. 556.

10. Ian Thomson, *Sunday Times*, 30 April 1989.
11. Warburg, *A Voice At Twilight*, p. 229.
12. Firestone, pp. 13–14.
13. Warburg, p. 230.
14. See Keuls, *The Reign of the Phallus*, pp. 79–82, for a full and fascinating discussion of 'Socrates' last words as a phallic joke'.
15. Holroyd, *Bernard Shaw*, vol. 2, p. 309.

12 KILLER MALE

1. Of child abusers, less than 3 per cent are female (*Child Abuse Trends in England and Wales 1983–87*, published by the NSPCC, 1989). For a discussion of 'female sadists' see Cameron and Frazer, pp. 23–6: 'we are forced to conclude that the "female sadists" are mere projections of a sexual double standard . . . in the great tradition of sadistic sexual murder, it seems that women are virtually non-existent.' Even the infamous Myra Hindley, Cameron and Frazer point out, acted for and with a male. Finally, the first female serial killer or mass murderer has yet to be apprehended.
2. Cameron and Frazer, p. 167.
3. Cameron and Frazer, p. 79, citing M. O. Casey *et al.*, 'Patients with Chromosome Abnormality in two Special Hospitals', *Special Hospitals Research Report* 2 (1971).
4. Mark Cooper, 'Welcome to LA', *The Sunday Correspondent*, 1 October 1989.
5. Kott, *Shakespeare Our Contemporary*, p. 72.
6. Renvoize, *Web of Violence*, p. 39.
7. See Annette Lawson, *Adultery*; *Sunday Telegraph*, 12 February 1989, gives more up-to-date statistics.

8. Jessie Bernard, *The Future of Marriage*, pp. 310–14; Hodson, p. 7.

9. 'Punching Judy', BBC Panorama Special, BBC1, 22 May 1989.

10. Dobash and Dobash, p. 93.

11. Renvoize, p. 36.

12. Borland (ed.), *Violence in the Family*, p. 6.

13. Anonymous contribution, *The Independent*, 28 November 1989.

EPILOGUE

1. Jean-Paul Sartre's comments on violence are taken from his preface to Frantz Fanon's *The Wretched of the Earth* (1961). For an interesting discussion of Sartre and Fanon, see Hannah Arendt, *On Violence* (1969).

2. For British figures, see HMSO Crime Statistics 1988–9, with analysis in *The Independent*, 17 March 1989, and Home Office Statistical Bulletins, *Notifiable Offences Recorded by the Police in England and Wales*, 1988 and 1989. For US statistics, see the US Department of Justice Report to the Nation, *Crime in the US*, UCR 1987 (1988), US Dept. of Justice, Washington DC. The future prediction of US murders comes from a 1990 study by the US Senate Judiciary Committee (*The Daily Telegraph*, 2 August 1990). Information on rape victims is taken from two Home Office research studies (105 and 106, 1989); for comment and analysis, see *The Daily Telegraph*, 22 February 1990, 22 February 1989, and *The Independent*, 31 May 1990: FBI figures for US rape victims corroborate. Information on female victims of domestic violence and murder again comes from Home Office figures (*The Times*, 14 April 1990) and a World In Action special report (*Observer*, 25 February 1990).

3. *The Daily Telegraph*, 15 April 1989.

Select Bibliography

Adams, John, 'Discourses on Davila: a series of papers on political history' (1790), in Charles Francis Adams (ed.), *The Works of John Adams* (6 vols, Chas. C. Little and Jas. Brown, Boston, 1851)

Altman, Denis *Homosexual Oppression and Liberation* (Avon Books, New York, 1973)

The Homosexualisation of America: the Americanisation of the Homosexual (St Martin's Press, New York, 1982)

Alvarez, A. *Scenes from a Divorce* (Macmillan, London, 1979)

Amis, Martin *Success* (Jonathan Cape, London, 1978)

Arendt, Hannah *On Violence* (Penguin, Harmondsworth, 1969)

Aronowitz, Alfred G., and Hamill, Peter *Ernest Hemingway: The Life and Death of a Man* (Lancer Books, New York, 1961)

Ayling, Stanley *George the Third* (History Book Club, London, 1972)

Badinter, Elisabeth *Man/Woman: The One is the Other*, tr. Barbara Wright, (Collins Harvill, London, 1989)

Bell, A. P., & Weinberg, M. S. *Homosexualities: a Study of the Diversity Among Men and Women* (Simon & Schuster, New York, 1978)

Belotti, Elena *Little Girls: Social Conditioning and its Effects on the Stereotyped Role of Women during Infancy* Readers & Writers Publishing Co-operative (London, 1975)

Bernard, Jessie *The Future of Marriage* (Penguin Books, Harmondsworth, 1976)

Blood, R. O., & Wolfe, D. M. *Husbands and Wives* (Free Press, New York, 1960)

Bloom, Allan *The Closing of the American Mind* (Simon & Schuster, New York, 1987)

Borkowski, Margaret, Murch, Mervyn, & Walker, Val *Marital Violence: The Community Response* (Tavistock Publications, London & New York, 1983)

Borland, Marie (ed.) *Violence in the Family* (Manchester University Press/Humanities Press, Atlantic Highlands, New Jersey, 1976)

Boswell, J. *Christianity, Social Tolerance and Homosexuality: Gay People in Western Europe from the Beginning of the Christian Era to the Fourteenth Century* (University of Chicago Press, Chicago, 1980)

Bresler, Fenton *The Mystery of Georges Simenon: a Biography* (Heinemann/Quixote Press, London, 1983)

Brian, Denis *The Faces of Hemingway: Intimate Portraits of Ernest Hemingway by those who knew him* (Grafton Books, London, 1988)

Brittan, Arthur, & Maynard, Mary *Sexism, Racism and Oppression* (Basil Blackwell, Oxford, 1984)

Brod, Harry 'A Case for Men's Studies', in Michael Kimmel (ed.), *Changing Men: New Directions in Research on Men and Masculinity* (Sage Publications, Beverly Hills, California, 1987)

Brownmiller, Susan *Against Our Will: Men, Women and Rape* (Simon & Schuster, New York, 1975)

Cameron, Deborah, & Frazer, Elizabeth *The Lust to Kill: A Feminist Investigation of Sexual Murder* (Polity Press, London, 1987)

Caro, Robert A. *The Years of Lyndon Johnson: The Path to Power* (Knopf, New York, 1982)

Clark, A. *Women's Silence, Men's Violence: Sexual Assault in England 1770–1845* (Pandora, London, 1987)

Clewlow, Carol *A Woman's Guide to*

Adultery (Michael Joseph, London, 1989)

Cowan, Connell, & Kinder, Melvyn *Women Men Love, Women Men Leave: Why Men are Drawn to Women, What Makes Them Want to Stay* (Sidgwick & Jackson, London, 1988)

Crick, Bernard *George Orwell: A Life* (Penguin Books, Harmondsworth, 1980)

Davies, Andrew *Getting Hurt* (Methuen, London, 1989)

Davis, Elizabeth Gould *The First Sex* (J. M. Dent and Sons Ltd, London, 1971)

de Mendelssohn, Peter *The Age of Churchill: Heritage and Adventure* (Thames & Hudson, London, 1961)

Dinnerstein, Dorothy *The Rocking of the Cradle and the Ruling of the World* (Souvenir Press, London, 1976)

Dobash, R. Emerson, & Dobash, Russell *Violence Against Wives: A Case Against the Patriarch* (Open Books, Shepton Mallet, Somerset, England, 1979)

Donaldson, Maureen *An Affair to Remember* (Macdonald, London, 1989)

Dover, K. J. *Greek Homosexuality* (Duckworth, London, 1978)

Ellmann, Richard *Oscar Wilde* (Hamish Hamilton, London, 1987)

Ellul, Jacques *Violence: Reflections from a Christian Perspective* (Mowbrays, London & Oxford, 1978)

Fanon, Frantz *The Wretched of the Earth* (Grove Press, New York, 1961)

Farb, Peter *Man's Rise to Civilisation as Shown by the Indians of North America from Primeval Times to the Coming of the Industrial State* (Secker & Warburg, London, 1969)

Fennell, Graham, Phillipson, Chris, & Evers, Helen *The Sociology of Old Age* (Open University Press, Milton Keynes, 1988)

Firestone, Ross (ed.) *A Book of Men: Visions of the Male Experience* (Mainstream Publishing, Edinburgh, 1979)

Ford, Anna *Men: A Documentary* (Weidenfeld & Nicolson, London, 1985)

Forman, Maurice Buxton *The Letters of John Keats* (2 vols, Oxford University Press, Oxford, 1931)

Franks, Helen *Goodbye, Tarzan: Men After Feminism* (Allen & Unwin, London, 1984)

French, Marilyn *Beyond Power: On Women, Men and Morals* (Jonathan Cape, London, 1985)

Freud, Sigmund *The Standard Edition of the Complete Psychological Works of Sigmund Freud*, ed. James Strachey (24 vols, London, 1954–73)

Gabler, Neil *An Empire of Their Own: How the Jews Invented Hollywood* (Anchor Books, Doubleday, New York, 1988)

Gary, Lawrence E. 'Predicting Interpersonal Conflict Between Men and Women: the Case of Black Men', in Michael Kimmel (ed.), *Changing Men: New Directions in Research on Men and Masculinity* (Sage Publications, Beverly Hills, California, 1987)

Gathorne-Hardy, Jonathan *The Public School Phenomenon* (Hodder & Stoughton, London, 1977)

The Rise and Fall of the British Nanny (Hodder & Stoughton, London, 1972)

Gayford, J. J. *Wife Battering: A Preliminary Survey of 100 Cases* (British Medical Journal, 1975)

Research on Battered Wives (Royal Society of Health Journal, December 1975)

Genet, Jean *Miracle of the Rose* (Penguin Books, Harmondsworth, 1971)

Gide, André *André Gide: Par Lui-Même* (ed. Claude Martin, Paris, 1963)

Goodman, Jonathan *Acts of Murder* (Harrap, London, 1986)

Gordon, Barbara *Jennifer Fever: Older Men, Younger Women* (Harper & Row, New York, 1988)

Gray, Muir, & Wilcock, Gordon *Our Elders* (Open University Press, Oxford, 1981)

Greengross, Sally *Ageing: An Adventure in Living* (Souvenir Press, London, 1985)

Greer, Germaine *The Female Eunuch* (McGibbon & Kee, London, 1970)

Hallet, Jean-Pierre *Pygmy Kitabu* (Souvenir Press, London, 1974)

Hanmer, J., & Saunders, S. *Well-Founded Fear* (Hutchinson, London, 1984)

Hartcup, Adeline *Love and Marriage in the Great Country Houses* (Sidgwick & Jackson, London, 1984)

Hayman, Ronald *Kafka: A Biography* (Open University Press, New York, 1982)

Hemingway, Ernest *A Moveable Feast* (Grafton Books, London, 1977) *The Old Man and the Sea* (New York, 1964)

Heymann, David C. *A Woman Named Jackie* (Signet, New American Library, New York, 1989)

Hibbert, Christopher *George IV, Prince of Wales* (RU Ltd, Newton Abbott, 1973)

Hodson, Philip *Men: An Investigation into the Emotional Male* (BBC Books, London, 1984)

Holroyd, Michael *Bernard Shaw* (2 vols, Chatto & Windus, London, 1988 and 1989)

Humphries, Steve, Mack, Joanna, & Perks, Robert *A Century of Childhood* (Sidgwick & Jackson, London, 1988)

Humphry, Derek, & Tindall, David *False Messiah: The Story of Michael X* (Hart-Davis McGibbon, London, 1977)

Huyck, Margaret Hellie *Growing Older* (Prentice-Hall, New Jersey, 1974)

Ingham, Mary *Men: The Male Myth Exposed* (Century Publishing, London, 1984)

Johnson, Robert A. *He: Understanding Masculine Psychology* (Perennial Library, Harper & Row, New York, 1986)

Jong, Erica *Fear of Flying* (Secker & Warburg, London, 1974)

Jukes, Adam *Men Who Hate Women* (Free Association Books, London, 1990)

Keeler, Christine *Scandal!* (Xanadu, London, 1989)

Keuls, Eva C. *The Reign of the Phallus: Sexual Politics in Ancient Athens* (Perennial Library, Harper & Row, New York, 1985)

Kimmel, Michael S. (ed.) *Changing Men: New Directions in Research on Men and Masculinity* (Sage Publications, Beverly Hills, California, 1987)

King, J. S. *Women and Work: Sex Differences and Society*, Manpower Paper No. 10 of the Department of Employment (HMSO, London, 1976)

Kirshner, Julius, & Wemple, Suzanne F. (eds) *Women of the Medieval World: Essays in Honor of John H. Mundy* (Basil Blackwell, Oxford, 1985)

Klein, Edward, & Erickson, Don (eds) *About Men: Reflections on the Male Experience* (Poseidon Press, New York, 1987)

Kohlberg, Lawrence, with Rita Devries et al. *Child Psychology and Childhood Education: A Cognitive-Development View* (Longman, London and New York, 1987)

Kott, Jan *Shakespeare Our Contemporary* (Methuen, London, 1965)

Kurtz, Irma *Malespeak* (Jonathan Cape, London, 1986)

Lawrence, D. H. *Lady Chatterley's Lover* (Penguin, Harmondsworth, 1960)

Lawson, Annette *Adultery* (Basil Blackwell, Oxford, 1988)

Lee, Carol *The Blind Side of Eden: The Sexes in Perspective* (Bloomsbury, London, 1989)

Lewis, Charlie *Becoming a Father* (Open University Press, Milton Keynes, 1986)

Llewellyn-Jones, Derek *Everyman* (Oxford University Press, Oxford, 1987)

Maccoby, Eleanor, & Jacklin, Carol *The Psychology of Sex Differences*

(Stanford University Press, Stanford, Oxford University Press, Oxford and London, 1974)

Marsh, Peter *Eye to Eye: How People Interact* (Andromeda, Oxford, 1988)

Metcalf, Andy, & Humphries, Martin *The Sexuality of Men* (Pluto Press, London, 1985)

Meyers, Jeffrey *Hemingway: A Biography* (Harper & Row, New York, 1985)

Miller, Henry 'My Life and Times' in Ross Firestone, *A Book of Men: Visions of the Male Experience* (Mainstream Publishing, Edinburgh, 1979)

Miller, Russell *Bunny: The Real Story of a Playboy* (Michael Joseph, London, 1984)

Millgate, Michael *Thomas Hardy: A Biography* (Oxford University Press, Oxford & New York, 1985)

Montagu, Ashley *The Natural Superiority of Women* (Macmillan, London, 1968)

Mullan, Bob *The Mating Trade* (Routledge & Kegan Paul, London, 1984)

Netter, Gwynn *Explaining Crime* (3rd edn, McGraw-Hill, New York, 1984)

Nicholson, John *Men and Women: How Different Are They?* (Oxford University Press, Oxford, 1984)

Nietzsche, Friedrich Wilhelm *The Will To Power* (Weidenfeld & Nicolson, London, 1968)

Nowra, Louis *The Cheated* (Angus & Robertson, Sydney & Melbourne, Australia, 1979)

Oakley, Ann *Subject Women* (Martin Robertson, Oxford, 1981)

O'Faolain, Julia, & Martines, Lauro *Not in God's Image: Women in History from the Greeks to the Victorians* (Maurice Temple Smith, London, 1973)

Olivier, Christiane *Jocasta's Children: The Imprint of the Mother*, tr. George Craig (Routledge, London & New York, 1989)

Ounsted, C., and Taylor, D. C. (eds) *Gender Differences: Their Ontogeny and Significance* (Williams and Wilkins, Baltimore, 1972)

Pagelow, Mildred Daly *Woman-Battering* (Sage Publications, London, 1981)

Phillips, W. J. *Maori Life and Custom* (A. H. & A. W. Reed, Wellington, New Zealand, 1966)

Pichois, Claude *Baudelaire*, tr. Graham Robb (Hamish Hamilton, London, 1989)

Pitcher, Evelyn Goodenough, & Schulz, Lynn Heckey *Boys and Girls at Play: The Development of Sex Roles* (Harvester Press, Brighton, 1983)

Plummer, K. (ed.) *The Making of the Modern Homosexual* (Hutchinson, London, 1981)

Prince, Peter *The Good Father* (Jonathan Cape, London, 1983)

Proust, Marcel *A la recherche du temps perdu, Swann's Way* (The Modern Library, New York, 1928)

Raven, Susan, & Weir, Alison *Women in History: Thirty-Five Centuries of Feminine Achievement* (Weidenfeld & Nicolson, London, 1981)

Reich, Wilhelm *Passion of Youth: An Autobiography* (Picador, London, 1989)

Renvoize, Jean *Web of Violence: A Study of Family Violence* (Routledge & Kegan Paul, London & Boston, 1978)

Report to the Nation on Crime and Justice (2nd edn, US Department of Justice, Bureau of Justice Statistics, Washington DC, March 1988)

Riess, Curt *Joseph Goebbels* (Ballantine Books, New York, 1960)

Roth, Philip *Portnoy's Complaint* (Corgi Books, London, 1971)

Rowse, A. L. *Homosexuals in History* (Macmillan, London, 1977)

Rutter, Peter *Sex in the Forbidden Zone: When Men in Power – Therapists, Doctors, Clergy, Teachers and Others – Betray Women's Trust* (Unwin Paperbacks, London, 1990)

Sanders, Deirdre *The Woman Report on Men* (Sphere Books, London, 1987)

Schneebaum, Tobias *Where the Spirits Dwell* (Weidenfeld & Nicolson, London, 1988)

Schreiber, Flora Rheta *The Shoemaker: Anatomy of a Psychotic* (Simon & Schuster, New York, 1983)

Shapiro, Evelyn, & Shapiro, Barry M. *The Women Say, the Men Say: Issues in Politics, Work, Family, Sexuality and Power* (Dell Publishing, New York, 1979)

Snitow, A., Stansell, C., & Thompson, S. *Desire: The Politics of Sexuality* (Virago, London, 1984)

Social Work Services Group *Violence in the Family* (Scottish Education Department, HMSO, Edinburgh, 1982)

Spence, J. T., & Helmreich, R. *Psychological Dimensions of Masculinity and Femininity: Their Correlates and Antecedents* (Austin University, Texas, 1978)

Stanko, E. *Intimate Intrusions: Women's Experience of Male Violence* (Routledge & Kegan Paul, London, 1985)

Staples, Brent 'A Brother's Murder', in Klein, Edward, & Erickson, Don (eds), *About Men: Reflections on the Male Experience* (Poseidon Press, New York, 1987)

Sutherland, James (ed.) *The Oxford Book of Literary Anecdotes* (Oxford University Press, Oxford, 1975)

Suttie, Ian D. *The Origins of Love and Hate* (Penguin Books, Harmondsworth, 1960)

Swiney, Francis *Women and Natural Law* (League of Isis, London, 1912)

Terkel, Studs *Working* (Pantheon, New York, 1974)
The Great Divide: Second Thoughts on the American Dream (Pantheon, New York, 1988)

Terman, L. M., & Miles, C. C. *Sex and Personality: Studies in Masculinity and Femininity* (McGraw-Hill, New York, 1936)

Theroux, Paul *My Secret History* (1989)

Trachtenberg, Peter *The Casanova Complex: Compulsive Lovers and their Women* (Angus & Robertson, London, 1989)

Vilar, Esther *The Manipulated Man* (Abelard-Schuman, London, 1972)

Walby, S. *Patriarchy at Work* (Polity Press, Cambridge, 1987)

Warburg, Tessa Lorant *A Voice at Twilight: Diary of a Dying Man* (Peter Owen, London, 1988)

Ward, Elizabeth *Father-Daughter Rape* (Women's Press, London, 1984)

Weeks, J. *Coming Out: Homosexual Politics in Britain, from 19th Century to Present* (Quartet, London, 1977)

Welldon, Estela V. *Mother, Madonna, Whore: the Idealization and Denigration of Motherhood* (Free Association Books, London, 1988)

West, D. J. *Sexual Crimes and Confrontations: A Study of Victims and Offenders* (Cambridge Studies in Criminology LVII, Gower, Aldershot, England, & Brookfield, Vermont, USA, 1987)

Wilde, Oscar *The Picture of Dorian Gray* (Ward Lock, London, 1891)

Williams, Tennessee *Memoirs* (Star/W. H. Allen, London, 1977)

Wilson, Jeremy *Lawrence of Arabia: The Authorised Biography of T. E. Lawrence* (Heinemann, London, 1989)

Yllo, Kersti, & Bograd, Michele (eds) *Feminist Perspectives on Wife Abuse* (Sage Publications, London, 1988)

Index